A Half-Forgotten Triumph

The Story of Kent's County Championship Title of 1913

A Half-Forgotten Triumph

*The Story of Kent's County
Championship Title of 1913*

Martin Moseling
&
Tony Quarrington

Foreword by Jonathan Rice

Published in Great Britain by
SportsBooks Limited
1 Evelyn Court
Malvern Road
Cheltenham
GL50 2JR

Cover designed by Alan Hunns.

A catalogue record for this book is available from
the British Library.

ISBN   9781907524400

Printed and bound in England by TJ International.

A Half-Forgotten Triumph

Contents

Chapter

Acknowledgements

THIS BOOK WOULD not have been possible without the kind assistance and advice of Kent County Cricket Club (KCCC) Honorary Statistician, Howard Milton and its Honorary Historian Derek Carlaw, whose respective "eyes" for detail, willingness to share their own research and unselfish encouragement is hugely appreciated. David Robertson, the Honorary KCCC Archivist, who, together with the two gentlemen already mentioned, has written a number of books on Kent cricket, kindly made the 1913 committee minutes, trials and scorebooks available to us to assist with research. Wise counsel and photographic material was also provided along the way by Roger Gibbons, Archivist and Board Member of Gloucestershire County Cricket Club.

We have taken extensive advantage of the improved and enhanced contemporaneous material now available in local libraries around the county. The Kent Library and History Centre in Maidstone enabled us to research original documents, primarily the *Kent Messenger & Maidstone Telegraph* newspaper and alerted us to the digital versions of other local and national publications of the era. Staff at the local libraries in Canterbury, Gravesend and Tunbridge Wells, as well as the MCC Library at Lord's, were also unfailingly helpful.

Immense gratitude is due to Richard and Helen Seymour. Richard is the grandson of one of Kent's premier professional batsmen of the era, James Seymour. They willingly laid at our disposal a treasure trove of photographs and other documents relating to the county club during his career. We should also acknowledge the role of Christopher Scoble, the author of *Colin Blythe – lament for a legend*, for providing us with this important contact.

We are indebted to Paul Lewis for the loan of his scrapbook containing newspaper reports of the 1913 season, and wish him well in his own researches on the war records of the cricketers of Kent.

KCCC Members Dan Simmons and Andrew Sim not only provided informed and valuable support, but gave of their time to proofread emerging drafts.

We would also like to thank Phil Brit, the Archivist of Warwickshire CCC, for his attempts to unearth the reason why Kent and Warwickshire had not played each other for 14 years, and Robert Brooke, the Warwickshire historian, for permission to quote from his excellent book, *Frank Foster: The Fields Were Sudden Bare*.

The photographs in this book come from The Roger Mann Collection, Kent County Cricket Club, Richard and Helen Seymour, Gloucestershire CCC archive and the authors' own private collections.

Foreword

IN RECENT YEARS Kent supporters have not had very much to cheer about on the pitch. Many of us, weaned on Kent's glory years of the 1970s, look wistfully back 40 years to the great days of Cowdrey, Underwood, Knott and co., while at the same time believing every April that this year could be the start of a new era for Kent cricket.

There is no point in harking back only as far as the days of our youth. The real glory days of Kent cricket were a century ago and more. That first decade and a bit of the twentieth century before the Great War has come to be known as cricket's Golden Age, but it was also Kent's Golden Age. Any team that could call on the skills of such as Blythe, Woolley, Fielder, Hardinge, Humphreys, Seymour, Huish and many others would be very difficult to beat, even for teams built around heroes of almost equal stature. To be a cricket watcher in 1913 meant the opportunity to see Jack Hobbs, Hayward, Rhodes, Hirst, Percy Fender, Pelham Warner, Patsy Hendren, Astill, Kennedy, Mead, Geary, "Croucher" Jessop, Braund, John Tyldesley, JWHT Douglas, Frank Foster, Sydney Barnes, Charlie Parker, Herbert Strudwick… the list of all-time greats goes on and on. No wonder so many people were eager to part with their sixpences and shillings to pack every county ground to watch such mighty players. And the Kent side was the best of all.

In 1913 there was no touring team playing Test matches in England, no knockout trophies or Sunday Leagues, and certainly no Twenty20. The County Championship was the be-all and end-all of cricket that year, and as in 1906, 1909 and 1910, Kent swept all before them. The 1913 Championship title was perhaps the most comprehensive success of them all, and it is impossible to say how many more titles Kent might have won had war not intervened. As it was, they had to wait until 1970 for their next Championship.

Martin Moseling and Tony Quarrington tell the story of this golden year well. It may be a tale of centuries (and five-fors) past, but it still has strong links with today. Many of the grounds used in 1913 are still played on today and cricket is still cricket even in the age of helmets, doosras and reverse sweeps. The more things change, the more they stay the same. Let us hope that in one hundred years' time, our great-grandchildren are reading of the marvellous exploits of Kent in 2013 and onwards, but in the meantime, let us enjoy a nostalgic wallow in the triumphant year of 1913.

Jonathan Rice
Saltwood, Kent
March 2013

Authors' Notes

IN WRITING ABOUT the 1913 season, we decided it was necessary to observe certain conventions regarding players' names and other matters. We thought it worthwhile to offer an explanation.

In the case of Kent players, as a general rule in the course of the match, we have referred to all the players by their surname alone. For the match scorecards, however, we have made the distinction between the amateur and professional, giving the amateurs the prefix of "Mr". Where we refer to opposition players, at their first mention in each chapter, we have included the first name or nickname. for example "Plum" Warner. Thereafter, we revert to surname alone.

In the Index to the book, we have excluded all Kent players who appeared during the 1913 season. We have decided that this should also be the case for the opposition. The exception to this rule is where we include information about a particular player in addition to simple match reportage or match information. For example SF Barnes, whom Kent met in the "festival" matches at the end of the season, and Albert Trott, who stood as umpire in the MCC match at the beginning of the season.

In the Statistical Section, the averages include only matches played for Kent. They therefore exclude runs scored and wickets taken in matches such as Gentlemen vs Players. The aggregate runs will not, therefore, accord with the national averages for the year as published in *Wisden*.

Because we have used the figures published in *Cricket Archive*, there may be some differences in the figures shown in this book from those published in *Wisden*. For example, in the chapter on the match Middlesex vs Kent at Lord's (page 246), we refer to Wilfred Rhodes as having taken 4,204 first-class wickets. The figure shown in *Wisden* is 4,187 and, because Rhodes took more wickets than any other bowler in the history of the game, the 4,187 figure is fairly well known. The difference is due to matches played in India in 1922/3 which are excluded from *Wisden*.

Preface

IT WAS MY father, one of four cricket-mad brothers from East Kent, who first stirred my interest in the cricketers of the Kent XI. His own heroes were those of the 1920s and 1930s, whom he first watched at Canterbury and Dover. Frank Woolley, "Tich" Freeman and Percy Chapman were particular favourites and I grew up listening to tales of their runs and wickets.

My specific interest in the "Golden Age" of cricket, was originally sparked by a 90-year-old gentleman called Eddie Chapman, who in the late 1960s shared with me his memories of three days he had spent at the Bat & Ball Ground, Gravesend watching Kent play Gloucestershire in the first match of the 1895 season. In that match, the Gloucestershire captain, WG Grace, spent every ball of the match on the field, scoring 257 and 73 not out as well as bowling 43 overs, taking 2-115. That conversation fired my curiosity about the cricket of the period, and sent me scuttling to the local library in search of more information, where I discovered that Dr Grace had eventually amassed 1,000 runs in the month of May, becoming the first man to accomplish that remarkable feat. That interest has remained with me ever since, surfacing at odd intervals when something new piqued my interest. When one combines the twin fascinations of the Golden Age with that of Kent cricket, it was, perhaps, inevitable that my focus should be on the first "golden era" of Kent cricket, 1905 to 1914.

In December of last year, it occurred to me that the story of Kent's 1913 Championship title had not yet been told, and that with the centenary upon us in a few months, it was the time to do so. A brief conversation with Tony decided the matter and we set to work. The process has been a fascinating and informative journey; hard work but, on the whole, enjoyable too.

Martin Moseling
Teddington, Gloucestershire
April 2013

Preface

BEING BORN IN Rochester, Charles Dickens is, understandably, one of my literary heroes. But I do think he missed a trick when, in *The Pickwick Papers*, he had the loquacious Mr Jingle say, *"Kent sir – everybody knows Kent – apples, cherries, hops and women."* Surely, he should have included "cricket" in that description?

While cricket historians will continue to debate where the first recorded game was played, there is little doubt that the Weald of Kent, along with the adjoining southern counties, is its true birthplace. I was brought up to be very conscious of that heritage and spent my summer weekends, from a very early age, visiting such exotic cricketing outposts as Marden, Hadlow, Nurstead and Addington to support, score, and ultimately play for, my father's team made up of shipwrights, plumbers and television repair men. The most popular game of the season, and I have never been able to fathom why, was at Warmlake where the hosts – Medway Brewery – supplied a free barrel of beer for the opposition players.

But on the Saturdays of the county cricket Weeks, and during the school holidays, you would find me sat behind the boundary rope, scorecard and pencil in hand, cheering on my Kent idols, especially the slightly portly but graceful Colin Cowdrey, whose extra cover drive to the pavilion gate at the St Lawrence Ground was the stroke of the gods.

It was there that I first learned of the legendary exploits of Ames and Freeman, Blythe and Woolley, and it triggered a lifelong fascination with the County Club's history. I am proud, therefore, with my first published book, to have added my own modest contribution to that history. And what better time than now to celebrate the centenary of the fourth Championship victory in eight years of arguably Kent's greatest era.

Finally, I would like to express my thanks to Martin for not only coming up with the idea for the book, but for helping to make the potentially risky process of collaboration at a distance a relatively painless one.

Tony Quarrington
Gillingham, Kent
April 2013

The Background to the 1913 Season

FOR THOSE OF us with an addiction to the cricket of Kent, the expression "The Glory Years" is usually associated with the period 1967 to 1978 when the county side won three Championship titles – 1970, 1977 (jointly with Middlesex) and 1978 – to accompany eight one-day victories in the Gillette Cup, Benson & Hedges Cup and John Player League. The foundation for that period of success was laid in the late 1950s when, with Les Ames as Secretary/Manager and Colin Cowdrey as the new captain, Kent built a side whose achievements are now legendary.

But there was an earlier period in the history of the County Club where they were equally as dominant as in the 1970s and similarly it covered a period of around ten seasons from 1905 to 1914. During that decade, Kent won the Championship title on four occasions, were runners-up twice and third twice. Cricket was undergoing significant changes at this time. The age of the amateur was on the wane and both batting and bowling were becoming more "scientific" for a variety of reasons, including the attitude to leg-side play, the development of the googly and swing bowling and, as a result, a new approach to field placing by captains and bowlers.

Kent dominated county cricket during the early years of Queen Victoria's reign (1837–49), "winning" the County Championship eight times. This was the era of "The Good Old Kent Eleven" when such giants of the game as Alfred Mynn, Fuller Pilch, William Hillyer, Ned Wenman and Nicholas "Felix" Wanostrocht were a match for the best in the land. But as these great players grew older and faded from the game, the county went into decline during the early 1850s. From regularly

Alfred Mynn

Fuller Pilch

William Hillyer

Nicholas Felix

beating the England team on a level basis, they were reduced to combining with other counties, or even playing with upwards of 16 men, in order to compete.

The foundations for revival were initially laid with the formation of the County Club in Maidstone in 1859, and then again with the amalgamation with the Beverley Club in Canterbury 11 years later to create the modern county-wide club we know today.

A reading of Lord Harris's reminiscences covering the period 1871–89 in Chapter 5 of *The History of Kent County Cricket Club* makes it clear that there could be no hope of a return to a position of dominance in the immediate future. When the County Championship was reconstituted in 1890 with Kent, Middlesex, Surrey, Sussex, Yorkshire, Lancashire, Nottinghamshire and Gloucestershire as the founding eight sides, Kent could finish no better than mid table. The addition of Derbyshire, Warwickshire, Somerset, Hampshire and Essex from 1895 made little difference, and it wasn't until 1898 that Kent settled into the top ten, where they remained until they eventually slipped to tenth in 1935.

Perhaps the most significant factor contributing to Kent's first "Golden Age" was the development of the Tonbridge Nursery under the sure eye of Captain William McCanlis. McCanlis had played for Kent between 1862 and 1877 and, like the man who helped shape the side of the 1970s – Colin Page – he was only a modest county performer. He played for Kent on 45 occasions and was described in Arthur Haygarth's *Scores & Biographies* as "*a fine and powerful hitter and likewise a good field*".

The other important contributor and influence on the Nursery was Tom Pawley, Kent's General Manager from 1881 to 1923. Educated at Tonbridge, Pawley was another who played a handful of matches for Kent – only four in total between 1882 and 1887 – possibly as a last-minute stand in, since he was also fulfilling the Manager's role at the time. *Wisden* describes him as "*a good batsman and useful bowler, being originally fast, but afterwards, taking to lobs.*"[1] The highlight of his administrative career came when he managed the MCC side to Australia in 1911/12 that regained

William McCanlis, Kent 1862 to 1877
Coach at The Tonbridge Nursery

Tom Pawley
Kent General Manager

the Ashes by four matches to one, largely due to the bowling of the Warwickshire captain, Frank Foster, and Sydney Barnes, who took 32 and 34 wickets respectively in the five Test matches.

Established in 1897, the Tonbridge Nursery was responsible for the development of a steady stream of young professionals, including Colin Blythe, Frank Woolley, James Seymour, Wally Hardinge, Jack Hubble, Ted Humphreys, Bill Fairservice, Tich Freeman and others who were to appear for Kent both before and after the Great War. These professionals came together with a crop of gifted amateurs such as Cuthbert Burnup, Kenneth Hutchings, Sammy and Arthur Day, Dickie Blaker, Jack Mason and Ted Dillon to produce sides that played a highly attractive brand of attacking and successful cricket which set the tone for the decades to come.

McCanlis's and Pawley's work began to bear fruit in the first year of the new century when the county came third in the Championship. This was largely due to the brilliant batting of the inspirational captain, Jack Mason, who scored 1,662 runs at 53.61, and the first hundred-wicket haul of his career for slow left-armer, Colin Blythe. Three years in mid table followed before third place was captured again in 1904. By this time Arthur Fielder had established himself as the spearhead of the pace attack, taking 84 wickets in support of Blythe's 121. The batting owed much to Mason and fellow amateur Sammy Day, who both averaged over 40. There was solid support from the two young professional batsmen, Ted Humphreys and James Seymour, who both made over 1,000 runs in a season for the first time.

Photo, *Mockford,*
Tonbridge.]   Humphreys,   Woolley,   Huish,   Seymour,   W. Hearne,
        Fielder,   Hubble.   R. N. R. Blaker,   C. H. B. Marsham, Capt.,   J. R. Mason,   Fairservice,   K. L. Hutchings.
                    KENT CRICKET TEAM, 1906.

Kent 1906

Here in 1906 – gone by 1913
Sammy Day, "Pinky" Burnup, "Dickie" Blaker, Alec Hearne and "Slug" Marsham

Kent finished sixth in 1905, when four of the players who were to figure in the 1913 Championship winning team were the outstanding contributors – Dillon (1,268 runs at 50.72), Arthur Day (1,050), Seymour (1,284) and Blythe (130 wickets). It was the lack of support for Blythe (only Bill Fairservice, with 62, took more than 50 wickets) that was the main factor in a disappointing season that saw Kent fail to win a single game in any of the traditional cricket "weeks".

Kent's first Championship title came a year later under the shrewd captaincy of Cloudesley Henry Bullock Marsham (who was generally known as Slug). The team combined brilliant amateur batsmen – Kenneth Hutchings, Ted Dillon, Jack Mason and Dickie Blaker – with reliable, skilled professionals – Seymour and Humphreys with the bat and Blythe and Fielder with the ball. Fielder took an incredible 158 wickets and Blythe, 90. This mixture of players created a perfect blend to deliver the county's first Championship.

But matters were far from straightforward. At the start of Tunbridge Wells cricket week on 16th July, Kent stood fifth in the table behind Surrey, Yorkshire, Lancashire and Nottinghamshire. They had played 11 matches, won five, lost two and drawn four. Kent's chances *"seemed little more than a forlorn hope."* [2] Thereafter, they won all of their 11 matches to top the table by 7.78 per cent from Yorkshire in second place. This was not dissimilar to Kent's situation in their first, modern, Championship in 1970 when, at the beginning of July, they were in 17th place in

Middlesex vs Kent at Lord's: *The Graphic* 1st September 1906

"The colt, Woolley deserves more than passing notice" – *Wisden* 1907

the table but went on to clinch the title in the final match at The Oval. It was a remarkable second half of the season in both years.

The 1906 season saw a memorable swansong from one of the country's most consistent batsmen. In his last full season, one of the less showy amateur batsmen, Pinky Burnup, topped the national averages, making 1,116 runs in the Championship at an average of almost 70. Another who finished his career in 1906 was Alec Hearne who, at the time of his retirement, had scored more runs (13,598) and taken more wickets (1,018) than any other Kent player. He is still one of only two Kent players to pass 10,000 runs and take 1,000 wickets – the other, of course, being Frank Woolley.

The same year also saw the emergence of a tall Tonbridge teenager, the son of a well-respected cycle and motor engineer, described in the Kent Trials Book as a "*fair bat*"[3] – Frank Edward Woolley. In 14 Championship games he scored 626 runs at 28.45 and took 42 wickets at 20.04 apiece – a solid enough debut season. *Wisden* in 1907 remarked "*The colt Woolley deserves more than passing notice.*" As

Champion County vs The Rest of England at The Oval 1906
Fielder to Haywood: from *The Graphic* 22nd September 1906

EW Swanton later suggested – something of an understatement. *Wisden* went on *"Good as he already is, Woolley will no doubt, with increased strength, go far ahead of his first season's doings. It is quite possible that within two or three years, he will be the best left handed batsman in England… he bowled uncommonly well but, as the summer advanced, he was regarded more and more as a batsman."*[4]

Kent slipped back to eighth in 1907 but came second in the following year, actually winning more games (17) than in their title-winning season. However, they were beaten three times and lost out to Yorkshire, who remained undefeated all season.

The appointment of a new captain in 1909, Edward Wentworth "Ted" Dillon, heralded back-to-back Championship victories. Dillon would turn out to be the most successful captain in Kent's history, leading the XI in 107 matches and winning an astonishing 69, including three Championships, one second and one third in his five-year tenure.

In 1909, Mason scored 738 runs in just 12 innings to finish top of the batting averages, Hutchings and Humphreys exceeded 1,000 runs and Woolley, Seymour and Arthur Day all fell just short of that milestone. In a season of wet wickets, Blythe had his best return with 178 wickets at 14.07 apiece, Fielder took 81 and Douglas Carr, a googly-bowling schoolmaster, took 51 wickets in eight matches in his debut

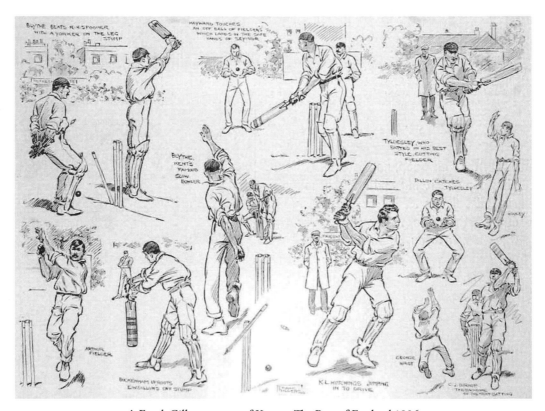

A Frank Gillett cartoon of Kent vs The Rest of England 1906

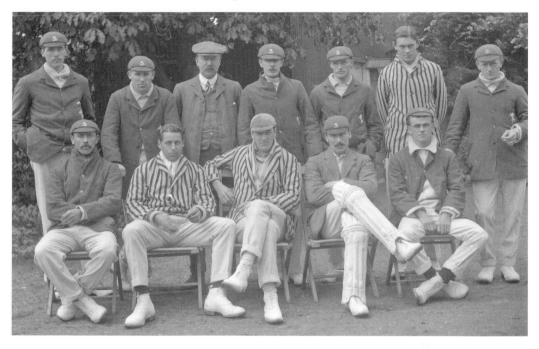

Kent: County Champions 1909
(left to right) back row: FE Woolley, E Humphreys, W Hearne (scorer), W Fairservice, J Seymour, Mr AP Day, W Hardinge. (front) A Fielder, Mr KL Hutchings, Mr EW Dillon (capt), F Huish, C Blythe

season at the age of 37. Carr is one of the more interesting characters of the Kent side between the years 1909 and 1914. Originally from Cranbrook, he attended Sutton Valance School and thereafter went up to Brasenose College in 1891. Playing little cricket at Oxford, he left to become a preparatory schoolmaster and played his club cricket in Kent for The Mote, Band of Brothers, Free Foresters and others. He was a decent club cricketer, who varied his style between leg breaks bowled at a decent pace and straightforward medium pace. Around 1906 he became fascinated with the googly, which he spent the next two years perfecting.

By 1909, Kent were sufficiently intrigued by his bowling that he was picked to play against his old university at the end of May 1909. He was immediately successful, taking 5-65 and 2-30. On the strength of this single performance he was selected to play for The Gentlemen against The Players at The Oval and Lord's in July. His figures were 3-58 and 5-80 at The Oval and, a few days later at Lord's, he took 6-71 and 1-57.

With just three first-class matches under his belt, he was included in the party for the fourth Test against Australia at Old Trafford but didn't play. In the meantime, with his teaching duties completed for the summer, he played three matches for Kent against Essex, Middlesex and Hampshire, collecting 20 wickets at 14.50 each.

He was again included in the side for the fifth Test at the Oval, becoming the first man ever to play Test cricket in his first year in the first-class game. His fellow

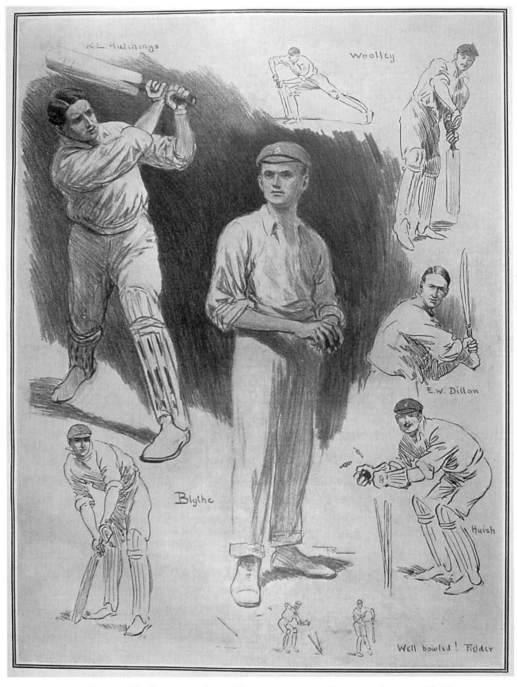

A Frank Reynolds illustration dated 6th August 1910 – Champion County v The Rest

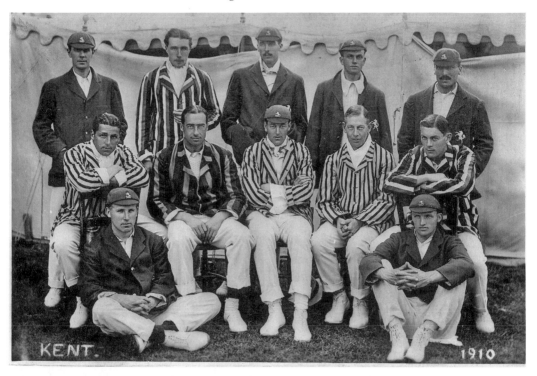

Kent: County Champions 1910
(back row: left to right) W Fairservice, Mr CVL Hooman, FE Woolley, C Blythe, F Huish
(middle row) Mr KL Hutchings, Mr JR Mason, Mr EW Dillon, Mr DW Carr, Mr AP Day
(front row) E Humphreys, J Seymour

England debutant in that match was Frank Woolley. Carr opened the bowling and reduced Australia to 55-3 by dismissing Sid Gregory, Monty Noble and Warwick Armstrong. Carr collected 5-146 in the first innings and 2-136 in the second but never played for England again.

A change in the points system did not deter Kent from retaining the title decisively in 1910. Hutchings, Seymour and Humphreys comfortably made their 1,000 runs and Woolley again narrowly missed out on his. But it was Woolley's bowling that was perhaps the major factor in winning the title. After just 173 wickets in his first four seasons, he took 124 at only 13.14 each, finishing above Blythe, who still took 149 wickets. Carr's nine appearances yielded another remarkable 60 wicket haul at 12.16. But it was Hutchings who not only headed the batting averages but the bowling too – with 1-5 in two overs.

In 1911 Kent were denied a hat-trick of titles when they were pipped at the post by 0.16 of a percentage point. They had to settle for second place when they failed to win their final match and Warwickshire beat Northamptonshire to secure their first title. (For more detail, see the chapter on the extraordinary Kent vs Warwickshire fixture at Tonbridge.) The professional batsmen, Seymour, Humphreys

Kenneth Lotherington Hutchings 1878–1916

and Woolley all exceeded 1,500 runs and Hardinge topped 1,000. Blythe (125) and Fielder (105) were chief wicket takers with Woolley completing a fine all-round season with 70 wickets. Carr collected his by now obligatory 55 wickets in just nine games.

After the frustration and disappointment of the previous year, Kent slipped one place to third in 1912, despite again winning more matches than the sides above them (Yorkshire and Northamptonshire). Runs were not as plentiful as in previous years, with only Woolley and Hardinge reaching 1,000 runs. Blythe accumulated 170 wickets, Woolley narrowly missed the double with 95 wickets and Carr collected 49 wickets in eight matches.

This was the last season in which Kenneth Hutchings appeared for Kent. Although he made his debut in 1902, following an outstanding schoolboy record at Tonbridge, it was not until 1906 that he was able to play on a regular basis. He then passed 1,000 first-class runs in each the six seasons up to 1911. Although some say he failed to fulfil his enormous potential, *"at his best, he was one of the most remarkable batsmen of his generation."*[1] In 1906, it was probably his dashing approach that made the difference, and brought Kent their first Championship. Never quite as spectacular again, he was, nevertheless, the brightest star in the constellation of Kent's amateur batsmen. His method was simple. When on the attack, he went forward and drove with a ferocity that caused the opposition fielders to retreat by an extra yard or so. Backfoot play was usually reserved solely for defence. He was a brilliant fielder, whether in the slips or the outfield, and had the strongest of arms. "*Reclining in a deck chair, he once threw to the far wicket at Canterbury without getting up. On another occasion, from a standing position at the Nackington Road wicket, he threw into the top of the pavilion six times and, taking a short run, threw over the pavilion for an encore.*"[5] In 1912, he made just seven first-class appearances for Kent and only two more for an England XI against the Australians and for MCC against the Champion County, at the end of the season.

Kent Amateurs & Kent Professionals

In the 1906 season, Kent had fielded 20 players in total, divided equally between amateurs and professionals but with appearances split on a 60/40 basis in favour of the professionals. As the years passed, the amateurs found it more difficult to devote their time to playing as much cricket as before, and their involvement steadily declined so that by 1913 amateur appearances had fallen to approximately 20 per cent overall. The only one to appear regularly was the captain, Ted Dillon. Eric Hatfeild and Arthur Day were the only other semi-regulars, appearing in 11 and ten matches respectively during the season. The policy of producing home-grown professionals in the Tonbridge Nursery had, by 1913, paid huge dividends with the graduates scoring 85 per cent of the runs and taking 83 per cent of the wickets.

Even allowing for this natural progression, there was still some controversy over amateurs being selected in the place of more able, professional players. Bill Fairservice and David Jennings in particular were usually the first casualties of amateur availability. Both were very good players who would have played a full Championship programme in just about any other side, including those of Yorkshire, Surrey, Middlesex and Nottinghamshire. Their places were usually rotated according to the availability of Day, Hatfeild and William Powell, the latter two being very much "bit part" players who made only minor contributions during the course of the season.

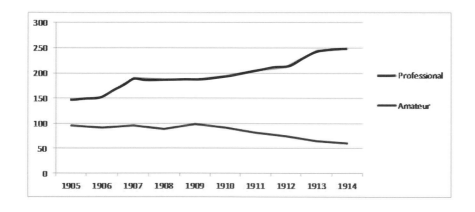

Kent player appearances per season – amateur against professional 1905–1914

Kent County Cricket Club: Analysis of Player Appearances 1905 to 1914

Year	1905	1906	1907	1908	1909	1910	1911	1912	1913	1914	Total	%
Position in Table	6th	1st	8th	2nd	1st	1st	2nd	3rd	*1st*	3rd		
Player												
C Blythe	22	15	22	23	25	23	25	25	*28*	27	235	8.38%
Mr CJ Burnup	1	12	3								16	0.57%
Mr AP Day	20	9	8	14	17	9	10	11	*10*	9	117	4.17%
Mr SH Day	9	1	7	8	9	1	2	8		8	53	1.89%
Mr EW Dillon	15	8	13	11	21	20	16	9	*26*		139	4.96%
WJ Fairservice	20	14	19	19	21	17	16	15	*19*	20	180	6.42%
A Fielder	12	22	25	17	20	16	22	14	*22*	23	193	6.88%
HTW Hardinge	2	4	17	24	15	5	19	26	*28*	27	167	5.95%
Mr WP Harrison	4										4	0.14%
A Hearne	19	10									29	1.03%
JC Hubble	1	9	3	2	2	16	16	21	*26*	25	121	4.31%
FH Huish	22	19	26	24	24	26	26	26	*28*	27	248	8.84%
E Humphreys	21	22	26	25	25	26	25	24	*27*	26	247	8.81%
Mr KL Hutchings	2	16	18	23	25	22	20	6			132	4.71%
Mr F Marchant	2										2	0.07%
Mr CHB Marsham	20	21	18	23	2						84	2.99%
Mr JR Mason	12	12	13	6	12	8	6		*3*	1	73	2.60%
HR Murrell	1										1	0.04%
Mr F Penn Jnr	1										1	0.04%
J Seymour	22	22	26	25	26	26	24	24	*28*	28	251	8.95%
FE Woolley		14	24	25	25	26	24	21	*26*	26	211	7.52%
Mr RNR Blaker	14	12	11								37	1.32%
R Munds			1	1							2	0.07%
Mr LHW Troughton			5	1	2	1	2	4		28	43	1.53%
HJN Preston			1	2	3	6		3	*1*		16	0.57%
Mr CS Hurst				2				3			5	0.18%
DW Jennings					1	2	3	6	*10*	11	33	1.18%
Mr HEW Prest					3		9	3			15	0.53%
Mr DW Carr					8	9	9	8	*8*	1	43	1.53%
Mr CE Hatfeild						2	6	14	*11*	6	39	1.39%
Mr CVL Hooman						14					14	0.50%
Mr FH Knott						6	1	1		2	10	0.36%
PE Morfee						5	4				9	0.32%
GC Collins							1	7	*1*		9	0.32%
Mr WA Powell								2	*6*	1	9	0.32%
Mr WGM Sarel								5		2	7	0.25%
AP Freeman										7	7	0.25%
WE Hickmott										1	1	0.04%
Mr GWE Whitehead										2	2	0.07%
Appearances	242	242	286	275	286	286	286	286	*308*	308		100.00%
Matches	22	22	26	25	26	26	26	26	*28*	28		
Players Used	21	18	20	19	20	22	22	24	*18*	22		
Amateur	96	91	96	88	99	92	81	74	*64*	60		
Professional	146	151	190	187	187	194	205	212	*244*	248		
Amateur %	40%	38%	34%	32%	35%	32%	28%	26%	*21%*	19%		
Professional %	60%	62%	66%	68%	65%	68%	72%	74%	*79%*	81%		

Day was certainly worth his place both as a forcing batsman and an occasionally devastating fast medium bowler with the ability to move the ball away from the batsman. Douglas Carr too was an automatic choice after he first appeared in 1909 in the unusual circumstances already described. Only available during school holidays, his career was telescoped into a mere five years. His leg-breaks and googlies were an invaluable addition to the Kent attack, otherwise packed with orthodox left-arm spin.

One of the difficulties in this area was the established policy that Kent should field a minimum of three amateurs in each game. This policy is referred to several times in the Minute Books of the period. In 1913, however, the minimum was only achieved in 12 out of 28 Championship matches, and in six matches there was only one amateur on the team sheet.

Although the debate about amateur and professional would continue to rage for another fifty years, Kent were one of the more enlightened counties when it came to the matter of amateurs entering onto the field through one gate while the professionals used another. Frank Woolley, in *Early Memories*, says, "*Like Hindu and Mohammedan, who do not drink from the same well, the amateurs entered the playing field by one gate and the professionals by another, a discrimination that wonderful Kent captain J.R. Mason quickly put an end to in our county.*"[6] This act of social egalitarianism by Mason was one of the things that fostered a happy and contented atmosphere in the Kent dressing room – a factor in the coming season's success as it had been in previous years – where the ethos of attacking cricket was paramount. Frank Woolley again, this time from *The King of Games*, says, "*It is in no boasting spirit that I state my belief that we in Kent do play cricket in a spirit rather characteristically our own. To us a defeat is not a case of the skies falling and of the near end of the world, but rather of 'Well done _____shire, good luck to you, you put us where you wanted us this time, next time, we hope to return the compliment'.*"[7]

The 1913 season dawned with Kent having won three Championships in seven seasons and a near miss in 1911. The side was experienced, with an average age of 31, well balanced, with adequate reserves in both batting and bowling. The only uncertainty was whether Arthur Fielder was worthy of his place and if, as was feared, his best days were now behind him, who would fill the need for a bowler of genuine pace on hard wickets? At the age of 35 when the season began, the odds were against him. As matters turned out, to Kent's relief, he still had a couple of good seasons in him.

Sources

1 *Wisden – The Book of Cricketers' Lives* – Benny Green: Macdonald Queen Anne Press, 1986
2 *Kent Cricket Champions 1906* – Clive Porter: Limlow Books 2000
3 Kent CCC Trials book
4 *Wisden* 1907 – Kent Matches
5 *100 Greats – Kent County Cricket Club* – Robertson, Milton & Carlaw 2005
6 *Early Memories* – Frank Woolley: The Cricketer 1976 pp 19
7 *King of Games* – Frank Woolley: Stanley Paul & Co Ltd circa 1935/1936

Sussex 1st Innings

Mr HL Simms	c Dillon b Blythe	3
RR Relf	c Woolley b Blythe	9
J Vine	c Woolley b Blythe	17
AE Relf	c Hardinge b Humphreys	29
Mr PGH Fender	b Fairservice	2
Mr HL Wilson	b Blythe	15
Mr HP Chaplin *	b Fairservice	40
GR Cox	c Dillon b Woolley	2
VWC Jupp	c Hatfeild b Blythe	2
JH Vincett	st Huish b Blythe	3
GB Street +	not out	12
Extras	(5 b, 2 lb)	7
Total	(all out, 66.1 overs)	141

Sussex 2nd Innings

[5] b Fairservice		17
[4] st Huish b Fairservice		4
[2] c Seymour b Fairservice		7
[3] c Fairservice b Humphreys		6
[6] lbw b Powell		0
[1] b Powell		33
run out		7
b Fairservice		20
st Huish b Fairservice		0
not out		3
run out		0
(2 b, 2 lb)		4
(all out, 54 overs)		101

FOW 1st Innings 1-12, 2-12, 3-53, 4-57, 5-64, 6-93, 7-102, 8-107, 9-112, 10-141
FOW 2nd Innings 1-28, 2-39, 3-46, 4-64, 5-68, 6-68, 7-82, 8-86, 9-101, 10-101

Kent bowling	O	M	R	W
Blythe	27	3	63	6
Woolley	19	2	42	1
Humphreys	14	4	25	1
Fairservice	6.1	2	4	2

Kent bowling	O	M	R	W
Blythe	3	0	5	0
Woolley	5	3	9	0
Humphreys	7	1	14	1
Fairservice	24	11	40	5
Powell	15	4	29	2

Kent 1st Innings

E Humphreys	c RR Relf b AE Relf	4
HTW Hardinge	lbw b Simms	43
J Seymour	b Simms	68
FE Woolley	b RR Relf	3
JC Hubble	b RR Relf	15
Mr EW Dillon *	b Simms	16
Mr CE Hatfeild	c Street b Vincett	29
Mr WA Powell	c Street b RR Relf	1
FH Huish +	b RR Relf	0
WJ Fairservice	b RR Relf	5
C Blythe	not out	8
Extras	(10 b, 5 lb)	15
Total	(all out, 94.1 overs)	207

Kent 2nd Innings

not out		18
b Simms		3
not out		14
did not bat		
did not bat		
did not bat		
did not bat		
did not bat		
did not bat		
did not bat		
did not bat		
(1 b)		1
(1 wicket, 10.3 overs)		36

FOW 1st Innings 1-4, 2-123, 3-126, 4-138, 5-157, 6-169, 7-182, 8-182, 9-193, 10-207
FOW 2nd Innings 1-10

Sussex bowling	O	M	R	W
AE Relf	15	7	22	1
Simms	26	7	68	3
Cox	12	1	30	0
Vincett	15	8	28	1
RR Relf	21.1	7	30	5
Fender	3	0	14	0
Jupp	2	2	0	0

Sussex bowling	O	M	R	W
AE Relf	5	1	14	0
Simms	5.3	0	21	1

Sussex vs Kent

The County Ground, Hove
Monday 12th, Tuesday 13th & Wednesday 14th May
Toss: Sussex
Kent won by 9 wickets
Points: Sussex 0 Kent 5

KENT GOT THEIR 1913 campaign off to the best possible start by winning their opening fixture inside two days against Sussex at Hove. The match was due to start on Whit Monday, but heavy rain fell for most of the day so that not a ball was bowled. Sussex were thereby robbed of one of their best gate receipts of the season – only August Bank Holiday Monday usually exceeded the May Bank Holiday crowd. *"Rain fell continuously for upwards of twelve hours, a drying wind sprung up and the ground made such a quick recovery that the delay in starting the match on Tuesday only amounted to a further half-hour."*[1] *Wisden* says that *"to a large extent, the rain of the previous day spoiled the wicket"* but, when Sussex won the toss, somewhat curiously, they decided to bat. Knowing folk shook their heads and predicted a very low score, particularly as the hot sun looked like turning the pitch into a real "sticky dog". As it happened, the wicket, while helpful right from the start, hadn't yet reached the state where it was really difficult.

Sussex, however, were soon in trouble against Blythe and Woolley. Harry Simms and Bob Relf were both dismissed in the same over from Blythe with the score on 12. Joe Vine and Albert Relf, the elder of the two brothers, batted well against the two left-armers to put on 41 for the third wicket in 50 minutes – *"Relf at intervals, bringing off*

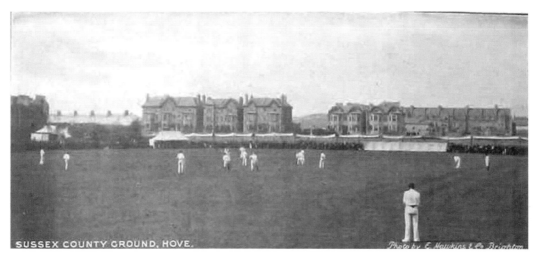

Hove circa 1910

some capital hits."[2] Blythe collected his third wicket by finding the edge of Vine's bat and Woolley took the catch at slip. Percy Fender went for just two, bowled by Fairservice, who had been tried to see if offspin might be more effective than orthodox left-arm spin. Briefly it was. There was some spirited resistance from Herbert Wilson making his first appearance for Sussex, and also from the captain, Herbert Chaplin, who kept out everything and was the last wicket to fall for a good, if somewhat charmed, 40. "*He withstood the bowling for an hour and a half. He gave a chance and was lucky with some of his other strokes. For all that, his innings was one of considerable merit.*" [1]

None of the remaining batsman could cope with Blythe, who made the most of the conditions to finish with 6-63 from 27 overs, despite not having had the best of luck. Fairservice had only bowled 6.1 overs but taken 2-4.

The Sussex total of 141 all out was considerably better than many had predicted when they began their innings, and they had kept Kent in the field for three hours "*because they had not made the most of their chances*".[2]

When Kent batted, they immediately found themselves in difficulty against Albert Relf and Simms, and took 20 minutes to reach four when Humphreys edged Albert Relf to his brother at slip. The bowlers, however, could not maintain this momentum. "*For the moment, the visitors looked likely to experience considerable difficulty in reaching the Sussex total but the bowling fell off and Seymour and Hardinge, seizing their opportunity, scored at a capital rate.*"[2]

Kent's main wicket tackers: Blythe (6-63) and Fairservice (2-4 and 5-40)

Albert Relf:
"some capital hits"

James Seymour:
"a sparkling 68"

Towards the close, the Sussex attack, led by Bob Relf, bowled better but by that time the batsmen were set, and reached the close without further loss at 108-1. Seymour had made 57 and Hardinge 39, adding 104 in less than two hours.

Next morning, the two not out batsmen did not survive long. Hardinge, *"who had batted with considerable skill and care for two hours and a half"*[3], was trapped lbw by Simms with the score at 123, and Seymour was bowled by the same man for *"a sparkling 68. His admirable innings was characterised by resolute driving and pulling and strong defence, included seven fours."*[3] The innings then fell away in much the same way the Sussex innings had done except for *"some vigorous work"* by Hatfield and lesser contributions from Dillon and Hubble. Kent lunched at 207-9 but lost their last wicket to the first ball of the afternoon session. Bob Relf had taken 5-30 from 21.1 overs, and although Kent had lost their last eight wickets for 84 runs, they still had a lead of 66 on first innings which, with the wicket still difficult, was significant.

In their second innings, Sussex lost half of their wickets in clearing the arrears, with Wilson the only batsman to look comfortable. Dillon switched his bowlers about quickly at the start of the innings. Fairservice was introduced after only six overs, and then bowled unchanged for the rest of the innings. The openers appeared to be simply intent upon survival. Nevertheless, they still scored 28 in 35

Robert Relf: 5-30 from 21.1 overs

minutes before Vine was caught in the slips by Seymour. The Relf brothers were next to go cheaply, reducing Sussex to 46-3. Simms remained with Wilson, who was then bowled for 33 by Powell and, in the next over, he hurried one on to Fender and trapped him lbw. The Sussex captain was then run out through some smart work in the field by Humphreys.

At tea, Sussex were only ten runs ahead with four wickets remaining. *The Times* correspondent was surprised that Kent had agreed to an interval (which they were entitled to deny, due to the playing regulations at that time) as "*Kent might easily have lost their victory… and they might have been very hard pressed for time had not two batsmen been run out on resuming.*"[4] *Cricket Magazine* however, attempted humour to emphasise that perhaps Kent were merely toying with their hosts: "*The Kent captain testified to the deplorable wickedness of his disposition by consenting to a tea interval, proposed by his fellow-criminal of Sussex, one gathers.*"[5]

The last resistance came from George Cox, who made a spirited 20 before being bowled by Fairservice. The Sussex innings ended at 25 minutes past five, leaving Kent just 36 runs to win. Fairservice had taken 5-40 from 24 overs, including 11 maidens. Kent made the required runs for the loss of Hardinge with 25 minutes to spare. Hardinge's failure was compensated by what *The Sportsman* called "*his brilliant fielding on the boundary that saved many runs.*"[6]

The season had started well for Kent but very poorly for the defending Champions, Yorkshire, who lost their opening match at Old Trafford against Lancashire by an innings and three runs. They were bowled out for scores of 74 and

Harry Simms: Sussex debutant

53 on a rain-affected wicket, with James Heap taking 11-39 in the match. Elsewhere, there were wins for Derbyshire, Middlesex and Nottinghamshire.

Sources

1 *Kent Messenger* 17th May 1913
2 *The Manchester Courier* 14th May 1913
3 *The Manchester Courier* 15th May 1913
4 *The Times* 15th May 1913
5 *Cricket Magazine* 17th May 1913
6 *The Sportsman* 15th May 1913

13th May 1913	P	W	L	DWF	DLF	NC	Max	Pts	PtsPC
Kent	1	1	0	0	0	0	5	5	100.00%
Nottinghamshire	1	1	0	0	0	0	5	5	100.00%
Middlesex	1	1	0	0	0	0	5	5	100.00%
Lancashire	1	1	0	0	0	0	5	5	100.00%
Derbyshire	1	1	0	0	0	0	5	5	100.00%
Northamptonshire	2	1	0	0	1	0	10	6	60.00%
Worcestershire	1	0	0	1	0	0	5	3	60.00%
Somerset	1	0	0	1	0	0	5	3	60.00%
Surrey	2	0	1	1	0	0	10	3	30.00%
Gloucestershire	1	0	0	0	1	0	5	1	20.00%
Warwickshire	1	0	0	0	1	0	5	1	20.00%
Yorkshire	1	0	1	0	0	0	5	0	0.00%
Sussex	1	0	1	0	0	0	5	0	0.00%
Hampshire	1	0	1	0	0	0	5	0	0.00%
Leicestershire	1	0	1	0	0	0	5	0	0.00%
Essex	1	0	1	0	0	0	5	0	0.00%

Kent 1st Innings

E Humphreys	lbw b Tarrant	1
HTW Hardinge	run out	20
J Seymour	b Douglas	15
FE Woolley	b Watson	5
JC Hubble	b Hearne	11
Mr EW Dillon *	lbw b Watson	4
Mr CE Hatfeild	c Whittington b Buckenham	20
Mr WA Powell	c Whittington b Hearne	8
FH Huish+	lbw b Tarrant	9
C Blythe	c and b Hearne	3
A Fielder	not out	0
Extras	(10 b, 1 lb)	11
Total	(all out, 35.1 overs)	107

FOW 1st Innings 1-1, 2-20, 3-44, 4-45, 5-57, 6-84, 7-86, 8-93, 9-107, 10-107

Kent 2nd Innings

c and b Douglas		0
lbw b Hearne		30
st Douglas-Jones b Douglas		3
c Doll b Tarrant		1
lbw b Douglas		4
c Thomson b Tarrant		30
b Hearne		25
b Tarrant		0
lbw b Tarrant		7
c Doll b Tarrant		1
not out		5
(9 b, 1 lb)		10
(all out, 45.4 overs)		116

FOW 2nd Innings 1-0, 2-10, 3-13, 4-19, 5-60, 6-96, 7-96, 8-100, 9-101, 10-116

MCC bowling	O	M	R	W
Douglas	7	1	25	1
Tarrant	13.1	3	25	2
Watson	5	1	23	2
Buckenham	4	0	15	1
Hearne	6	5	8	3

MCC bowling	O	M	R	W
Douglas	10	4	19	3
Tarrant	15.4	5	30	5
Buckenham	6	2	16	0
Hearne	13	1	36	2
Haig	1	0	5	0

MCC 1st Innings

Mr JWHT Douglas * Essex	b Fielder	0
FA Tarrant Middlesex	c Huish b Powell	29
JW Hearne Middlesex	b Blythe	0
Major EP Thomson MCC	st Huish b Blythe	25
Mr NE Haig Middlesex	run out	3
Mr TAL Whittington MCC	b Humphreys	30
Capt. SD Douglas-Jones + MCC	c Seymour b Blythe	7
Mr MHC Doll Middlesex	b Blythe	4
CP Buckenham Essex	not out	5
H Watson MCC	c Fielder b Humphreys	5
Mr JE Raphael Surrey	absent hurt	
Extras	(7 b, 2 lb, 1 w)	10
Total	(all out, 51.1 overs)	118

FOW 1st Innings 1-0, 2-7, 3-52, 4-56, 5-78, 6-102, 7-106, 8-110, 9-118

MCC 2nd Innings

run out	1
c Huish b Powell	31
did not bat	
b Humphreys	2
not out	39
[2] ct Huish b Powell	31
[6] not out	7
did not bat	
did not bat	
did not bat	
did not bat	
(1 nb)	1
(4 wickets, 33.4 overs)	111

FOW 2nd Innings 1-1, 2-44, 3-47, 4-85

Kent bowling	O	M	R	W
Fielder	12	2	31	1
Blythe	15	1	38	4
Powell	7	4	4	1
Woolley	10	2	18	0
Humphreys	7.1	1	17	2

Kent bowling	O	M	R	W
Fielder	6	0	16	0
Blythe	11	4	34	1
Powell	3	1	9	1
Woolley	3	1	17	0
Hatfeild	1.4	0	11	0

MCC vs Kent

Lord's Cricket Ground, St John's Wood
Thursday 15th & Friday 16th May
Toss: MCC
MCC won by 6 wickets

KENT ARRIVED AT Lord's to play against the Marylebone Club who were captained by Johnny Douglas. His side included seven amateurs, of which two were current serving army officers neither of whom had previously played first-class cricket. Also making his first-class debut was Harold Watson, who had previously played for Norfolk before joining the Lord's Ground Staff for the 1913 season.

Kent made one change to the side that won in the Championship at Hove the previous day, leaving out Fairservice for Fielder. The weather was fine but there was a cold wind blowing down the ground from the north east, "*the sort of day that often comes at this time of year, when fielding is not an unmixed blessing and the ball hurts.*"[1] The wicket was slow, as might be expected in the very early season, but it also produced some variable bounce. Douglas won the toss and invited Kent to bat "*and as events proved, he was well rewarded. The Kent batsmen could not do very much.*"[1] Hardinge and Dillon were the top scorers with 30 each but the best innings came from "*Mr CE Hatfeild, who is a much improved cricketer.*"[1] Woolley was dismissed by Watson with his first ball in first-class cricket and Kent were bowled out for a meagre 116 shortly after lunch. It was a thoroughly mediocre total on a surface that *The Times* described as "never really difficult".

Fielder made an impressive start to his first match of the season by clean bowling Douglas without a run on the board and then, with the score at seven, Blythe bowled "Young" Jack Hearne for a duck. Frank Tarrant, Major Thompson and Tom Whittington[2] were the mainstays of the MCC innings, which was barely

Lord's Cricket ground: home of the MCC

more impressive than that of their opponents. Kent eventually conceded an 11-run deficit on first innings with Blythe taking 4-38 from 15 overs. Only ten men batted in the MCC innings as Mr Rafael *"had the misfortune to put his shoulder out during the Kent innings in throwing up the ball from the deep field and he was, of course, unable to bat."*[1]

The MCC innings closed at approximately ten minutes to six, leaving Kent an awkward half hour to bat before stumps. As so often happens in cricket, it was this short session that virtually determined the outcome of the match. *"Mr Douglas, bowling from the pavilion end, at once caught and bowled Humphreys. With 10 on the board, Seymour was stumped down the leg side, so far as could be seen, the ball coming off the wicket keeper's pads. Four runs later, Woolley was caught off Tarrant's bowling and before half past six, Mr Douglas got Hubble out lbw."*[1] The score was 19-4 at the close with Dillon, Hatfeild and possibly Powell as the only recognised batsmen remaining.

The following morning, Kent improved on their bad start of the previous evening by adding a further 92 for their remaining six wickets with Hardinge and Dillon each contributing 30 and Hatfeild, 25 but nobody else reached double figures. Tarrant was the most successful bowler for MCC with 5-30. The most interesting

Eric Hatfeild and Ted Dillon

The Lord's Pavilion circa 1908 and the means of cropping the grass

feature of the Kent innings was a "Grace-like" refusal, by Dillon, to leave the wicket when given out caught by Hearne off the bowling of Buckenham.

"Off a rising ball from Buckenham, Mr Dillon looked to have been caught close to the ground by JW Hearne at third slip. Butt, the umpire at the bowler's end, had his view somewhat obstructed and referred to Trott who gave the batsman out. Hearne, however, in reply to a direct question from Mr Dillon expressed a doubt as to whether he had taken the catch and, notwithstanding the the umpire's ruling, Mr Douglas said "Not Out" and Mr Dillon continued batting."[4]

With MCC needing 106 to win, and with the wicket now dry and good for batting, Kent quickly removed Douglas, who was run out by a direct hit from third man with the score on one. Hearne with 30 and Capt. Douglas-Jones with 31 batted sensibly while Nigel Haig attacked. The match was won for MCC when Haig hit Hatfeild into the pavilion for six with the ball striking the wall just below the first balcony – a significant blow but nowhere near that struck by the watching umpire, Albert Trott, some 14 years previously.[4]

The winning margin was six wickets.

Sources

1   *The Times* 16th May 1913
2   Tom Whittington was one of the main influences on the cricket of Glamorgan and had first played for them in 1901. He continued to turn out for them until 1923, captaining the side for his last two years. It was his hard work on behalf of the Welsh county that led to their entry into the County Championship in 1929. In honour of his services to the Club, he was elected as Glamorgan's first ever Life Member – Dr A Hignell Hon Statistician to Glamorgan CCC
3   *The Times* 17th May 1913
4   The umpire was Albert Trott, the Australian-born all-rounder, who played for both Australia and England in Test match cricket. Trott first represented Australia in 1894/5 when he played against England at Adelaide, taking 8 for 43 and scoring 38 and 72 (both not out) – a remarkable debut. In the second Test at Sidney, he scored 85 not out but, inexplicably, didn't bowl. He was omitted from the Australian touring party to England in 1896 despite his brother, GHH "Harry" Trott, being included in the side, although at the time the side was selected, Harry Trott had not been appointed as captain. Albert Trott

Lord's Cricket Ground 1911: Eton vs Harrow

then travelled independently to England and qualified for Middlesex, for whom he first appeared in 1898. In 1899, he was selected for MCC to play against the Australian tourists, and in the course of his innings, he hit Monty Noble over the pavilion and out of the ground with the ball landing in the garden of a house in Grove End Road. In 1907, Trott was awarded a Benefit Match against Somerset at Lord's. In the second Somerset innings on the final morning, Trott ran through the batting to take 7-20 so that Somerset were all out for 97 before the luncheon interval. In those days, the gentry left their offices in the City and West End at lunchtime to watch their cricket during the afternoon and early evening. In producing this inspired spell, Trott had done himself out of a sizeable collection that may well have changed the subsequent course of his life. One of the foremost all-rounders of the day, his life ended tragically. He retired in 1910 and became an umpire for a few years. In 1914, he was living alone in Willesden. By this stage, he was suffering from dropsy (oedema) and melancholia. He wrote out his Last Will & Testament on the back of an old laundry ticket, leaving his entire worldly possessions, consisting of his wardrobe and the sum of £4 in cash, to his landlady. On 30th July 1914, he took a revolver and shot himself through the head.

Trott the umpire

Trott the bowler

Trott the batsman

Kent 1st Innings

E Humphreys	lbw b Melle	22
HTW Hardinge	c Herring b Davies	19
J Seymour	b Davies	96
FE Woolley	not out	224
Mr EW Dillon *	b Hosie	39
Mr LHW Troughton	lbw b Hosie	0
Mr CE Hatfeild	c Peat b Hosie	0
WA Powell	b Hosie	1
FH Huish +	b Peat	18
C Blythe	c Fraser b Peat	7
A Fielder	run out	2
Extras	(38 b, 14 lb)	52
Total	(all out, 96.1 overs)	480

FOW 1st Innings 1-47, 2-49, 3-259, 4-386, 5-386, 6-390, 7-397, 8-445, 9-452, 10-480

OUCC bowling	O	M	R	W
Melle	22	2	88	1
Peate	22	0	90	2
Davies	26	2	98	2
Fraser	9.1	0	63	0
Wilkinson	6	0	54	0
Hosie	11	3	35	4

OUCC 1st Innings

Mr FH Knott	c and b Blythe	24
Mr EF Herring	run out	9
Mr IPF Campbell *	lbw b Blythe	70
Mr GRR Colman	c Huish b Powell	17
Mr WAC Wilkinson	c Woolley b Humphreys	12
Mr AL Hosie	c Seymour b Fielder	3
Mr BGV Melle	b Blythe	14
Mr EA Shaw +	not out	44
Mr PH Davies	st Huish b Blythe	3
Mr JN Fraser	lbw b Blythe	4
Mr CU Peat	b Humphreys	2
Extras	(11 b, 9 lb, 2 nb, 1 w)	23
Total	(all out, 72.5 overs)	225

OUCC 2nd innings

c Huish b Fielder	0
b Humphreys	21
lbw b Humphreys	23
b Fielder	29
c Hatfeild b Humphreys	7
c and b Blythe	15
not out	28
lbw b Blythe	18
st Huish b Blythe	0
run out	3
lbw b Blythe	0
(1 b, 9 lb)	10
(all out, 54.3 overs)	154

FOW 1st Innings 1-22, 2-39, 3-70, 4-99, 5-115, 6-149, 7-182, 8-188, 9-222, 10-225
FOW 2nd Innings 1-0, 2-43, 3-50, 4-68, 5-99, 6-106, 7-149, 8-149, 9-152, 10-154

Kent bowling	O	M	R	W
Fielder	18	5	51	1
Blythe	25	8	68	5
Powell	14	2	57	1
Humphreys	6.5	1	13	2
Woolley	9	4	13	0

Kent bowling	O	M	R	W
Fielder	11	2	34	2
Woolley	10	4	12	0
Humphreys	12	2	36	3
Hatfeild	7	1	22	0
Powell	5	0	13	0
Blythe	9.3	2	27	4

Oxford University vs Kent

The University Parks, Oxford
Monday 19th, Tuesday 20th & Wednesday 21st May
Toss: Kent
Kent won by an innings and 101 runs

KENT SHRUGGED OFF their defeat at the hands of the MCC at Lord's and consoled themselves by pummelling the University attack for 480 on the first day, largely with the hands of Frank Woolley and James Seymour.

Oxford had high hopes for their cricket in 1913 but, "*considering the number of good cricketers in residence, Oxford proved a disappointing side. In May, there seemed to be all the material to build a side of more than ordinary strength and totals of 445 against MCC and 407 against the Free Foresters suggested the batting would be quite formidable. However, from various causes, including accidents to the players, things went wrong and the result was a very poor season.*"[1]

Kent arrived at The Parks the day after Oxford had roundly beaten HK Foster's XI by 157 runs at a time when their expectations were still high. The visitors made one change from the side that played at Lords, bringing in Lionel Troughton for Jack Hubble.

Kent won the toss and made excellent use of a perfect batting wicket. Oxford's task was made no easier when "*play was interrupted occasionally by small showers which made the ball difficult to hold.*"[2] The Kent openers, however, were out for a fairly moderate opening partnership within two runs of each other to leave the score at 49-2. This brought together the main batsmen of the day in Seymour

The University Parks, Oxford, circa 1910

and Woolley. "*Both batsmen played delightful cricket, Woolley in particular playing with characteristic freedom. Mr IPF Campbell tried several changes of bowling and placed his field well, but when two batsmen of this type get set on a perfect wicket, it is impossible to stop the scoring.*"[1] The partnership for the third wicket was worth 210 before Seymour was bowled by Davies, four short of his hundred, from a ball he made no attempt to play. Woolley was dropped on 78 by Freddie Knott, who had gone up to Oxford in 1911, having already played six matches for Kent in 1910. This generosity to his Kent professional was to prove costly as Woolley went on to make his highest score of the season, being not out at the end of the innings with 224 scored in 270 minutes, including 31 fours and a six. "*The feature of the day's play was Woolley's innings. Except for the chance referred to he never looked like getting out and drove and cut with delightful freedom. It is always a pleasure to watch Woolley bat and his display yesterday was no exception.*"[1]

The next day, the weather was very cold, and it may well have been the cause of the Kent fielding falling below their normal standard. The temperature would also have been of concern to the exhibitors at the RHS Great Spring Show which was being staged in the grounds of the Royal Hospital at Chelsea for the first time that morning.

Top scorer for the students was their captain, Ion Campbell, who played his county cricket for Surrey between 1910 and 1927. Campbell made 70 before falling lbw to Blythe but was missed three times. He received his best support from Edward Shaw, the wicketkeeper, who made 44 which contained "*several lucky strokes which*

Woolley and Seymour: a partnership of 219 at Oxford

The Pavilion as originally proposed at The Parks, Oxford

fell out of harm's way… Oxford should have made more runs. They are too uneven and tend to get out to reckless strokes."[3] The innings closed on 225 with Blythe taking 5-68 from 25 overs. Asked to follow on, Oxford reached 99-5 by stumps with Humphreys collecting three of the wickets to fall.

On the third morning, Kent took the remaining Oxford wickets for 55 runs. *"Oxford gave a disappointing display and with the exception of Mr BG von Melle, who made a few good drives and Mr GRR Coleman who played steadily, no one offered any resistance to the Kent bowling."*[4]

Wisden says, *"The Dark Blues found themselves quite unequal to the task of holding their own against Kent, an hour's cricket on Wednesday finishing the match in favour of the county by an innings and 101 runs.*"[5] The last three wickets were taken by Blythe for five runs to give him match figures of 9-95.

While Kent were providing a tutorial for Oxford's dreaming squires, Sussex had bounced back from their defeat by Kent to win their match against Middlesex at Lord's by 33 runs. Among the other sides expected to do well in the Championship in 1913, Surrey had an easy victory over Gloucestershire by 260 runs.

Sources

1	*Wisden* 1914 p 337
2	*The Times* 20th May 1913
3	*The Times* 21st May 1913
4	*The Times* 22nd May 1913
5	*Wisden* 1914 p 344

Kent 1st Innings

E Humphreys	c & b King	77
HTW Hardinge	c Wood b Geary	56
J Seymour	c Geary b Astill	1
FE Woolley	c & b Shipman	71
JC Hubble	lbw b Skelding	13
Mr EW Dillon *	c King b Skelding	49
Mr CE Hatfeild	c Geary b Skelding	22
FH Huish+	c Whitehead b Geary	2
WJ Fairservice	c Whitehead b Shipman	9
C Blythe	b Shipman	5
A Fielder	not out	2
Extras	(4 b, 3 lb, 3 nb, 1 w)	11
Total	(all out, 101.3 overs)	318

FOW 1st Innings 1-92, 2-95, 3-192, 4-214, 5-260, 6-287, 7-290, 8-305, 9-313, 10-318

Kent 2nd Innings

not out		1
c Shields b Shipman		0
not out		8
did not bat		
did not bat		
did not bat		
did not bat		
did not bat		
did not bat		
did not bat		
did not bat		
Extras	(1 b, 1w)	2
Total	(1 wicket, 2.2 overs)	11

FOW 2nd Innings 1-2

Leicestershire bowling	O	M	R	W
Shipman	22.3	2	73	3
King	28	9	52	1
Skelding	22	3	67	3
Astill	11	1	46	1
Geary	18	2	69	2

Leicestershire bowling	O	M	R	W
Shipman	1.2	1	3	1
Skelding	1	0	6	0

Leicestershire 1st Innings

Mr CJB Wood	c Hubble b Fairservice	3
Major EL Challenor	c Huish b Fielder	0
H Whitehead	c Hubble b Fielder	10
W Shipman	c Woolley b Fielder	1
Mr J Shields *+	c Hubble b Fielder	5
JH King	c Dillon b Fielder	20
A Monteney	c Huish b Fielder	0
A Lord	c Huish b Woolley	22
WE Astill	c Huish b Fielder	14
G Geary	c Seymour b Fairservice	42
A Skelding	not out	5
Extras	(9 b, 1 nb)	10
Total	(all out 53.3 overs)	132

FOW 1st Innings 1-3, 2-5, 3-8, 4-16, 5-27, 6-27, 7-42, 8-69, 9-103, 10-132

Leicestershire 2nd Innings

c Dillon b Fielder		13
b Fielder		10
run out		43
[9] b Humphreys		43
[8] c Huish b Fielder		35
[4] c Fielder b Fairservice		13
[5] st Huish b Woolley		1
[6] c Huish b Fielder		20
[7] c Hubble b Fielder		0
not out		1
c Huish b Fielder		0
(5 b, 4 lb, 7 nb)		16
(all out 61 overs)		195

FOW 2nd Innings 1-19, 2-37, 3-60, 4-61, 5-95, 6-95, 7-126, 8-186, 9-194, 10-195

Kent bowling	O	M	R	W
Fielder	18	4	50	7
Fairservice	17.3	8	24	2
Blythe	9	3	25	0
Humphreys	5	0	14	0
Woolley	4	1	9	1

Kent bowling	O	M	R	W
Fielder	18	2	69	6
Fairservice	19	3	45	1
Blythe	11	4	25	0
Humphreys	4	0	27	1
Woolley	9	3	13	1

Leicestershire vs Kent

Aylestone Road, Leicester
Thursday 22nd & Friday 23rd May
Toss: Kent
Kent won by 9 wickets
Points: Leicestershire 0 Kent 5

THE EARLY FINISH at The Parks allowed the Kent side to take an earlier train to Leicester for their Championship fixture the next day.

The match was played at Aylestone Road, Leicester, and not the current home of Leicestershire cricket, Grace Road. The position is, however, confusing to say the least. Up to the 1890s, what we now know as the Grace Road ground was the home of the county club, but was sometimes known as Aylestone Road because that was the nearest major road to the ground. In 1901, Leicestershire moved to the new Aylestone Road ground, and Grace Road only became known as Grace Road when Leicestershire returned to the ground in 1946, by which time there was a housing estate separating it from Aylestone Road. Between 1901 and 1946, Aylestone Road was the home of Leicestershire CCC. The ground still exists today and is the home ground of Leicester Electricity Sports Cricket Club, although there is no longer a connection with the Electricity Board.[1]

Turning to the match itself, *Wisden* tells us that Leicestershire lost this match *"chiefly because of their indiscretion in dealing with Fielder's fast bowling"*.[2] which in view of the fact that he took 13 wickets in the match, might not only seem to be stating the obvious, but also unfair on Fielder. He had been seriously out of form during the previous season, taking only 28 wickets at 35.75 each with his best analysis being 4-58. His return to form was most welcome, as in his previous matches in this season, at Lord's and Oxford, he had been ineffective, taking only four wickets in four innings.

Aylestone Road, Leicester

Kent won the toss and had no hesitation in batting first on a hard wicket. Their first innings total of 318 was thought only moderate and Leicestershire "*seemed to have done fairly well in dismissing Kent on a hard pitch before 6 o'clock.*"[2] Three batsman reached fifty – Humphreys, Hardinge and Woolley with Dillon falling just one short. The pick of these was Woolley, who scored his runs in just 70 minutes in brilliant fashion, whereas Humphreys and Hardinge had both given chances during their innings. In the last half hour of the day, Kent made quick inroads into the Leicestershire top order by removing Cecil Wood, Major Edward Challenor and Bill Shipman to leave them on 11-3 at stumps.

The following morning, there was little respite for Leicestershire with Fielder bowling at great pace which the batsmen clearly didn't relish, and "*they followed the example of those already out by playing half-heartedly at Fielder's very quick, short pitched bowling.*"[2] They were reduced to 69-8 when Albert Lord, who was missed before scoring, came together with the 20-year-old George Geary to put on 34 for the ninth wicket. Geary and Alec Skelding then added another 29 for the final wicket to improve the score significantly to 132 all out. Geary finished as the top scorer with 42. Fielder had taken 7 for 50 from 18 overs, with all but one of his wickets coming from catches behind the wicket and in the slips. The only time he hit the stumps was when Challenor got a thick inside edge and played on.[2]

With a lead of 186, Kent asked Leicestershire to follow on. Second time round the home side fared better, but still found themselves six wickets down for 95 and unable to find any real answer to Fielder's pace. It was left to the captain, John Shields, Shipman and Harry Whitehead to offer real resistance as they put on 60 for the eighth wicket. Shields was finally caught behind to give Fielder his fifth wicket, and his sixth followed shortly when he dismissed Skelding in the same manner to finish off the innings for 195. This left the Kent batsmen to score only 11 for victory. Shipman secured a small consolation prize in getting Hardinge out for a duck. The match was completed inside two days.

Another view of Aylestone Road, Leicester circa 1925

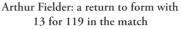

Arthur Fielder: a return to form with
13 for 119 in the match

Ewart Astill: who in 1935 was to become the
first professional to captain a county side[4]

Fielder's fine form prompted the *Kent Messenger* to ponder that, if he could continue to produce this form, *"It should make all the difference to Kent, for without him on hard wickets, the Kentish attack is not very formidable at this point of the season.*[3]*"* An apt qualification given the potency of Blythe and Woolley on soft and wet wickets, but probably referring to the need for some variation in the form of Douglas Carr, who would only become available from July.

Sources

1   Leicester Electricity Sports CC
2   *Wisden's Cricketer's Almanack* 1914 – Sidney Pardon
3   *The Kent Messenger* 31st May 1913
4   Ewart Astill had the distinction of becoming the first professional to captain a first-class county in 1935. He first played for Leicestershire as a 16-year-old in 1904. He was commissioned during his military service in World War I. His career lasted until 1939 and included 9 appearances for England. During World War II he was employed as a coach at Tonbridge School where one of his charges was Colin Cowdrey.

Kent 1st Innings

E Humphreys	c Daniell b Hylton-Stewart	53
HTW Hardinge	c and b White	38
J Seymour	c Chidgey b White	5
FE Woolley	c Braund b White	36
JC Hubble	b White	9
Mr AP Day	b White	7
Mr EW Dillon *	c Braund b White	14
Mr CE Hatfeild	b Robson	11
FH Huish +	not out	24
C Blythe	b Robson	19
A Fielder	c Robson b White	5
Extras	(5 b, 6 lb, 1 nb)	12
Total	(all out, 62.5 overs)	233

FOW 1st Innings 1-80, 2-90, 3-112, 4-140, 5-150, 6-157, 7-176, 8-178, 9-222, 10-233

Kent 2nd Innings

	c Robson b White	70
	b Hardy	105
	c Robson b White	118
	b Hylton-Stewart	60
	b Hylton-Stewart	31
	not out	1
	did not bat	
	did not bat	
	did not bat	
	did not bat	
	did not bat	
	(1 lb, 1 nb, 1 w)	3
	(5 wickets dec, 94.3 overs)	389

FOW 2nd Innings 1-118, 2-250, 3-330, 4-374, 5-389

Somerset bowling	O	M	R	W
Hylton-Stewart	13	0	73	1
Robson	18	1	54	2
White	25.5	7	83	7
Hardy	6	2	11	0

Somerset bowling	O	M	R	W
Hylton-Stewart	18.3	2	98	2
Robson	22	0	87	0
White	32	5	96	2
Hardy	21	0	95	1
Braund	1	0	10	0

Somerset 1st Innings

Mr J Daniell	run out	33
Mr MP Bajana	c Dillon b Day	10
Mr PR Johnson	b Blythe	15
LC Braund	c and b Woolley	28
Mr ESM Poyntz *	b Blythe	0
Capt. LES Ward	b Fielder	0
E Robson	run out	1
Mr BD Hylton-Stewart	b Fielder	1
FP Hardy	c Huish b Fielder	42
Mr JC White	not out	1
H Chidgey +	c Seymour b Fielder	3
Extras	(8 b, 1 lb, 3 nb)	12
Total	(all out, 58.5 overs)	146

FOW 1st Innings 1-13, 2-57, 3-58, 4-58, 5-59, 6-61, 7-70, 8-139, 9-143, 10-146

Somerset 2nd Innings

	c Woolley b Humphreys	30
	b Blythe	29
	run out	0
	c Woolley b Fielder	6
	c Hubble b Woolley	24
	c Dillon b Woolley	3
	b Blythe	8
	c Seymour b Woolley	1
	not out	10
	c Huish b Woolley	5
	c Fielder b Woolley	0
	(2 b, 3 nb, 1 w)	6
	(all out, 32.1 overs)	122

FOW 1st Innings 1-58, 2-58, 3-60, 4-77, 5-82, 6-100, 7-104, 8-110, 9-116, 10-122

Kent bowling	O	M	R	W
Fielder	16.5	5	37	4
Day	12	1	40	1
Blythe	10	4	31	2
Woolley	15	7	20	1
Humphreys	5	1	6	0

Kent bowling	O	M	R	W
Fielder	9	0	24	1
Day	4	0	16	0
Blythe	8	1	43	2
Woolley	7.1	2	21	5
Humphreys	4	0	12	1

Kent vs Somerset

Private Banks Sports Ground, Catford
Monday 26th, Tuesday 27th & Wednesday 28th May
Toss: Kent
Kent won by 354 runs
Points: Kent 5 Somerset 0

THE TWO-DAY victory at Leicester had earned the players an extra day off before they met Somerset at Catford. Kent had first played at The Private Banks Sports Ground in 1875 when the town was still, technically, part of Kent. At that time, Kent had not settled on St Lawrence as their headquarters and there was some discussion as to whether Catford should become a permanent base. In 1899, Catford was absorbed into the newly formed London County Council. Looking at the matter a hundred years later, there is an argument that Kent would have been better served, in financial terms at least, by having their headquarters in Metropolitan Kent – although having a London postal address might be seen as carrying matters slightly too far.

Kent made one change as Day came into the side for Fairservice. Winning the toss, they batted on a hard, fast wicket which, traditionally, gave assistance to the spinners in the later stages of the match as the surface deteriorated. Kent faced what was considered *"a strong Somerset side"*[1] which might have been better described as "the strongest side Somerset could field", that included no fewer than seven amateurs. By 1913, this was very much the exception rather than the rule – particularly this early in the season. They had already lost two of their three matches and drawn the other.

The Private Banks Sports Club Cricket Pavilion circa 1910

"The young Stegumber amateur", Jack White: 7-83 & 2-96 in the match from 56 overs

There were 1,895 paying customers[2] for their county's opening home fixture and they watched Kent score 233, with only Humphreys, Hardinge and Woolley, assisted by a late partnership between Huish and Blythe, making real contributions. This was largely due to *"some remarkable bowling by Mr J.C. White, the young Stegumber amateur"*[3] who, at just turned 22, took 7-83 from 25.5 overs. White joined the attack with Kent at 62-0 and dismissed five of the first six in the order. At one time, he had 5-38, and it was only the late order hitting of Huish and Blythe that spoiled his figures. *Wisden* found his bowling *"one of the most interesting features of the contest."*[3]

The bowler who made such a good impression on both *The Times* and *Wisden* was to become known as "Farmer" Jack White, who later captained England against Australia in one Test in 1928/9 as a stand-in for Percy Chapman. The following summer, he led England in his own right against South Africa. He played 15 Tests in all and on the 1928/9 trip to Australia, took 25 wickets including dismissing Don Bradman on his Test debut.[3] He was a slow left-arm bowler who used variation in pace rather than spin to deceive batsmen. White made his debut for Somerset in 1909 aged just 18, but didn't secure a regular place until the current season when he took 93 wickets in all matches.

By close of play, Kent had made significant inroads into the Somerset batting, which was mainly due to some indifferent running between the wickets. *The Times* said, *"There is little doubt that Somerset would have made a good fight if two of their best wickets had not been thrown away by bad judgement in running. Kent really gained the upper hand when Mr Daniell broke up Somerset's promising 2nd wicket partnership by losing his wicket in this way."*[5] When stumps were drawn, Kent were the better placed with the visitors on 139-8, 94 runs behind their first innings total. Eighteen wickets had fallen on that first day and the general view was that the batsmen were discomfited by the pace of the wicket – *"most of the batsmen found the ball left the wicket too quickly."*[5]

The following morning, Kent snapped up the remaining two wickets for the addition of only seven runs. Percy Hardy, 42 overnight, feathered one to Huish and wicketkeeper Harry Chidgy edged one to Seymour at slip, both off Fielder's bowling, to give him 4-37 and end the Somerset innings at 146.

Kent, in their second innings, found no difficulty with the pace of the pitch and decided they quite liked it. The Somerset bowling was fairly collared as they scored 389-5 in only 250 minutes. Hardinge took an hour and 45 minutes over his first 50 but doubled his score in the next hour. His 105 came up in three hours. Humphreys was caught for 70 at mid on shortly after lunch, having been the more aggressive batsmen while Hardinge was finding his touch. This brought Seymour to the wicket in supreme form – *"Seymour played very bright cricket and … was full of confidence from the first; he timed his pulls and drives perfectly and was most successful in placing the ball beyond the reach of the fieldsmen."*[6]

One hundred and thirty-two were added in 85 minutes as Seymour stepped up his assault on the bowlers. His 118 came in 120 minutes with 12 fours and a six. When he was out to White, Woolley bludgeoned a tired attack *"unmercifully".*[6]

Dillon declared around a quarter past five to leave Somerset just over an hour's batting plus a full day– approximately 420 minutes in all to score 477. By the time poor light caused the players to leave the field at 20 minutes past six, Somerset had reached 72-3. The openers had *"hit out splendidly with a courage born, perhaps of desperation."*[6] Daniell was caught by Woolley at cover and then there was a mix-up in running which involved Randall Johnson and the Indian Prince Manek Pallon

Wally Hardinge, Jim Seymour and Ted Humphreys: Kent's run makers at Catford

Prince Manek Pallon Bajana

Bajana. It was Johnson who made his way back to the pavilion for a duck, probably on the basis that an Indian Prince out-ranks a "gentleman" even if he had been educated at Eton.[7] Seven runs later, Bajana was deceived by the flight by Blythe, missed the ball and was bowled. It was left to the veteran Len Braund and the captain, Massey Poyntz, to play out the few remaining deliveries and to contemplate the enormity of their task, which was to score 405 runs for victory with seven wickets remaining while keeping Blythe, Woolley and Humphreys at bay on a pitch that was, by now, showing signs of wear.

As matters turned out, Kent had already encountered the best of the Somerset resistance as, with the exception of Poyntz (24), the rest of the visitors' batting crumpled in a heap. Fielder had Braund caught by Woolley at slip with his first delivery, and then Woolley and Blythe set to work on the rest of the Somerset batting, which was described by *The Times* as "*lamentably weak*".[8] Woolley took 5-21 and Blythe 2-43 to complete Kent's victory by 364 runs before lunchtime.

A short piece, published in *The Bath Chronicle* a week after the match was played, appeared strangely prophetic given that, a hundred years later, Somerset are still seeking their first Championship title. *The Bellman* lamented the fact "*that it is not yet possible to indulge in that shout for joy which shall hail some meritorious performance by the Somerset team. To suffer defeat, even by as fine a side as Kent by 354 runs after Kent had declared with only 5 wickets down in the second innings, does not inspire us with confidence in the future. Let it be noted that Somerset had as good a team as the county is likely to field this season. This was no weak team this time. However, we won't despair. I am sure the Somerset Spirit is willing if the flesh is weak. The time may come!*"[1]

Sources

1   *Bath Chronicle* Saturday 31st May 1913
2   Kent Messenger 30th May 1913
3   Jack White – Bradman c Chapman b White 1 in the 1st Test of the 1928/9 series in the second innings. Bradman was lbw b Tate 18 in the first innings.
4   *Wisden* 1914
5   *The Times* 27th May 1913

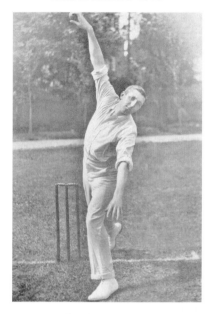

Len Braund, the veteran of the Somerset XI, played 23 Tests for England with three hundreds. Braund was 38 at the time of this match. He had played three seasons for Surrey before moving to the West Country to join Somerset in 1899, for whom he played until 1920. He also played for London County from 1900 to 1904.

6   *The Times* 28th May 1913
7   Prince Manek Bajana had toured England with the Indian side of 1911 which played 23 fixtures against various opponents throughout the summer with three of the matches being first class (Surrey, Somerset and Kent). The Kent match saw Lord Harris make his return to the Kent side for only the second time since 1897. It was to be his final first-class match at the age of 60. He made 36 in his only innings. It is not known if Bajana was a real Indian Prince or was simply known as "Prince". He played for Somerset between 1912 and 1920, scoring a total of 1,975 first-class runs at 20.78 with three hundreds and seven fifties. He died aged only 41 in Bethnal Green.
8   *The Times* 29th May 1913

28th May 1913	P	W	L	DWF	DLF	NC	Max	Pts	PtsPC
Kent	3	3	0	0	0	0	15	15	100.00%
Middlesex	2	2	0	0	0	0	10	10	100.00%
Derbyshire	3	3	0	0	0	0	15	15	100.00%
Yorkshire	5	4	1	0	0	0	25	20	80.00%
Nottinghamshire	4	3	1	0	0	0	20	15	75.00%
Surrey	5	3	1	1	0	0	25	18	72.00%
Northamptonshire	4	2	1	0	1	0	20	11	55.00%
Warwickshire	4	2	1	0	1	0	20	11	55.00%
Lancashire	5	2	2	1	0	0	25	13	52.00%
Worcestershire	2	0	1	1	0	0	10	3	30.00%
Somerset	3	0	2	1	0	0	15	3	20.00%
Leicestershire	5	0	4	1	0	0	25	3	12.00%
Essex	3	0	2	0	1	0	15	1	6.67%
Gloucestershire	4	0	3	0	1	0	20	1	5.00%
Hampshire	4	0	3	0	1	0	20	1	5.00%
Sussex	4	0	4	0	0	0	20	0	0.00%

Northamptonshire 1st Innings

W East	c Huish b Fielder	43			
CN Woolley	c Huish b Blythe	4			
RA Haywood	b Fielder	2			
Mr SG Smith *	c Fielder b Fairservice	133			
GJ Thompson	c Fairservice b Blythe	2			
Mr JS Denton	b Powell	39			
J Seymour	b Fielder	7			
Mr JHA Ryan	b Blythe	2			
FI Walden	c Powell b Fairservice	38			
W Wells	c Seymour b Humphreys	5			
WA Buswell +	not out	1			
Extras	(11 b, 7 lb, 4 nb)	22			
Total	(all out, 106 overs)	**298**			

FOW 1st Innings 1-21, 2-23, 3-86, 4-100, 5-202, 6-222, 7-225, 8-283, 9-296, 10-298

Northamptonshire 2nd Innings

c Seymour b Fielder	9	
c Seymour b Fielder	5	
c Huish b Woolley	1	
[6] c Hubble b Blythe	21	
b Fielder	26	
[7] lbw b Blythe	5	
c Hubble b Fielder	27	
not out	5	
[4] c Dillon b Fielder	2	
b Blythe	12	
c Huish b Fielder	1	
(5 b, 2 lb, 20 nb)	27	
(all out, 46.1 overs)	**141**	

FOW 2nd Innings 1-16, 2-19, 3-21, 4-24, 5-85, 6-85, 7-110, 8-121, 9-138, 10-141

Kent bowling	O	M	R	W
Fielder	25	4	68	3
Blythe	24	7	47	3
Fairservice	14	2	44	2
Powell	17	1	63	1
Woolley	18	7	31	0
Humphreys	8	2	23	1

Kent bowling	O	M	R	W
Fielder	22.1	4	50	6
Blythe	14	3	46	3
Fairservice	3	0	6	0
Powell	1	0	6	0
Woolley	6	3	6	1

Kent 1st Innings

E Humphreys	c East b Wells	11
HTW Hardinge	c Walden b East	71
J Seymour	c Wells b East	91
FE Woolley	c Buswell b Wells	33
JC Hubble	c Woolley b Thompson	37
Mr EW Dillon *	c Buswell b Smith	53
WA Powell	c Walden b Smith	48
FH Huish +	not out	29
WJ Fairservice	c Thompson b Smith	0
C Blythe	c Buswell b Wells	9
A Fielder	b Wells	1
Extras	(1 b, 1 lb, 16 nb, 2 w)	20
Total	(all out, 114.1 overs)	**403**

Kent 2nd Innings

not out	19
not out	13
(4 b, 1 lb, 2 nb)	7
(0 wicket, 9.1 overs)	**39**

FOW 1st Innings 1-30, 2-141, 3-214, 4-223, 5-235, 6-336, 7-368, 8-368, 9-386, 10-403

Northants bowling	O	M	R	W
Wells	35.1	5	110	4
Thompson	19	3	67	1
Smith	31	5	103	3
Denton	3	0	18	0
East	17	4	45	2
Ryan	3	0	9	0
Woolley	3	0	14	0
Seymour	3	0	17	0

Northants bowling	O	M	R	W
Wells	5	1	10	0
Ryan	4.1	1	22	0

Northamptonshire vs Kent

The County Ground, Northampton
Thursday 29th, Friday 30th & Saturday 31st May
Toss: Kent
Kent won by 10 wickets
Points: Northamptonshire 0 Kent 5

IN 1912, NORTHAMPTONSHIRE had inflicted two rather embarrassing defeats on Kent. The first encounter at The County Ground was by four wickets when, set 224 for victory, the Trinidad-born Sydney Smith scored a fine hundred which carried the day for the home side. At Tonbridge, Kent were defeated by 240 runs, Smith again proving more than useful by taking five wickets in Kent's second innings. In reality, it was outstanding knocks of 96 by the captain, George Vials, and 86 by John Seymour (brother of the Kent batsman Jim Seymour), in a stand of 150 for the seventh wicket that really placed the match beyond Kent's reach. Set to make 402 in the fourth innings, they were bowled out for 161. Northamptonshire finished second in the Championship table to Yorkshire in 1912 with Kent third.

Sydney Smith was the son of a Scottish father and English mother. He played for Trinidad from 1899/1900 to 1905/6 and first came to the notice of George Thompson, the Northamptonshire all-rounder, when he toured the West Indies with Lord Brackley's side in 1906. He came to England later that year with HGB Austin's West Indian team, and topped both the batting and bowling averages for all matches. He first appeared for Northamptonshire in 1907 as an amateur and stayed for seven seasons, becoming captain in 1913 when Vials fell ill. He was described by Wisden as *"a capital left-handed all-rounder … generally a hard hitting batsman strong in cutting, driving and leg-side strokes."* After the War, he played for Auckland and represented New Zealand against Australia in 1922/23.[1]

The 1913 match at Northampton was notable for the fact that the home county fielded the brothers of two Kent players in Claud Woolley and John Seymour. This is believed to be the first time four brothers have played against each other in county cricket in the same match. The second (and only other occasion as far as we can tell) was the return fixture, later in the season at Dover when the Woolleys and Semours were joined by the Denton twins for Northamptonshire.

Claud Woolley had been taken on to the Kent Ground Staff in 1906 and played only 2nd XI cricket for his native county until 1908. Released by Kent, he moved to Gloucestershire but only played one first-class match for them against the Australian Tourists in 1909. In 1911, he joined Northamptonshire where he remained until 1931 when he retired as a player, became an umpire and went on to officiate in the Ashes clash at Lord's in 1948, his only Test match.

Trinidad-born Sydney Smith

John Seymour, like his brother, was born in West Hoathly, Sussex. He played for Sussex from 1904 to 1907 when he moved to Northamptonshire, where he remained until 1919. A right-handed batsman, he was also a useful slow left-arm bowler. The Seymours were regular opponents, first playing against each other in 1904 when John played for Sussex against Kent.

Kent made two changes to the side that had beaten Somerset at Catford with Hatfeild and Day giving way to Powell and Fairservice. When Northamptonshire won the toss and decided to bat, William East and Claud Woolley opened the batting. East was the dominant partner, playing fluently from the start of his innings, until Claud Woolley got an edge to Blythe and was caught by Huish. Two runs later at 23, Fielder bowled Robert Haywood, whose father had played one game for Kent in 1878 against MCC at Lord's, failing to score a single run or take a wicket.[2] This brought the new captain, Smith, to the middle and *"but for his magnificent batting, they would have fared no more than moderately on a wicket that was hard and true... he played the bowling with confidence ... both stylish and free."*[3]

Smith's partnership with East was worth 63 when East was caught by Huish off Fielder for 43. When Thompson was deceived by Blythe, Smith shared another good partnership of 102 with John Denton. Later on that afternoon, when John Seymour and James Ryan had gone cheaply, he found another useful partner in Fanny Walden, the Tottenham and England footballer. Together, they put on 59 in less than even time for the eighth wicket before Smith's fine effort came to an end on 133 and with Northamptonshire on 283. His innings had occupied four hours and 20 minutes and contained eleven fours and a six.

The last two wickets fell for 15 as Fairservice had Walden caught by Powell and John Seymour caught by Buswell off Humphreys to conclude the innings for 298. Unusually, the wickets were shared among five Kent bowlers. With the last wicket falling at the end of the day, there was no time for Kent to open their innings that evening.

On Friday morning, in bright sunshine, and with the wicket still true, Kent set about the Northamptonshire bowling with intent. By ten minutes to six, they had bludgeoned 403 runs and established a lead of 105. This fine exhibition of stroke play was played out in front of a very poor crowd, despite the respectable score made by the home side on the previous day.

Humphreys went early for 11, which brought Hardinge and Seymour together for a partnership of 111. Hardinge *"played faultlessly for two hours for his 71 … Seymour's innings had not nearly so much merit for he was missed on 11 and gave a hard chance on the leg-side when 41."*[4] Hardinge was the first to go when he was caught at cover by Walden off the medium pace of East at 141. Woolley, dropped before scoring, made 33 before being caught behind off Wells. By this stage of the match, the home side had already dropped four catches and with the pressure being applied by the Kent batsmen, their ground fielding began to suffer too as the middle order piled on the pressure. Hubble made 37, Dillon a hard-hit 53, Powell a brutal 48 (his highest score in Championship and first-class matches) and Huish a cheeky 29 not out before the tail folded conveniently at around ten minutes to six, in time to allow the Kent bowlers half an hour at the Northamptonshire batsmen. Both Wells and Smith had got through more than 30 overs, taking 4-110 and 3-103 respectively.

The last 30 minutes saw Kent establish a clear advantage as Fielder had both East and Woolley caught by Seymour at slip and Claud's brother, Frank, found the edge of Haywood's bat with Huish taking the catch. Walden, who had been

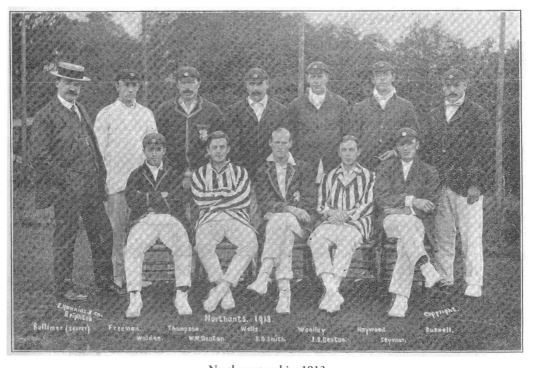

Northamptonshire 1913

Arthur Fielder: 3-68 and 6-50 at Northampton

promoted in the order from number nine, to bat at four, was not out two at the close with Northamptonshire on 21-3. Although Kent were in firm control of the match, they would have been aware that the Northamptonshire skipper had held himself back and, given his recent performances against them, victory was by no means assured.

The home side resumed their innings on Saturday still 84 runs behind and with seven wickets in hand. A great deal depended on their remaining batsmen, especially Smith. Three runs later, however, they lost Walden, caught by Dillon off Fielder. This brought together the veteran Thompson and his captain. The pair put on 61 in an hour. Kent must have been getting slightly concerned that they had dropped Thompson in the slips when he was on two.

A shower of rain interrupted their partnership at a quarter past twelve and the players were off the field for an hour. After the break, the batsmen raised the total to 85, "*at which point, both left. Thompson being bowled and Smith caught at slip.*"[5] Thompson had made a stoic 26 in 70 minutes. Rain fell again as the players left the field for lunch with the score at 107-6, but it was only a quick shower and did not delay the resumption.

With only three runs added to the score, Blythe trapped Denton lbw to reduce Northamptonshire to 110-7. It was only some lucky resistance by Seymour that prevented a quick end to the innings. Blythe bowled Wells, and Fielder collected his fifth and sixth wickets as Northamptonshire were finally out for 141, leaving Kent 39 to score for a well-earned win.

With the exception of one over from Powell, Fielder had bowled unchanged for the entire innings and was rewarded with 6-50. He did, however, deliver 20 no balls which, under today's Laws, would have seen his figures at 6-70. In those days, it was Mr Extras who was held responsible.

Humphreys and Hardinge made light work of scoring the 39 needed for victory in 9.1 overs in 25 minutes. Those with a mathematical bent will have quickly calculated that this was an over rate of 22 per hour, and this with two fast men who had longish runs sharing the new ball.

The match finished at four o'clock, allowing the players a leisurely tea before Kent started out for Bradford that evening.

Sources

1   *The Wisden Book of Cricketers' Lives* Benny Green 1986
2   MCC beat Kent by an innings and 104 runs. MCC scored 199 in their innings and then dismissed Kent for 39 and 56. Kent were bundled out in the first innings by Arnold Rylott, who took 14 for 34 in the match. The other wicket taker was Derbyshire's William Mycroft, whose name was borrowed by Sir Arthur Conan Doyle for Sherlock Holmes' elder and, sometimes, smarter brother.
3   *Derby Daily Telegraph* 30th May 1913
4   *The Dundee Evening Courier* 31st May 1913
5   *Derby Daily Telegraph* 31st May 1913

31st May 1913	P	W	L	DWF	DLF	NC	Max	Pts	PtsPC
Kent	4	4	0	0	0	0	20	20	100.00%
Middlesex	2	2	0	0	0	0	10	10	100.00%
Derbyshire	3	3	0	0	0	0	15	15	100.00%
Nottinghamshire	5	4	1	0	0	0	25	20	80.00%
Yorkshire	5	4	1	0	0	0	25	20	80.00%
Surrey	6	3	1	1	1	0	30	19	63.33%
Warwickshire	5	2	1	1	1	0	25	14	56.00%
Lancashire	5	2	2	1	0	0	25	13	52.00%
Northamptonshire	5	2	2	0	1	0	25	11	44.00%
Worcestershire	2	0	1	1	0	0	10	3	30.00%
Somerset	3	0	2	1	0	0	15	3	20.00%
Gloucestershire	5	0	3	1	1	0	25	4	16.00%
Leicestershire	6	0	5	1	0	0	30	3	10.00%
Essex	3	0	2	0	1	0	15	1	6.67%
Hampshire	4	0	3	0	1	0	20	1	5.00%
Sussex	5	0	4	0	1	0	25	1	4.00%

Kent 1st Innings

E Humphreys	lbw b Booth	42
HTW Hardinge	c Dolphin b Booth	11
J Seymour	b Booth	14
FE Woolley	lbw b Hirst	81
JC Hubble	c Booth b Rhodes	55
Mr EW Dillon *	c Dolphin b Rhodes	2
Mr WA Powell	b Rhodes	4
FH Huish +	c Dolphin b Booth	11
WJ Fairservice	c and b Booth	2
C Blythe	c Tasker b Booth	14
A Fielder	not out	7
Extras	(5 b, 2 lb, 1 nb)	8
Total	(all out, 69.5 overs)	251

FOW 1st Innings 1-40, 2-68, 3-88, 4-196, 5-208, 6-212, 7-228, 8-230, 9-232, 10-251

Kent 2nd Innings

run out		52
c Booth b Hirst		5
c Denton b Booth		69
c Rhodes b Booth		6
c Wilson b Booth		4
[7] b Booth		62
[6] c and b Booth		26
c Dolphin b Hirst		27
not out		7
st Dolphin b Hirst		10
run out		0
(1 b, 6 lb)		7
(all out, 111 overs)		275

FOW 2nd Innings 1-11, 2-129, 3-135, 4-135, 5-141, 6-204, 7-237, 8-263, 9-275, 10-275

Yorkshire bowling	O	M	R	W
Hirst	20	3	53	1
Booth	24.5	1	108	6
Drake	5	1	5	0
Rhodes	10	0	55	3
Haigh	10	4	22	0

Yorkshire bowling	O	M	R	W
Hirst	21	7	54	3
Booth	33	3	103	5
Rhodes	21	4	42	0
Haigh	17	5	23	0
Haigh	17	5	23	0
Drake	11	1	39	0
Kilner	8	4	7	0

Yorkshire 1st Innings

W Rhodes	c Hubble b Fielder	17
BB Wilson	c Dillon b Fielder	0
D Denton	c Hubble b Powell	85
A Drake	c Hubble b Blythe	0
GH Hirst	c Seymour b Powell	15
R Kilner	c Seymour b Powell	5
Mr J Tasker	c Hardinge b Blythe	15
E Oldroyd	c Fielder b Blythe	4
MW Booth	not out	38
S Haigh	c Seymour b Blythe	0
A Dolphin +	run out	29
Extras	(2 b, 2 lb, 3 nb, 2 w)	9
Total	(all out, 69.2 overs)	217

FOW 1st Innings 1-0, 2-61, 3-62, 4-101, 5-125, 6-130, 7-135, 8-161, 9-162, 10-217

Yorkshire 2nd Innings

c Huish b Fielder		4
lbw b Blythe		7
b Fielder		7
b Fielder		7
not out		102
not out		50
did not bat		
did not bat		
did not bat		
did not bat		
did not bat		
(6 b, 5 lb, 3 nb, 1 w)		15
(4 wickets, 83 overs)		192

FOW 2nd Innings 1-15, 2-23, 3-23, 4-41

Kent bowling	O	M	R	W
Fielder	22	6	61	2
Fairservice	3.2	0	15	0
Blythe	22	6	64	4
Woolley	9	1	27	0
Powell	12	3	37	3
Humphreys	1	0	4	0

Kent bowling	O	M	R	W
Fielder	18	5	44	3
Blythe	27	10	44	1
Powell	1	0	9	0
Fairservice	17	9	30	0
Woolley	20	9	50	0

Yorkshire vs Kent

Park Avenue, Bradford
Monday 2nd, Tuesday 3rd & Wednesday 4th June
Toss: Kent
Match Drawn
Points: Yorkshire 0 Kent 3

THE FIRST MATCH against Yorkshire was always going to be Kent's sternest test of the season so far, particularly as it was played away from home. Whereas Kent were unchanged, Yorkshire made one change to the team that had beaten Sussex at Sheffield the previous week, with Edgar Oldroyd replacing the captain, Sir Archibald White, who was unavailable. John Tasker took over as captain and was the only amateur in the side.

Kent won the toss and batted in glorious sunshine and, at one stage, looked as if they might run up a big total on a fast wicket, but the batting was very uneven. Humphreys opened well but lost Hardinge and Seymour before he too fell to William Booth for 31 to leave the visitors 88-3. This brought Hubble in to join Woolley, who took the attack to the bowlers, and in one over from Booth hit five fours – "*three drives, a cut and a clever stroke to the leg side.*"[1] Together they put on 108 for the fourth wicket, but at 196, Hubble cut at a ball from Rhodes and was caught single handed, high and to his right by Booth. *The Times* described it as a "*clever catch*" that "*brought about a complete change in the game.*" Woolley's first 50 had come at a run a minute but, once Hubble departed, he became more circumspect. Dropped

Park Avenue, Bradford circa 1920

Frank Woolley, top scorer for Kent and William Powell, career best bowling at Bradford

on 58 by Drake, he went on to 81 before being trapped lbw by Hirst. The last six Kent wickets went down for 55 runs with Booth, making excellent use of the new ball, taken with the score at 228, returning 6-108. Apart from an early savaging by Woolley, "*he bowled in splendid form, keeping a very accurate length and making the ball get up and swing away awkwardly. The Yorkshire fielding was excellent, only one catch being missed.*"[1] Kent had taken almost 70 overs to score their 251 runs, leaving Yorkshire two hours to bat before close of play.

The home side got off to a poor start, losing Ben Wilson in the first over caught by Dillon at point off Fairservice, but Wilfred Rhodes blocked whilst David Denton attacked brilliantly. 61 runs were added in 50 minutes before Rhodes edged Fielder to Hubble. He was quickly followed by Alonzo Drake, caught by the same fielder off Blythe to leave Yorkshire at 62-3. George Hirst gave Denton some support before he and Roy Kilner were out in quick succession to Powell. The Kent captain had been obliged to leave the field during this session after being hit on the head in attempting to stop a powerful shot.

Kent picked up one more wicket from the last ball of the day when Powell found the edge of Denton's bat and Hubble took a smart catch at slip. Yorkshire would have been pleased that there was no more play as Powell was clearly threatening and had snapped up the last three wickets for next to nothing to secure his best ever bowling figures of 3-29. The 6,000 crowd had seen a splendid day's cricket despite their side ending it 121 in arrears, with only four wickets remaining.

Next morning, an even larger crowd of 7,000[2] saw Oldroyd caught by Fielder off Blythe, then, after 27 were added, two further wickets fell to leave Yorkshire teetering on 162-9 with little chance of overhauling Kent's first innings score. But, as so often happens, a last-wicket partnership came to the rescue. Booth and future

England wicketkeeper Arthur Dolphin managed to get Yorkshire within 34 of the visitors' total with 55 in 40 minutes *"much to the jubilation of the crowd"* before Dolphin was run out.

When Kent set out on their second innings, they soon lost Hardinge to George Hirst, but Humphreys and Seymour mastered the bowling to put on 118 for the second wicket. *"Seymour drove the ball beautifully on both sides of the wicket and Humphreys made the most of his runs by drives and leg hits."*[2] Then came a small collapse as firstly Humphreys was run out by the combined efforts of Dolphin and Kilner, and then Booth produced another fine spell to remove Seymour, Woolley and Hubble in quick succession. *"Woolley was brilliantly caught by Rhodes who ran a long way back from short leg"*[2] to take the catch which reduced Kent to 141-5.

Things looked serious for Kent but the two amateurs, Dillon and Powell batted well together and put on 63 runs in even time. *The Times* referred to Dillon's chanceless innings as the best of the day, being played against *"formidable bowling"*. The partnership was broken towards the end of the day when Powell gave a sharp return catch to Booth, who shortly after got one through the captain's defence with the score at 237. Huish and Fairservice were left to keep the dangerous Yorkshire attack at bay until the close came on 240-7 with Kent 274 runs ahead. *"So far, this has been as good a county match as any this season,"* praised *The Times*.

On the final morning, the last three Kent wickets fell in half an hour for the addition of 35 runs to set Yorkshire a victory target of 310 in around five hours.

The original scorecard for Kent at Bradford 1913

George Hirst:
century maker for Yorkshire

Ted Dillon:
"best of the day against
formidable bowling"

Booth was again the pick of the Yorkshire bowlers with 5-103 from 33 overs, giving him 11-211 in the match which, with his valuable 38 not out in the first innings, underlined his value as an all-rounder.[3]

The *Kent Messenger* reported an unusual incident towards the end of the Kent innings which illustrates the sportsmanship of Blythe. He was "*confidently appealed against for a catch at the wicket and, apparently, had no doubt he was out for he walked away towards the pavilion but, as the umpire made no sign, Fairservice called his colleague back. Blythe deliberately ran down the pitch the next ball and was easily stumped.*"[4]

The prospect of a home victory was quickly dispelled as Fielder snapped up three early wickets (Rhodes, Denton and Drake) and Blythe trapped Wilson in front to reduce Yorkshire to 41-4. At this point, Kent looked almost certain to achieve their fifth consecutive Championship victory but George Hirst and the young Roy Kilner showed "*stout resistance*". During the afternoon, the light deteriorated sufficiently to halt play, but fortunately, they were only off for 15 minutes. When the players returned, Kent could make no further impression on the two batsmen, who took their partnership to 151 by the time rain arrived at around five o'clock. This was fine batting by this pair, particularly as the light throughout the afternoon was barely playable. This probably accounted for Hirst's "*inability to time the ball to perfection on many occasions*", but didn't prevent his finishing with a chanceless 102 not out with Kilner, also unbeaten, on 50. Kent's attack wasn't at full strength as Powell had split a finger and bowled only one over in the second innings. *Wisden* also refers to Fielder being "handicapped", although no details are given as to why he was only able to bowl 18 overs. *Wisden* suggested that when the match was called off, the position favoured Yorkshire although *The Times* said "*the fine defensive batting of Hirst and Kilner saved Yorkshire from defeat.*"[5] A total of 16,000 spectators attended the game, adding the princely sum of £476 to the Yorkshire coffers.

This heroics on the part of Hirst and Kilner, and the inability of the Kent bowlers to force victory meant that Kent's 100 per cent record took a knock. The failure to gather the additional two points reduced their percentage of maximum points to 92. Because Middlesex had played only three fixtures and won all three, they maintained their 100 per cent record. As a result, they went to the top of the table for the only time.

Sources

1   *The Times* 3rd June 1913
2   *The Times* 4th June 1913
3   The consistent performances by Major William Booth (Major being a rather unusual Christian name rather than military rank) throughout the 1913 season earned him a place as one of *Wisden*'s Cricketers of the Year in 1914 and a place on the 1913/14 MCC tour to South Africa. In 1913, he scored 1,228 runs and took 181 wickets and was one of the leading all-rounders that year and the highest wicket taker for the season. Although George Hirst scored more runs (1,540) than Booth, he was significantly in arrears with his tally of wickets (101). Booth was another casualty of the Great War. Shortly after he had received a field commission to become (rather confusingly) 2nd Lt Major William Booth, he was fatally injured in an attack on German trenches on 1st July 1916. He died in a shell hole in no-man's land where he had taken refuge alongside another, later, Yorkshire and England cricketer, Abe Waddington, who was rescued later that day by stretcher bearers. Booth's body, however, remained in the shell hole until the following Spring when his body was recovered and was buried in the Sarre Road No. 1 Cemetery.
4   *The Kent Messenger* 7th June 1913
5   *The Times* 5th June 1913

4th June 1913	P	W	L	DWF	DLF	NC	Max	Pts	PtsPC
Middlesex	3	3	0	0	0	0	15	15	100.00%
Kent	5	4	0	1	0	0	25	23	92.00%
Nottinghamshire	5	4	1	0	0	0	25	20	80.00%
Derbyshire	4	3	1	0	0	0	20	15	75.00%
Yorkshire	6	4	1	0	1	0	30	21	70.00%
Surrey	7	4	1	1	1	0	35	24	68.57%
Lancashire	6	3	2	1	0	0	30	18	60.00%
Northamptonshire	6	3	2	0	1	0	30	16	53.33%
Warwickshire	6	2	2	1	1	0	30	14	46.67%
Worcestershire	2	0	1	1	0	0	10	3	30.00%
Somerset	3	0	2	1	0	0	15	3	20.00%
Gloucestershire	5	0	3	1	1	0	25	4	16.00%
Leicestershire	6	0	5	1	0	0	30	3	10.00%
Essex	4	0	3	0	1	0	20	1	5.00%
Hampshire	5	0	4	0	1	0	25	1	4.00%
Sussex	5	0	4	0	1	0	25	1	4.00%

Kent first innings

E Humphreys	c JT Tyldesley b Huddleston	61
HTW Hardinge	c MacLeod b Dean	16
J Seymour	c Hornby b MacLeod	107
FE Woolley	c Heap b Dean	77
JC Hubble	c Blomley b Dean	26
Mr EW Dillon *	b Dean	12
DW Jennings	c Hornby b Heap	30
FH Huish +	run out	19
WJ Fairservice	c Blomley b Dean	0
C Blythe	c Blomley b Dean	0
A Fielder	not out	0
Extras	(2 b, 4 lb)	6
Total	(all out, 102.3 overs)	354

FOW 1st Innings 1-27, 2-144, 3-240, 4-281, 5-296, 6-319, 7-352, 8-354, 9-354, 10-354

Kent 2nd Innings

[2]not out		0
[1]not out		4
did not bat		
did not bat		
did not bat		
did not bat		
did not bat		
did not bat		
did not bat		
did not bat		
did not bat		
Extras		0
Total	(no wicket, 0.1 overs)	4

Lancashire bowling	O	M	R	W
Dean	27	5	93	6
Whitehead	24	5	71	0
Huddleston	34	3	107	1
Sharp	6	0	29	0
Heap	7.3	1	29	1
MacLeod	4	1	19	1

Lancashire bowling	O	M	R	W
MacLeod	0.1	0	4	0

Lancashire 1st Innings

Mr AH Hornby *	c Huish b Fielder	8
JWH Makepeace	c Huish b Fielder	0
JT Tyldesley	st Huish b Woolley	65
J Sharp	lbw b Fairservice	45
GE Tyldesley	c Humphreys b Woolley	0
H Dean	c Huish b Fairservice	12
Mr KG MacLeod	b Fairservice	21
JS Heap	lbw b Fairservice	4
R Whitehead	c Jennings b Woolley	11
W Huddleston	not out	23
B Blomley+	c Humphreys b Fairservice	1
Extras	(5 b, 1 lb)	6
Total	(all out, 61.1 overs)	196

FOW 1st Innings 1-3, 2-18, 3-97, 4-108, 5-132, 6-133, 7-155, 8-158, 9-187, 10-196

Lancashire 2nd Innings

b Fairservice		43
lbw b Fairservice		17
b Fairservice		7
b Blythe		17
c Seymour b Fairservice		0
[10] b Blythe		3
Woolley		21
[7] b Blythe		6
[8] st Huish b Blythe		4
[9] b Fairservice		34
not out		0
(1 b, 2 lb, 4 nb)		7
(all out, 75.4 overs)		159

FOW 1st Innings 1-50, 2-62, 3-87, 4-87, 5-100, 6-114, 7-122, 8-126, 9-137, 10-159

Kent bowling	O	M	R	W
Fielder	7	0	25	2
Blythe	18	2	58	0
Woolley	18	5	46	3
Fairservice	17.1	3	58	5
Humphreys	1	0	3	0

Kent bowling	O	M	R	W
Blythe	27	12	42	4
Woolley	19	8	40	1
Fairservice	20.4	9	44	5
Humphreys	9	2	26	0

Lancashire vs Kent

Old Trafford, Manchester
Thursday 5th, Friday 6th & Saturday 7th June
Toss: Kent
Kent won by 10 wickets
Points: Lancashire 0 Kent 5

FRUSTRATED IN THEIR quest for victory at Bradford, the Kent players made the 45-mile journey across the Pennines to Old Trafford to play Lancashire on Thursday morning. As the players set out on Thursday evening, news came through of an incident at Epsom Racecourse during the running of the Derby Stakes, which had resulted in the serious injury of a woman who, as far as people knew at that time, had attempted to cross the racecourse before all the horses had passed. By the following morning, further details were published in the national press naming the woman as the well-known Suffragist, Emily Wilding Davison who, it was now revealed, had stepped out in front of Anmer, the horse owned by King George V. She died of her injuries four days later on Sunday 8th June.

There was one enforced change to the Kent side in that William Powell was left out because of the injury to his hand sustained at Bradford, and David Jennings

SENSATIONAL DERBY.

SUFFRAGIST'S MAD ACT.

KING'S HORSE BROUGHT DOWN.

WOMAN AND JOCKEY INJURED.

An extraordinary incident marked the race for the Derby yesterday afternoon. As the horses were making for Tattenham Corner a woman rushed out on the course in front of the King's horse Anmer, and put her hands above her head. The horse knocked her down, and then turned a complete somersault on its jockey, Herbert Jones. When the animal recovered itself Jones was dragged a few yards. He is suffering from concussion, and the woman, who had a Suffragist flag wrapped round her waist, and whose name is Emily Wilding Davison, is in a very serious condition in Epsom Cottage Hospital. The King made immediate inquiries regarding his jockey, who has no bones broken.

The Morning Post, 5th June 1913

ABOYEUR'S DERBY.

DESPERATE ACT OF A SUFFRAGIST.

FALL OF THE KING'S HORSE.

DISQUALIFICATION OF THE FAVOURITE.

The race for the Derby yesterday was marked by two incidents for which it will be long remembered, not only by the vast gathering at Epsom, but by all who take an interest in English sport. The King's horse was brought to the ground by a woman suffragist, who rushed from the crowd at Tattenham Corner, apparently with the object of seizing the reins. The horse fell and rolled on the jockey, who, however, was not severely hurt. The woman was knocked down and received such serious injuries that it was reported at first that she had been killed. The second inci-

The Times 5th June 1913

Old Trafford, Manchester circa 1910

came in for his first match of the season. Fielder's fitness remained a cause for concern and he bowled only seven overs in Lancashire's first innings and not at all in the second. His injury was reported in the *Manchester Courier* to have been the result of a "*strain*" and Henry Preston came on as twelfth man when Fielder left the field.

Kent won the toss and made best use of a very good batting wicket, and in the three hours before the rain arrived, scored 240 for the loss of only two wickets. This was largely due to Seymour and Humphreys, and also the generosity of the Lancashire fielders who "*gave a splendid exhibition of how not to take catches*".[1] Humphreys and Hardinge put on 27 for the first wicket before Hardinge was wonderfully caught low down at short leg for 16, but that was Lancashire's last success until ten minutes to two when Humphreys was caught by Johnny Tyldesley at slip. In between times, the home side put down four catches. The main beneficiary seems to have been Seymour, who was dropped at 43, 62 and then again before he reached his hundred. So incensed was "Mancunian", the cricket correspondent of the *Manchester Courier,* that he devoted a full paragraph of over 200 words of his report to the shortcomings of the fielders and the good fortune of the Kent batsmen. *The Times* was not nearly so partisan and observed that "*This splendid start will very likely give them the match as the pitch, after the rain, is almost certain to be difficult.*"[2]

By lunch, Kent had scored 153 but the players did not take the field again until just after three o'clock due to a rain shower. The wicket was still playing well but the bowlers and fielders were handicapped by the wet ball. The mood of "Mancunian" seems to have changed once Woolley came to the crease and set about the bowling with his usual élan. He headed his next paragraph "*The Sparkle of Woolley*" and said "*Anything in the scoring line hitherto seen was quite eclipsed when Frank Woolley joined Seymour … but the first over after resuming, he hit Dean for 13 … and after 57 minutes play, he reached his 50, he had sent the ball no fewer than 11 times to the confines.*" Seymour then reached his second hundred of the season which, although flawed by giving several chances, came up in only 125 minutes and included 13 fours.

At around four o'clock, with Kent on 240-2, a huge thunderstorm struck Old Trafford and before long, the ground was awash with puddles all over the outfield which, unsurprisingly, brought a halt to play for the rest of the day.

"Mancunian", having paused for a little customary Woolley worship, sums up the day: "*The facility with which Kent made their runs will be realised if it is stated that the rate of scoring was a hundred per hour. But fancy, fielders missing precious catches with the conditions all on the side of the batsmen, and with such a team as Kent in opposition. The chances are Lancashire will have to pay dearly for these lapses.*"[1]

The next morning, the effects of the storm of the previous evening were accompanied by a dramatic drop in temperature, so that conditions were described as being "*of almost Arctic severity*".[3] The small crowd of Thursday was numbered only in hundreds on Friday and those who did brave the elements had to wait until a quarter to three to see any play. When play resumed, with Seymour on 107, Kent tried to push on with the wicket significantly changed in character. Seymour was caught by the Lancashire captain Albert Hornby[5] off Kenneth MacLeod without adding to his score, and Woolley went to 77 before falling to Dean. Hubble and Jennings, with 26 and 30 respectively, were the major contributors from the lower middle order, and there was a bright 19 from Huish before he was run out. Kent lost their last four wickets for a mere two runs, finishing on 354.

Lancashire opened their innings on the stroke of five o'clock and, very soon, Fielder had removed the openers, Hornby and Harry Makepeace, for 18. The veteran Johnny Tyldesley and Jack Sharp then steadied matters to put on 79 in 70

Bill Fairservice: 10-102

minutes and take the score to 97-3. Tyldesley was dropped on 13 by Blythe at mid on as he chanced his arm, doubtless on the principle that the wicket would produce an unplayable ball sooner rather than later. By this stage, Fielder had suffered a recurrence of his injury after bowling just seven overs, and he took no further part in the match.

Tyldesley reached 50 in even time but, when on 65, he left his ground in an attempt get at Woolley to repeat the huge six he had just hit off Fairservice, only to be beaten and stumped by Huish. His brother George went immediately for a duck, caught by Humphreys. Two overs later, play ended for the day with the home side steadier, but by no means safe from the follow on. "Mancunian", however, had his doubts and said *"a hundred and one runs have to be made by the six remaining batsmen for this to be averted. And the sun may shine… If that should be the case, Lancashire had better look out for squalls."* [3]

Much to the regret of the Lancashire side, Saturday dawned bright, clear and sunny and the Old Trafford wicket began to dry nicely under an ever warming sun. By half past eleven, the turf was in the ideal condition to offer considerable help to the Kent bowlers in the form of Blythe, Woolley and Fairservice. A crowd of around four thousand Lancastrians turned up to see if their side could thwart the visitors in their push for victory. Unfortunately, it wasn't to be, as Fairservice, relishing the additional responsibility afforded him in Fielder's absence, captured five of the six remaining Lancashire wickets in his medium pace style. The *Manchester Courier* made the comment: *"Truth to tell, they could make little of Fairservice's fast medium bowling, this trundler, in the absence of Fielder… doing the bulk of the work and capturing five*

Frank Edward Woolley:
The Pride of Kent

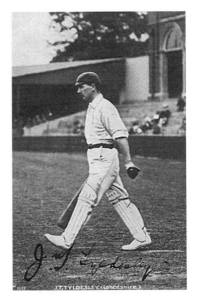

Johnny Tyldesley:
Lancashire's top scorer

James Seymour – centurion at Old Trafford

wickets at a cost of 58 runs, though all his wickets were captured on Saturday morning for 34 runs."[4] The Kent bowlers, however, did not have matters all their own way as the home side managed to add 92 runs to their overnight score and only failed to avoid the follow-on (and, thereby, probable safety) by nine runs. *Cricket* magazine, however, thought "*on the whole, Lancashire did very well to score as many as they did.*"

Sharp added 20 to his overnight score before falling lbw ("Mancunian" says "*given out*") and MacLeod, playing in his first match for over a year following a serious injury during the 1911 season, made 21. Whitehead hit out at Woolley and was caught by Jennings, who took a "*magnificent running catch in the long field which probably had a deal to do with Lancashire having to go in a second time with a minority of 158 runs*".[4] Huddleston played aggressively in scoring 23 not out, and his rough handling of Fairservice spoiled the latter's figures. Lancashire's brave effort to avoid batting a second time was thwarted when Fairservice dismissed wicketkeeper Benjamin Blomley at 196.

Second time round, things went better for the home side at the start and Hornby and Makepeace put on 50 in 90 minutes together before Makepeace went lbw to Fairservice – "*the professional was adjudged 'leg before', a decision he apparently didn't agree with.*"[4] After that, Hornby had difficulty finding batsmen to stay with him as he compiled 43 in two hours. Ernest Tyldesley collected a pair in the match

Albert, Son of "Monkey"   Bill Huddleston   Harry Dean 6-93

"and except for MacLeod, no one showed much power of resistance until Huddleston went in ... Huddleston was evidently bent on avoiding the ignominy of an innings reverse if an effort would accomplish it ... his methods would have done credit to Jack Lyons[6] or a Jessop." His 34, made in quick time, was the only real resistance in the end and entertained the crowd enormously. "Mancunian" then puts aside his usual home bias and aknowledges that *"The Kent team, like good sportsmen, joined in the general cheering which greeted the Earlstown man's great hit and Frank Woolley, the victim, was in no way behind the rest in his display of enthusiasm."[4]* Huddleston's second six of the innings had landed in a tennis court on the opposite side of the Warwick Road *"much to the dismay of the occupants."[4]*

"Mancunian's" piece that day is headed

A MIGHTY HIT
HUDDLESTON'S
JESSOPIAN TACTICS
(and then)
Kent Win by 10 Wickets

Kent wrapped up the innings when Fairservice bowled Huddleston[7] as he attempted another mighty blow, leaving them needing 4 to win. This they did from the first ball of the innings and, with 30 minutes to spare, the five points were secured. Fairservice had taken 5 for 44 to give him 10 for 102 in the match. "Mancunian"'s final observation in his piece was that only eight Lancashire players took the field for the Kent second innings. Whether the deficiency of numbers was as a result of injury, indifference or resignation isn't related.

Sources

1   *Manchester Courier* 6th June 1913
2   *The Times* 6th June 1913
3   *Manchester Courier* 7th June 1913
4   *Manchester Courier* 9th June 1913
5   Albert Henry Hornby was the Lancashire captain from 1908 to 1914. He was the son of Albert Neilson "Monkey" Hornby who captained Lancashire from 1880 to 1893 and then again in 1897 and 1898. "Monkey" was also the captain of the England side when they lost to Australia at The Oval in 1882 by seven runs, in the match which gave birth to The Ashes. Albert Henry was a Cambridge man who didn't get a Blue but subsequently toured India with the Oxford University Authentics in 1902/03. He played 292 first-class matches scoring 9,784 runs at 24.58 including eight hundreds and 56 fifties. He took three wickets in his career at nearly 90 runs apiece.
6   Jack Lyons, the Australian batsman who developed a reputation as a fierce hitter in the late 1880s and 1890s in the course of his 14 Test matches.
7   Bill Huddleston took 685 wickets at 17.57 for Lancashire with a best of 9-36 against Nottinghamshire at Aigburth, Liverpool. He first appeared for Lancashire in 1906 but didn't play again after the Great War. He was principally known as a fast bowler who formed part of the fearsome Lancashire attack that included Walter Brearley, Walter Dean, Willis Cuttell and Alex Kermode. He played 185 matches, taking 685 wickets at 17.57 each. His batting was not scientific but, when it came off, it usually did so in spectacular manner as Kent found at only relatively small cost at Old Trafford in 1913. His career batting record was 2,765 runs at 12.23 with a highest score of 88 made in very quick time.

7th June 1913	P	W	L	DWF	DLF	NC	Max	Pts	PtsPC
Middlesex	3	3	0	0	0	0	15	15	100.00%
Kent	6	5	0	1	0	0	30	28	93.33%
Nottinghamshire	6	4	1	0	1	0	30	21	70.00%
Yorkshire	7	4	1	1	1	0	35	24	68.57%
Surrey	7	4	1	1	1	0	35	24	68.57%
Derbyshire	5	3	2	0	0	0	25	15	60.00%
Northamptonshire	6	3	2	0	1	0	30	16	53.33%
Worcestershire	3	1	1	1	0	0	15	8	53.33%
Lancashire	7	3	3	1	0	0	35	18	51.43%
Warwickshire	6	2	2	1	1	0	30	14	46.67%
Somerset	4	1	2	1	0	0	20	8	40.00%
Sussex	6	1	4	0	1	0	30	6	20.00%
Gloucestershire	6	0	4	1	1	0	30	4	13.33%
Leicestershire	7	0	6	1	0	0	35	3	8.57%
Essex	4	0	3	0	1	0	20	1	5.00%
Hampshire	5	0	4	0	1	0	25	1	4.00%

Worcestershire first innings

FL Bowley	c Hardinge b Woolley	72
FA Pearson	c Hubble b Blythe	37
Mr HK Foster *	c Huish b Blythe	0
Mr WB Burns	c Seymour b Woolley	2
EG Arnold	c Jennings b Woolley	0
CGA Collier	c Dillon b Woolley	22
JA Cuffe	c Preston b Woolley	14
F Chester	not out	5
RD Burrows	run out	0
EW Bale +	b Woolley	1
AJ Conway	c Jennings b Blythe	0
Extras	(3 b)	3
Total	(all out, 49 overs)	156

FOW 1st Innings 1-95, 2-99, 3-112, 4-112, 5-112, 6-144, 7-148, 8-148, 9-151, 10-156

Worcestershire 2nd Innings

c Dillon b Woolley	5
c Seymour b Blythe	8
b Blythe	9
c Hubble b Blythe	3
c Seymour b Blythe	5
c Humphreys b Woolley	0
b Woolley	0
c Humphreys b Blythe	10
c Hardinge b Blythe	2
not out	0
b Blythe	0
(1lb)	1
(all out, 31 overs)	43

FOW 2nd Innings 1-5, 2-16, 3-25, 4-26, 5-26, 6-26, 7-39, 8-43, 9-43, 10-43

Kent bowling	O	M	R	W
Blythe	25	10	56	3
Fairservice	9	1	31	0
Preston	5	0	35	0
Woolley	10	2	31	6

Kent bowling	O	M	R	W
Blythe	16	6	21	7
Woolley	15	7	21	3

Kent 1st Innings

E Humphreys	lbw b Burrows	7
HTW Hardinge	lbw b Burrows	50
J Seymour	c Bowley b Chester	6
FE Woolley	b Chester	99
JC Hubble	b Chester	13
EW Dillon*	b Burrows	5
DW Jennings	b Chester	12
FH Huish+	c Conway b Chester	0
WJ Fairservice	c Cuffe b Chester	32
C Blythe	c Burns b Cuffe	12
HJB Preston	not out	8
Extras	(4 b, 5 lb, 1 nb)	10
Total	(all out, 61.4 overs)	254

FOW 1st Innings 1-13, 2-31, 3-134, 4-182, 5-189, 6-191, 7-192, 8-206, 9-237, 10-254

Worcestershire bowling	O	M	R	W
Burrows	16	1	64	3
Burns	2	0	13	0
Chester	25.4	0	95	6
Pearson	5	1	16	0
Cuffe	13	3	56	1

Worcestershire vs Kent

War Memorial Ground,
Amblecote, Stourbridge
Monday 9th, Tuesday 10th & Wednesday 11th June
Toss: Kent
Kent won by an innings and 55 runs
Points: Worcestershire 0 Kent 5

KENT ARRIVED AT Amblecote with just enough players to field a full side following the injuries sustained at Bradford. Powell's hand prevented his playing and Fielder was also omitted due to the injury he had been carrying at Bradford and Manchester. In Fielder's absence, Henry Preston, a right-arm medium pacer, played his only game of the season and what also turned out to be his final match for Kent. He had first played for the 2nd XI in 1904 and made his first-team debut in 1907 against Essex at Leyton. Preston ended the season playing in the Second XI, and in 1914 signed as Professional for Nelson in the Lancashire League.[1]

The match started on a rain-damaged pitch after heavy overnight rain, and on winning the toss, Dillon asked the home side to bat first. For a while it looked as if this had been a misjudgement as the Worcestershire openers, Fred Bowley and Fred Pearson, scored easily, firstly against Blythe and Fairservice and then Blythe and

The immaculate Henry Knollys Foster,
brother of RE, GN, MK, BS, NJA & WL Foster

Henry John Berridge Preston:
who played his only match of the season
and his final game for Kent at Amblecote

Ted Arnold:
Worcestershire & England all-rounder
who played ten Test matches for England
(1903-07), eight of them against Australia

Preston. Their opening stand was worth 95 in 80 minutes. After 29 overs with the score at 82, Dillon introduced Woolley to the attack. From that moment onwards, the batsmen could find no answer to the Kent spinners. Blythe dismissed Pearson, caught by Hubble at slip, and Woolley collected his first wicket when Bowley, who *Wisden* says had batted with *"marked skill"*, despite being dropped at 13 and 40, holed out to Hardinge in the deep for 72. After that, only Christopher Collier, and briefly, the Australian John Cuffe, provided any real resistance as nine wickets fell for 61 runs. Woolley had taken 6-31 in ten overs while Blythe had bowled unchanged throughout the innings and collected 3-56.

Kent lost Humphreys lbw early on to Robert Burrows, the right-arm fast opening bowler, and Frank Chester, bowling his off breaks, had Seymour caught by Bowley to leave Kent on 31 for 2. Hardinge and Woolley led a recovery with 103 for the third wicket with Woolley *"hitting delightfully .... 2 sixes and 10 fours"*[2] while Hardinge concentrated on defence. Woolley eventually went for 99. This was not untypical for a man who seemed to care little for personal landmarks. In his career, he made 35 scores in the nineties (32 times dismissed and three times not out). He was out five times on 99 alone. Of those 35, seven were in matches at Lord's. He also made three scores in the 190s.

By close of play, Kent were 51 runs ahead with three wickets remaining. Next morning Fairservice, with assistance from Blythe, raised the score to 254 all out. Chester had been the most successful bowler taking 6-95 from 25.4 overs.

Worcestershire's second innings was nothing short of a procession as Blythe and Woolley once more got to work on a wicket offering help for the spinners. *The Times* was moved to compare the home county's performance of the previous week when they had *"scored 529 runs for four wickets against Gloucestershire ... the conditions prevailing were, of course, very different from those which obtained at Worcester last week, but that hardly accounts for so complete a failure of the Worcestershire batsmen."*[3] The innings folded for 43 – Blythe took 7-21 (at one time he had bowled eight overs for seven runs and taken six wickets) and Woolley 3-21. Their match figures were 10-77 and 9-52 respectively.

This was Kent's easiest win of the season to date and had been achieved well inside two days. This gave the players five whole days before their next match against Essex at Tonbridge. For a side accustomed to playing six days a week and probably travelling on the seventh, the break was no doubt very welcome. This season, the players had probably left their homes on Sunday 25th May to travel to Catford for the Somerset match. Leaving Catford on the afternoon of the 28th, they journeyed to Northampton to play on the following morning. On Sunday 1st June, they went by rail to Bradford and thence over the Pennines to Old Trafford. The following Sunday (8th June) they made the journey from Manchester to Stourbridge. By the time they returned to Kent, none of them had slept in their own beds for 18 nights, and it is likely that those who lived in East Kent would have been away since the season started on 12th May.

The Kent firm of Blythe & Woolley: purveyors of orthodox left-arm spin to the gentry
From a photograph taken at Leyton in 1913

Fred Bowley: top scorer for Worcestershire

At the time of this match, Frank Chester was only 18 years of age, having made his debut the previous year against South Africa and remained in the side for 14 Championship matches in total. In 1913 he scored 703 runs, including three hundreds with a highest score of 148 not out. At that time, he was the youngest player to score a championship hundred; a record which stood until it was broken in the fifties by Peter May. In addition to his runs, he also took 44 wickets with a best of 6-43. Although his 1914 season wasn't quite as good, he was considered one of the most promising young players of the time and many commentators thought he would go on to represent his country in due course.

On the outbreak of War, he volunteered and joined the Royal Field Artillery in a battery commanded by Major Frederick Allsop, who had captained him in two of only three 2nd XI matches he had played for Worcestershire. In July 1917, his unit was transferred to Salonika and he was seriously wounded in his right arm. The wound turned gangrenous and the arm had to be amputated below the elbow which, of course, ended his playing career. When Chester returned to England, he was fitted with an artificial arm and then turned to umpiring. He stood in his first match at Leyton for the Essex vs Somerset match in 1922 and very soon gained an excellent reputation so that two years later, he stood in his first Test match when England played South Africa at Lord's. He was acknowledged by the best Test players as their first choice because of his uncompromising fairness and ability to get the important decisions right.

Frank Chester as an umpire

Chester stood in a total of 48 Test matches between 1924 and 1955. This total could well have been higher had he not declined to officiate in any further matches of the 1953 Ashes series as a protest against what he saw as excessive appealing on behalf of the tourists – something he had also complained of in the 1948 Ashes series. Towards the end of his career, he was not in the very best of health. He suffered from stomach ulcers which caused him to become rather irascible. He retired from umpiring after the 1955 season, and a year later Hutchinson published his autobiography which was entitled *How's That*. He died two years later in Bushey, Hertfordshire aged 62.

Sources

1 Henry Preston had an excellent season for the 2nd XI. He appeared in 14 matches taking 41 wickets at an average of 14.58. He was second in the bowling averages behind Tich Freeman who took 44 wickets at 13.72 each.

2 *Wisden* 1914

3 *The Times* 10th June 1913

11th June 1913	P	W	L	DWF	DLF	NC	Max	Pts	PtsPC
Middlesex	4	4	0	0	0	0	20	20	100.00%
Kent	7	6	0	1	0	0	35	33	94.29%
Yorkshire	8	5	1	1	1	0	40	29	72.50%
Nottinghamshire	6	4	1	0	1	0	30	21	70.00%
Surrey	8	4	2	1	1	0	40	24	60.00%
Northamptonshire	7	4	2	0	1	0	35	21	60.00%
Warwickshire	7	3	2	1	1	0	35	19	54.29%
Lancashire	8	3	3	2	0	0	40	21	52.50%
Derbyshire	7	3	4	0	0	0	35	15	42.86%
Worcestershire	4	1	2	1	0	0	20	8	40.00%
Somerset	4	1	2	1	0	0	20	8	40.00%
Sussex	8	3	4	0	1	0	40	16	40.00%
Gloucestershire	7	0	4	1	2	0	35	5	14.29%
Leicestershire	8	0	7	1	0	0	40	3	7.50%
Essex	5	0	4	0	1	0	25	1	4.00%
Hampshire	6	0	5	0	1	0	30	1	3.33%

Kent 1st Innings

E Humphreys	lbw b Douglas	4
HTW Hardinge	c Clark b Buckenham	83
J Seymour	c Louden b Buckenham	47
FE Woolley	b Tremlin	72
JC Hubble	b Buckenham	4
Mr EW Dillon *	b Tremlin	12
Mr AP Day	c Clark b Douglas	26
Mr CE Hatfeild	b Tremlin	29
FH Huish+	run out	3
C Blythe	b Tremlin	1
A Fielder	not out	0
Extras	(1b, 2lb, 1 nb)	4
Total	(all out, 69.3 overs)	285

FOW 1st Innings 1-4, 2-80, 3-195, 4-199, 5-220, 6-231, 7-277, 8-284, 9-285, 10-285

Kent 2nd Innings

	b Russell	53
	b Louden	50
	c Tremlin b Louden	46
	lbw b Tremlin	2
	not out	97
	not out	26
	did not bat	
	did not bat	
	did not bat	
	did not bat	
	did not bat	
Extras	(2 lb, 3 w)	5
Total	(4 wickets dec, 68 overs)	279

FOW 2nd Innings 1-105, 2-105, 3-108, 4-239

Essex bowling	O	M	R	W
Douglas	17	1	58	2
Buckenham	21	2	112	3
Tremlin	22.3	4	70	4
Louden	7	0	29	0
Russell	2	0	12	0

Essex bowling	O	M	R	W
Douglas	3	0	16	0
Buckenham	19	2	75	0
Tremlin	24	3	101	1
Russell	7	0	33	1
Louden	15	4	49	2

Essex 1st Innings

Mr JWHT Douglas*	c Seymour b Day	3
CAG Russell	c Seymour b Day	2
JR Freeman	b Day	5
Mr PA Perrin	st Huish b Blythe	34
Mr FL Fane	b Humphreys	15
Mr CD McIver +	st Huish b Blythe	19
Rev FH Gillingham	c Blythe b Fielder	45
CP Buckenham	c Huish b Blythe	4
RD Clark	c Dillon b Blythe	4
B Tremlin	b Blythe	12
Mr GM Louden	not out	5
Extras	(9 b, 4 nb)	13
Total	(all out, 59 overs)	161

FOW 1st Innings 1-3, 2-13, 3-16, 4-45, 5-81, 6-96, 7-102, 8-112, 9-149, 10-161

Essex 2nd Innings

[6] b Fielder		23
lbw b Blythe		21
c Huish b Fielder		27
lbw b Fielder		57
c Day b Fane		33
[1] c Day b Woolley		76
b Fielder		6
c Huish b Fielder		7
[11] c Huish b Fielder		14
[9]not out		0
[10]b Fielder		2
Extras (2lb, 9 nb)		11
Total (all out, 106.5 overs)		277

FOW 1st Innings 1-70, 2-119, 3-146, 4-218, 5-230, 6-236, 7-259, 8-260, 9-263, 10-277

Kent bowling	O	M	R	W
Fielder	20	2	55	1
Day	15	5	39	3
Blythe	21	4	46	5
Humphreys	2	0	6	1
Woolley	1	0	2	0

Kent bowling	O	M	R	W
Fielder	30.5	6	120	8
Day	19	6	30	0
Blythe	27	8	60	1
Humphreys	9	1	22	0
Woolley	21	8	34	1

Kent vs Essex

The Angel Ground, Tonbridge
Monday 16th, Tuesday 17th & Wednesday 18th June
Toss: Kent
Kent won by 126 runs
Points: Kent 5 Essex 0

KENT RETURNED FROM their "Northern Tour" which "*was the most successful they ever had*",[1] having beaten Leicestershire, Northamptonshire, Lancashire and Worcestershire as well as having the best of a draw with Yorkshire. In between they popped back home to the Kent borders to beat Somerset in two days. They made three changes from the side that had made short work of Worcestershire, with Jennings, Fairservice and Preston making way for Hatfeild, Day and Fielder who was fit again. At first reading of the scorecard, this looks a fairly comfortable victory for Kent over their local rivals, who had yet to win a game, and had secured just a single point from six matches. Although the final margin of 126 runs was substantial, the result was in some doubt up to half past three on the final day.

Winning the toss, Kent took first use of a true, hard wicket. "*The wicket at Tonbridge is something like a Lord's wicket. The ball comes off the pitch very fast and occasionally, one or two keep low. The fast bowler always has a chance and it is against fast bowling that Kent have failed.*"[1] This was the somewhat harsh opinion of *The Times* correspondent who, in his next sentence, makes an attempt to soften his previous criticism by saying, "*Yesterday there was a marked improvement in the batting for they were not afraid to go out to meet the ball.*"[1]

Losing Humphreys early on, there then followed the most "*glorious session*" of cricket when 177 runs were scored before lunch for the loss of one further wicket. "*Seymour made his runs very well and both Hardinge and Woolley played finely. Woolley scored all round the wicket and it was no easy matter to set a field to stop his shots; his driving and hooking were both quite beautiful to watch.*" Seymour was only dismissed through "*a magnificent one-handed catch by Mr Louden.*"[1]

After lunch, Bert Tremlin stemmed the onslaught by varying his pace and flight and was eventually rewarded with Woolley's wicket. There were other useful contributions from the amateurs, Hatfeild and Day, but *The Times* did not altogether approve their method – "*Mr Hatfeild's defence does not look sound*" – but was prepared to concede "*he hits finely with his wrists and he made some splendid drives.*" Then, still in coaching mode, "*Mr Day's was a valuable innings, but he did not get his leg across in his offensive strokes.*"[1]

The innings was wrapped up quickly for 285 with Tremlin returning 4-70. The Essex captain, Johnny Douglas, had bowled well but had little luck, beating the bat on several occasions. Despite missing three catches in the innings, the Essex fielding had stood up well to the pre-lunch onslaught by Hardinge, Seymour and Woolley and Ron Clark, the Essex wicketkeeper, was singled out for special praise by *The Times*.

When Essex batted, they were soon in trouble with Day, exacting prodigious swing, taking the wickets of Douglas, Jack Russell and John Freeman, the brother of future Kent legend "Tich" Freeman, to reduce them to 16-3. The first two were caught by Seymour at slip and the third was bowled all ends up. Peter Perrin and Fred Fane then made "*a useful little stand*" of 29, but in Humphreys' first over, Fane played at a wide ball that was swinging away still further, got an under edge and the ball came back to hit his stumps. Perrin and Colin McIver then saw Essex safely through to the close at 72-4.

The first hour's play on the second morning was crucial in settling the match. "*Essex collapsed badly before the bowling of Blythe – or rather before the combination of Blythe's bowling and Huish's wicket-keeping*"[2] – Perrin and McIver were both stumped, Claude Buckenham was caught behind and Tremlin was bowled. In contrast, the "Vicar of Leyton",[3] Frank Gillingham, provided some resistance, but had Fielder taken a difficult chance at mid off, Essex might very well have had to follow on. The innings finished on 161. Blythe grabbed both the bowling and fielding headlines with 5-46 and an extraordinary catch to dispose of Gillingham. Day finished with

The "Vicar of Leyton", The Rev F H Gillingham – drawn by Sir Leslie Ward as "Cricketing Christianity"

Charlie Blythe: 5-46:
as portrayed by ALS in *Vanity Fair* 1910

Jack Hubble:
"robbed" of a hundred

3-39 from 15 overs, and it was his excellent bowling at the start of the innings which removed Douglas, Russell and Freeman.

When Kent started their second innings, at around ten minutes to one, there were fifties for Humphreys and Hardinge (dropped before scoring) in an opening stand of 105 in 80 minutes. Seymour and Hubble gave "*an exhibition of wonderful hitting.*"[2] to continue the attack. Although the batsmen did not quite achieve the dominance of the first morning of the match, they still scored at over four runs an over. "*There were one or two dangerous strokes behind the wicket and two of them to 'the box'[2] went to hand but they were travelling very fast… Hubble made some beautiful strokes off the fast bowlers; he is a short man but he uses all the height he has and some of his hits through cover point travelled at great pace.*"

Dillon declared at 279-4. Hubble was unbeaten on 97 and Kent had set Essex 404 to win with a day and about eight overs to go. *Wisden* described it as a "*sporting declaration*",[4] which made it all the more strange that he should leave Hubble stranded three short of his century. Asked about this, he said he was unaware of Hubble's impending milestone, provoking the *Kent Messenger* to pronounce that "*an up to date scoreboard is evidently wanted at Tonbridge.*"[5] Essex finished the day on

32 without loss, leaving 372 to score on the final day with the wicket still favouring the batsman.

The next morning, Essex set off with a will led by McIver with sound contributions from all the top six batsmen. At half past three, they had scored 200 for the loss of only three wickets, with Perrin and Douglas going well. A victory for the visitors looked more than a possibility until Fielder began an inspired spell. At 218, he trapped Perrin lbw and then bowled Douglas. Fane was caught by Day and Gillingham was bowled to bring an end to the Essex victory attempt. The remaining wickets went down quickly and Kent won by 126 runs with plenty of time to spare. Fielder had taken 8-120 in 30.5 overs and hit the stumps on two other occasions only to hear the umpire call "*No Ball!*" It was to be his best bowling return of the season.

Kent's victory saw them move back to the top of the Championship table because Middlesex had secured only a single point from their last game. Kent were to remain on top for the rest of the 1913 season.

Two ground records were broken at Tonbridge – the Benefit collection for Ted Humphreys amounted to £45 1s 0d[7] (perhaps due to the collection boxes being taken round the ground by well-known Kent players past and present), while a record 158 motor vehicles ringed the boundary edge.[5]

Sources

1   *The Times* 17th June 1913
2   *The Times* 18th June 1913
3   Canon Frank Hay Gillingham (born in Tokyo in 1875) was educated at Dulwich and Durham University and ordained in 1899. He made his debut for Essex in 1903 and continued to play until 1928. Described as a "fine preacher" by TN Pearce, his Essex team-mate, he put that talent to good use when he was involved in the first ever outside broadcast of cricket on 14th May 1927 when the BBC covered the Essex vs New Zealand match from Leyton. He continued to commentate occasionally for the BBC until he managed to

Peter Perrin (57), Colin McIver (76) and the destroyer of Essex, Arthur Fielder (8-120)

Wally Hardinge: 83 & 50 at Tonbridge   Frank Woolley: 72 in Kent's 1st innings

upset Lord Reith by reading the advertising hoardings that appeared on the ground during a particularly
long rain break during a broadcast from The Oval. He died, aged 77 in 1953.

4   *Wisden* 1914
5   *Kent Messenger* 19th June 1913
6   One other interesting aside in this match was that the Essex team included two Olympic gold medal
       athletes in the form of Claude Buckenham and Johnny Douglas the Essex captain. Buckenham was part
       of the Upton Park FC team that represented GB in the inaugural Olympic tournament in 1900 and
       Douglas was the Olympic Middleweight Champion in 1908 when he beat the Australian Snowy White
       in controversial circumstances in the final.
7   Kent CCC Miniutes book 1913

18th June 1913	P	W	L	DWF	DLF	NC	Max	Pts	PtsPC
Kent	8	7	0	1	0	0	40	38	95.00%
Middlesex	6	5	0	0	1	0	30	26	86.67%
Yorkshire	10	7	1	1	1	0	50	39	78.00%
Northamptonshire	8	5	2	0	1	0	40	26	65.00%
Surrey	9	5	2	1	1	0	45	29	64.44%
Nottinghamshire	7	4	1	0	2	0	35	22	62.86%
Lancashire	10	3	3	4	0	0	50	27	54.00%
Warwickshire	9	3	3	2	1	0	45	22	48.89%
Somerset	4	1	2	1	0	0	20	8	40.00%
Sussex	9	3	4	0	2	0	45	17	37.78%
Derbyshire	8	3	5	0	0	0	40	15	37.50%
Worcestershire	6	1	4	1	0	0	30	8	26.67%
Leicestershire	9	1	7	1	0	0	45	8	17.78%
Hampshire	8	1	6	0	1	0	40	6	15.00%
Gloucestershire	8	0	5	1	2	0	40	5	12.50%
Essex	6	0	6	0	1	0	30	1	3.33%

Warwickshire 1st Innings

C Charlesworth	c Hatfeild b Woolley	47
Rev JH Parsons	b Day	0
Mr F R Foster*	b Fielder	13
WG Quaife	c Seymour b Blythe	31
CS Baker +	c Dillon b Humphreys	59
P Jeeves	b Woolley	30
Mr G Curle	b Woolley	1
Mr W.C. Hands	lbw b Blythe	21
S Santall	c Dillon b Woolley	31
LTA Bates	lbw b Woolley	4
JD Brown	not out	0
Extras	(14 b, 9 lb, 2 nb)	25
Total	(all out, 87.5 overs)	**262**

FOW 1st Innings 1-2, 2-33, 3-83, 4-118, 5-179, 6-190, 7-192, 8-255, 9-259, 10-262
FOW 2nd Innings 1-5, 2-6, 3-6, 4-12, 5-12, 6-12, 7-12, 8-12, 9-15, 10-16

Warwickshire 2nd Innings

[3] c Seymour b Blythe		1
[1] st Huish b Woolley		5
[5] c Hubble b Blythe		2
b Blythe		0
[2] c Humphreys b Woolley		4
c Blythe b Woolley		0
st Huish b Blythe		0
b Woolley		0
ct Huish b Woolley		3
not out		0
st Huish b Blythe		1
		0
(all out, 10.2 overs)		**16**

Kent bowling

	O	M	R	W
Fielder	21	4	56	1
Day	18	4	61	1
Blythe	22	4	50	2
Woolley	16.5	4	44	5
Humphreys	10	2	26	1

Kent bowling

	O	M	R	W
Blythe	5.2	1	8	5
Woolley	5	1	8	5

Kent 1st Innings

E Humphreys	c Baker b Jeeves	11
HTW Hardinge	c Jeeves b Foster	15
J Seymour	c Hands b Jeeves	24
FE Woolley	c Hands b Jeeves	8
JC Hubble	c Bates b Foster	24
Mr EW Dillon*	c Baker b Foster	15
Mr AP Day	b Foster	0
Mr CE Hatfeild	b Foster	10
FH Huish+	not out	7
C Blythe	c Quaife b Jeeves	6
A Fielder	b Foster	0
Extras	(8 lb 4 w)	12
Total	(all out, 59 overs)	**132**

FOW 1st Innings 1-23, 2-27, 3-40, 4-66, 5-104, 6-104, 7-113, 8-116, 9-129, 10-132
FOW 2nd Innings 1-1, 2-16, 3-73, 4-93

Kent 2nd Innings

lbw b Santall		1
b Foster		27
c Jeeves b Foster		9
not out		76
b Charlesworth		10
not out		18
did not bat		
did not bat		
did not bat		
did not bat		
did not bat		
(5b, 1lb)		6
(4 wickets, 37.4 overs)		**147**

Warwickshire bowling

	O	M	R	W
Foster	29	8	62	6
Hands	8	2	14	0
Jeeves	12	5	27	4
Santall	10	5	17	0

Warwickshire bowling

	O	M	R	W
Foster	10	1	44	2
Hands	3.4	0	27	0
Jeeves	7	0	20	0
Santall	11	0	27	1
Charlesworth	6	0	23	1

Kent vs Warwickshire

The Angel Ground, Tonbridge
Thursday 19th, Friday 20th & Saturday 21st June
Toss: Warwickshire
Kent won by 6 wickets
Points: Kent 5 Warwickshire 0

THIS WAS A historic match in more ways than one. To begin with, it was the first time in 14 years that Kent had played Warwickshire, and secondly the visitors' score of 16 in their second innings remains the lowest score made against Kent to this day.

There is some mystery as to why Kent had not played Warwickshire since 1899, which neither Kent nor Warwickshire are able to explain. At that time, there were many petty feuds within county cricket stretching back into the mists of time. Essex had refused to play Warwickshire because of some slight, either real or imagined, years previously, while Sussex had only resumed their fixture in 1911 after a gap of some years. Doubtless the reason for the Midland county's absence from Kentish fixture lists was something similar, although it is often assumed it was simple southern sniffiness. One would like to think this wasn't the case, but it remains a possibility.

Warwickshire were latecomers to the revised County Championship which started in 1890 when, along with Derbyshire, Essex, Hampshire, Leicestershire and Somerset, they competed for the first time in 1895. They performed respectably in their first decade when they finished consistently mid table. They fell away in 1908 (12th), 1909 (12th) and 1910 (14th) before coming from nowhere to win the competition in 1911 when they pipped Kent to the title by 0.16 of a percentage point.

The Angel Ground, Tonbridge, circa 1907

Warwickshire were not the wealthy club they are today, and in the first decade of the century stumbled from crisis to crisis. By 1910, their membership stood at a mere 1,700. Finishing two off the bottom in that season, they cobbled together a new side under the reluctant captaincy of the 22-year-old Frank Foster, whose mind at that time was bent more on marriage than cricket. After missing the first match, when Warwickshire where annihilated by Surrey, he was persuaded by his father, the founder of Foster Brothers, the men's outfitters, that he should, after all, concentrate on cricket. Foster then took his band of *"motley replacements"*,[1] and melded them into an attractive side that quickly discovered they could win cricket matches after all.

The new points system was introduced in 1911 and the fact that Warwickshire played only 20 matches, winning 13 against Kent's 17 from 26, seems to have created some resentment in Kent. The main reason was that in 1911, Warwickshire did not play a fixture against Kent – who were probably the strongest side in the Championship at that time. Neither did they play fixtures against Nottinghamshire, Middlesex or Essex – four of the first eight in the table that year. In fairness, Warwickshire didn't play Somerset either and they finished bottom.

The History of Kent Cricket (Appendix F) grumbled: *"Kent, who were by general consent, the strongest team of the year, being second … by any of the systems formerly in use the latter would have headed the list."*[2] Whether this was a valid complaint or just sour grapes probably depends on your county affiliation. The Kent case was based on the apparent absurdity of the negligible difference between the points for a win (five) and those for a draw (three points for a lead on first innings and one for a loss on first innings), and the fact that Warwickshire had not played matches against the above counties. In their defence, Warwickshire argued that it was no fault of theirs that their fixture list didn't include these counties – they wanted to play against them but their invitations had been rejected. Middlesex and Nottinghamshire hadn't played the Midlanders at any time since Warwickshire first competed in 1895 and Kent had "dropped" them for the 1900 season in favour of Worcestershire.

One Warwickshire cricket historian, Robert Brooke in his book *FR Foster – The Fields Were Sudden Bare* says, *"It seemed out of the question that a challenge could be mounted to the old counties. Kent, Middlesex and Surrey in the south, Lancashire, Nottinghamshire and Yorkshire up north seemed resentful of the Midland interlopers – why else the reluctance to arrange fixtures? Middlesex and Notts had never yet played the Edgbaston side in the Championship, while Kent had not done so since 1899. Kent had won successive titles – perhaps it's easier if one is allowed to pick and choose opponents."*[3] This excerpt appears in a chapter entitled *"Tell Kent from me she hath lost…"*, which, for a Kent supporter, must be one of the least favourite out of context quotations from *Henry VI Part II*, which, of course was written by another

Percy Jeeves and Willie Quaife

Warwickshire-born "player". The full version reads more agreeably: "*Tell Kent from me, she hath lost her best man, and exhort all the world to be cowards; for I, that never feared any, am vanquished by famine, not by valour.*"[4] Although, in truncated form, this is a "red rag" to the Kentish bull, there seems to be little point in encouraging further inter-county strife, and it is best to let the case stand or fall on the strength of the arguments already aired above. However, at this distance of time, it is surprising to find Kent's success in this period attributed to nothing more than being able to select their opponents at will. One hundred years is a very long time to fret over such things.

This was the second match of Kent's week at The Angel Ground following immediately after the win against Essex, where over 1,000 runs had been scored on a good, hard, pitch. They fielded an unchanged side. Warwickshire, however, were not at full strength. "*Jack of all trades Charles Barker deputised for the injured Smith. Kinnear, Field, Langley and the Stevens twins were unable to turn out.*"[3]

Warwickshire won the toss and scored a very respectable 262 with only Charles Baker passing 50. He was assisted by the waif-like Willie Quaife and Percy Jeeves in robust style. These were two of the more interesting members of the Warwickshire side. Jeeves was the inspiration for PG Wodehouse's famous gentleman's gentleman and Quaife was once described by a bowler as "*like bowling at a 4th stump.*"[5] Later in the afternoon there was a stand of 63 between William Hands and Sydney Santall.

TWO GENTLEMEN OF WARWICKSHIRE.

Mr. F. R. Foster (*Captain of the Warwickshire XI., who have just won the Cricket Championship*).
"TELL KENT FROM ME SHE HATH LOST."—*II. Henry VI., iv. 10.*
William Shakspeare. "WARWICK, THOU ART WORTHY!"—*III. Henry VI., iv. 6.*

The cartoon that appeared following Warwickshire's 1911 Championship

Crowther Charleshurst and Sydney Santall, Warwickshire's run makers in the first innings

Woolley was the most successful Kent bowler with 5-40, which he regarded as one of his best ever bowling performances.[6]

When Kent batted, they were in early trouble losing Humphreys, Hardinge and Woolley to Jeeves and the England all-rounder, Foster, to reach 40-3 by stumps. *The Times* remarks that Woolley was "*caught by Hands in the box*" which, for the modern reader, might create some confusion, and cause them to enquire whether he made a full recovery or, perhaps, whether charges were preferred by the Tonbridge constabulary. That is until they discover the great all-rounder had been caught at gully by the Warwickshire opening bowler.[7]

The second day of the match was badly interrupted by the weather and only an hour's play was possible. Kent were still able to score at a run a minute to put on 64 for the loss of Seymour's wicket.

When play started on Saturday in front of a crowd of 3,000,[8] with Kent on 104-4, a draw seemed the most likely result but, due to the state of the rain-affected wicket, which was by now drying quickly under a hot sun, the remainder of the Kent wickets fell for a mere 28 runs in 45 minutes to concede the visitors a huge first innings advantage of 130. Dillon was the first to depart when he "*lashed out at Foster's first ball and was caught by Baker standing back.*"[8] Day was bowled by a beautiful delivery first ball and Hatfeild was lucky to avoid becoming the hat-trick victim when he was beaten all ends up, with the ball missing his leg stump by the proverbial coat of varnish.

The score gradually crept up over the next few overs and Hubble eventually avoided the follow-on with an off drive, before being caught at short leg off the very

Frank Foster:
Warwickshire captain

next ball. Hatfeild's charmed innings came to an end when Foster produced another fine delivery to bowl him. At this point, Foster had bowled four overs, taking four wickets without conceding a run. Huish and Blythe added 12 runs together but the innings was over quickly when Jeeves had Blythe caught by Quaife and, in the very next over, Foster collected his sixth wicket by bowling Fielder with the last ball.

Towards the end of the Kent innings but, presumably, before Blythe batted, Woolley and Blythe sat in the pavilion contemplating a Kent follow-on: "*We thought we saw Kent following on, making a recovery, knocking the cover off Mr Foster and all that kind of thing and setting them 160 or so to get; we two getting our own back, and winning the match, on a cut up surface in the fourth innings.*"[6] It didn't quite work out that way but it wasn't that far wide of the mark.

Warwickshire must have been fairly confident going in to bat for the second time at a quarter past twelve with that sort of lead, and when someone asked Foster if he was intending to enforce the follow-on, he responded: "*No fear – We've got you where we want you, we're going in again and you can have fourth innings on that stuff.*"[6]

Both Foster and his interrogator appear to have overlooked the fact that the follow-on deficit was 150. Foster's remark was apparently overheard by Fred Huish, whose Sybil-like response was "*You know, I've seen sides out for next to nothing on such a pitch with two left handers bowling.*"[6]

In an attempt to subdue the wicket, Foster asked for the heavy roller to be used, which appears to have been a misjudgement because 62 balls and 43 minutes later, Warwickshire were all out for the unbelievable score of 16. The wicket was described by *Wisden* as "*quite unplayable*", and including the four Kent second innings wickets, 20 wickets fell on that final day. *The Times* said: "*On sticky wickets, Blythe and Woolley are a terrible proposition. Blythe is probably as clever a bowler of his type as has ever been seen. No one, it is said, makes the batsman think more, and Woolley, with his height and spin, on such wickets is almost as formidable. The batsman gets no rest at either end and with the slips standing almost in reach of the bat, they are indeed terrors to face.*"[9]

This was a very telling comment as Kent not only had the most potent form of attack for a "sticky dog" wicket such as they encountered in their second innings, but they also had three other left-arm bowlers in the form of Humphreys, Hardinge and Hatfeild in reserve. This was something *The Times* also remarked upon in their summary of the weekend results printed the following Monday, and added that Huish was also left handed as a wicketkeeper despite batting right

The Tonbridge scoreboard at the close of the Warwickshire second innings

Frank Woolley, the top scorer and 10-48 with the ball

handed. Warwickshire's attack in the form of the fastish left-arm seam of Foster, the right-arm seam of Jeeves, Hands and the 40-year-old Santall was much less suited to the conditions that existed at Tonbridge on that warm June afternoon in 1913.

Blythe and Woolley each took five wickets for eight runs and Huish picked up four victims, three of them stumped. Although he had conceded 14 byes in the first innings, his keeping was reported as being "*particularly brilliant*" in the second. From first to last, none of the Warwickshire batsmen could find an answer to their bowling and, at one time, it looked as if the previous record lowest score of 12 by Northamptonshire against Gloucestershire, at The Spa Ground in Gloucester in 1907, might be lowered. It wasn't to be, however, because with the score at 11, Santall snicked one through the slips off Woolley to secure the run which tied the record. The innings subsided to its sad conclusion four runs later when the final batsman, Leonard Bates, went down the track to get at Blythe, only to see the ball turn past him, leaving Huish to remove the bails. Despite this miraculous performance by the two left-arm spinners, *Wisden* had thought that the target of 147 was "*impossible given that the wicket was still treacherous.*"[10]

Dillon, knowing that Foster had used the heavy roller only an hour before, decided to rely on the light roller and a good sweeping so as not to make matters

Colin Blythe:
5-8 in the Warwickshire second innings

Fred Huish:
four victims in the Warwickshire second innings

worse and *"the turf was allowed to recover in a perfectly natural way"*.[9] Even so, Kent lost Humphreys and Seymour almost immediately to be 16-2. Woolley and Hardinge steadied the ship, putting on 57 for the third wicket before Hardinge was bowled by Foster for a valuable 27.

Meanwhile, Woolley had set about the Warwickshire attack with what *Wisden* described as *"dazzling brilliancy"*.[10] He lost Hubble with the score on 93 and was joined by his captain, Dillon, who was content to keep an end up, take the odd single and marvel at the genius at work the other end. *"Woolley continued to hit in the most delightful fashion"*[9] and the winning runs were scored without further loss after 37.4 overs. *"Woolley scored his 76 runs in 80 minutes and throughout he drove and hit to leg with great power"*[9] to secure Kent's unlikely victory by six wickets and earn the full five points for their efforts. Had the match petered out into the draw, which at the start of the day seemed the best they could hope for, Kent would have only added a single point to their total by virtue of having "lost" on the first innings.

This result was a fine example of the "never say die" attitude of the very high-quality Kent sides of the era who maintained their belief in attacking cricket whatever the circumstances, even when the odds appeared stacked against them.

Time and again they snatched victories from situations where the match could well have been lost but for this spirit.

It was also typical that the match winner should have been Frank Woolley, who often seemed to make the difference with either bat or ball. In this match he not only took 10-48, but there was probably no other player in the country who could have played the innings he did to win the match on such a wicket. Opinions differed as to whether Woolley's innings was chanceless. One report claimed it was, whilst another referred to him having been dropped at mid on when he had scored only 23.[11]

When the match finished at 20 minutes to four, large crowds gathered outside the pavilion to cheer the Kent side for having achieved this remarkable victory. Newspapers reported some four to six thousand spectators in the ground at the end of the match and, if the initial estimates were correct, then two thousand of these arrived during the day as word of Kent's position spread in the locality of Tonbridge. This wasn't an unusual occurrence, as Chris Arnot remarked in the opening paragraph of the chapter on The Angel Ground in his book *Britain's Lost Cricket Grounds* – *"Frank Woolley could empty Tonbridge High Street. All he had to do was stride from the pavilion across the nearby Angel Ground and take guard for Kent. Tobacconists and butchers would bolt their doors and not expect to open them any time soon."*[12]

Blythe, who took only one wicket in the first innings, was overheard to say *"Well perhaps I can bowl after all."*[11]

The match made headlines in many of the national newspapers even if their local correspondent hadn't actually been at the match. The *Evening News,* for example, said *"A truly wonderful achievement. Under such conditions as prevailed the odds against almost any side making 147 runs must have been enormous, and that they should have been obtained for the loss of four batsmen was nothing short of marvellous... Woolley rose to the occasion in such grand style that on resuming the 131 runs which Kent still required were hit off in less than an hour and a half."*[13]

At the end of that day, the Championship table saw Kent extend their lead as Yorkshire had been unable to capture the last four Middlesex wickets to force a win at Lord's. In that match, there was a fine all-round performance from William Booth, who scored 107 and 30 not out, as well as taking 5-72 and 3-64.

Sources

1   *Breaking the Big Six: Warwickshire's first county championship title*: David Mutton Cricket Web.net
2   *The History of Kent Cricket* (Appendix F)
3   Robert Brooke – *Frank Foster The Fields Were Sudden Bare* ACS Publications 2011
      Although Frank Foster subsequently went on to have an excellent summer in 1914, he never fulfilled his true promise and his life ended in tragedy. In 1915 he was involved in a motor cycle accident which ended his playing career and, thereafter, his life drifted. His attempts at a career in the family business ended with him being sacked in 1928 and he then based himself in London, living off an

allowance from his father. In 1931, he was involved in a murder investigation when one of his cheques was discovered in the flat of a young prostitute who had been found dead in an empty shop. He escaped formal charges when the coroner accepted his rather eccentric version of events but, nevertheless, it caused a significant scandal. Matters then started to go from bad to worse. He separated from his wife and family and, following his incurring significant gambling debts, he was made bankrupt. The first signs of psychiatric problems began to manifest themselves when, in 1934, he publicly declared that he should be selected for England to play against Australia as he "*knew how to bowl to Australians*". After the war, he was banned from Edgbaston "*for his disgraceful conduct in the past season, notably towards amateur players and the catering staff.*" In 1949, he was charged with larceny and fraud and was interned in the Northamptonshire County General Lunatic Asylum, where he died in 1958. It was, perhaps, more than ironic that Warwickshire should have achieved the 1911 Championship title at Northampton when Foster said "*My joy was unbounded. I will always remember Northampton for giving me the greatest day of my life.*" It was a sad end for such a talented cricketer.

4　*Henry VI Part II* – Act 4 Scene 10. This quotation was also used by Paddy Briggs in his book, *John Shepherd – The Loyal Cavalier*, when he describes Shep's last match for Kent – "Tell Kent from me, she hath lost her best man."

5　*A Cricketers' Companion* – C Martin-Jenkins

6　*Frank Woolley: King of Games*: Stanley Paul 1936

7　"The box" being an alternative term for the "gully" at that time, and in fairly common usage in the various press reports consulted in researching these matches.

8　*The People* Sunday 21st June 1913

9　*The Times* 23rd June 1913

10　*Wisden* 1914 – Kent Matches p10

11　*The Kent Messenger* 27th June 1913

12　Christopher Arnot: *Britain's Lost Cricket Grounds*: Arum 2011

13　*The Evenings News* 21st June 1913

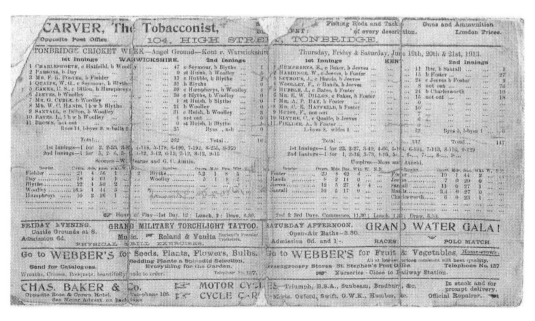

The original printed scorecard of the match that would have been sold on the ground
at the end of the day's play showing the adverts placed by local businesses in the Tonbridge area

Kent 1st Innings

E Humphreys	c Barnett b Cranfield	32
HTW Hardinge	c Smith b Jessop	20
FE Woolley	c Smith b Dipper	50
J Seymour	c and b Jessop	62
JC Hubble	c Cranfield b Jessop	24
Mr EW Dillon *	c and b Jessop	0
Mr CE Hatfeild	c Sewell b Dennett	13
FH Huish +	c Jessop b Dennett	1
WJ Fairservice	lbw b Dennett	4
C Blythe	b Dennett	5
A Fielder	not out	0
Extras	(3 b, 4 lb, 2 nb)	9
Total	(all out, 71.2 overs)	220

FOW 1st Innings 1-48, 2-58, 3-142, 4-177, 5-177, 6-200, 7-208, 8-212, 9-219, 10-220

Kent 2nd Innings

	c Smith b Dennett	52
	c Smith b Parker	3
	c Green b Dennett	11
	c Barnett b Dennett	0
	b Dennett	6
	c Barnett b Dennett	7
	c Nason b Parker	0
	b Dennett	10
	not out	7
	c Green b Dennett	0
	c and b Dennett	16
	(1 w)	1
	(all out, 49.5 overs)	113

FOW 2nd Innings 1-7, 2-7, 3-23, 4-40, 5-58, 6-65, 7-83, 8-90, 9-90, 10-113

Gloucs bowling	O	M	R	W
Parker	12	5	29	0
Dennett	22.2	5	57	4
Jessop	21	3	64	4
Cranfield	15	3	54	1
Dipper	1	0	7	1

Gloucs bowling	O	M	R	W
Parker	17	6	40	2
Dennett	24.5	5	63	8
Jessop	8	3	9	0

Gloucestershire 1st Innings

AE Dipper	c Woolley b Blythe	4
Mr CS Barnett	c Seymour b Blythe	0
Mr COH Sewell *	c Dillon b Blythe	37
Mr GL Jessop	c Hatfeild b Woolley	1
T Langdon	c Woolley b Humphreys	22
Mr JWW Nason	c Seymour b Humphreys	20
Mr MA Green	b Fairservice	2
H Smith +	run out	54
LL Cranfield	c Fairservice b Blythe	33
CWL Parker	b Blythe	26
EG Dennett	not out	0
Extras	(2 lb, 1 nb)	3
Total	(all out, 67.1 overs)	202

FOW 1st Innings 1-2, 2-42, 3-42, 4-43, 5-81, 6-84, 7-88, 8-146, 9-188, 10-202

Gloucestershire 2nd Innings

	c Huish b Fielder	29
	not out	49
	c Blythe b Humphreys	21
	lbw b Fairservice	10
	b Fairservice	1
	not out	18
	did not bat	
	did not bat	
	did not bat	
	did not bat	
	did not bat	
	(1 b, 1 lb, 1 nb, 1 w)	4
	(4 wickets, 50.1 overs)	132

FOW 2nd Innings 1-52, 2-93, 3-94, 4-104

Kent bowling	O	M	R	W
Blythe	24	5	65	5
Woolley	16.1	5	50	1
Fairservice	16	6	38	1
Humphreys	7	1	25	2
Fielder	4	0	21	0

Kent bowling	O	M	R	W
Blythe	7	3	14	0
Woolley	3	1	7	0
Fairservice	20	6	44	2
Humphreys	10	3	26	1
Fielder	8	1	36	1
Hatfeild	2.1	1	1	0

Gloucestershire vs Kent

Ashley Down Ground, Bristol
Monday 23rd & Tuesday 24th June 1913
Toss: Kent
Gloucestershire won by 6 wickets
Points: Gloucestershire 5 Kent 0

KENT MUST HAVE travelled to Bristol in high spirits to meet Gloucestershire, who were reclining in 12th position in the table having played eight matches, won two and lost three. There seemed to be little to worry them and indeed, it was described in some newspapers as a David and Goliath contest. But, as happens every once in a while, it was David's pebble that found its mark and Kent suffered their first defeat of the season by six wickets inside two days.

Kent made one change from the game at Tonbridge with Fairservice returning for Arthur Day. Kent won the toss and elected to bat. The start was delayed by a sharp shower which had an effect on the already soft wicket. The batsmen set off in positive mood and were at first successful without being able to dominate. The openers put on 48 for the first wicket with Humphreys dropped in Charlie Parker's first over by the captain, Cyril Sewell.

When Gilbert Jessop replaced George Dennett, he immediately had Hardinge caught behind for 20. Humphreys followed ten runs later, bringing together Seymour and Woolley, who attacked knowing the wicket was getting more

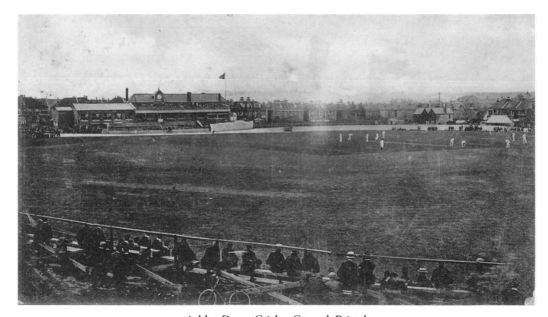

Ashley Down Cricket Ground, Bristol

Left – Harry Smith who made the top score of 54 in the Gloucestershire first innings
Centre – "CS" Barnett, known by his initials alone. The father of Gloucestershire legend, Charlie Barnett,
and the rock of the Gloucestershire second innings at Bristol in 1913
Right – George Dennett, 4-67 and 8-63

difficult as it dried. *"Woolley hit merrily sending the ball seven times to the boundary and completing his 50 in as many minutes"*.[1] They added 84 in 50 minutes but at 177, the 39-year-old Jessop picked up wickets with successive balls. With the wicket now more favourable to spin, Dennett was reintroduced to the attack and took the remaining four wickets. The last six wickets had fallen for just 43 runs and Kent's innings had subsided to 220 all out.

Gloucestershire started poorly against Blythe and Woolley and lost "CS" Barnett (usually known by his initials to distinguish him from his better known son who was also Charles, but more commonly Charlie), with only two runs scored. Whilst Sewell hit out, Alf Dipper played quietly at the other end. At 42, Blythe induced an edge from Dipper which was well caught by Woolley at slip, and when "Croucher" Jessop had made only one, he fell to a smart catch by Hatfeild to leave the home side struggling at 43-4. Tom Langdon and John Nason contributed a useful fifth wicket partnership of 38 but both fell to Humphreys within a few minutes of each other. Michael Green was then bowled by Fairservice to leave Gloucestershire on 88-7. Harry Smith and Lionel Cranfield batted patiently during the final overs so that Gloucestershire were 116-7 at the close, with the visitors comfortably in the driving seat.

The next morning, Kent would have been keen to pick up the remaining wickets cheaply, score a quick 250-odd runs and set Gloucestershire 300 plus to win on a wicket that they hoped would still favour the bowlers. Nothing "*seemed less likely when play was begun in the morning that Kent would suffer their first defeat this season.*"[2] But things did not go quite as Kent wished, largely because the wicket had recovered and was now good for batting.

Smith and Cranfield took up where they had left off the previous evening, steadily taking the score to 146 when Cranfield was caught by Fairservice off Blythe for 33. Smith and Parker batted aggressively in adding 45 in 25 minutes before Smith was run out for a very good 54. Parker's enthusiastic knock was ended when he was bowled by Blythe to wrap up the Gloucestershire innings for 202, only 18 runs behind the Kent total. Blythe was the main wicket taker with 5-65 from 24 overs.

The Times stated: "*as the wicket was in excellent condition, it was fully expected that Kent, on going in a second time, would make a large score but, in a little over two hours they were dismissed for 113.*"[3]

Those then are the bald facts, but whether it was poor batting on the part of the Kent side (with the exception of Humphreys who made 52), or just brilliant cricket by Gloucestershire, isn't completely clear, but some excellent bowling by George Dennett in particular, coupled with some wonderful catching and fielding, were major factors.

Wisden implies that it was down to poor batting by most of the batsmen. "*While so many of his colleagues failed to steady themselves, Humphreys batted admirably going in first and being eighth man out. Undoubtedly, the majority of the Kent batsmen played in a manner unworthy of their reputations.*"[2] *The Times*, on the other hand, gives the credit to the Gloucestershire fielding. "*Everything came off for Gloucestershire, Dennett, who bowled in his best form, being splendidly supported in the field. The catches in the long field that dismissed Woolley and Blythe, and the one at square leg from which Mr Dillon was out, were alike brilliant.*"[2]

The clue is probably in the reference to the catches being taken from aggressive strokes which implies that, on this occasion, the characteristically dashing Kentish approach came unstuck, and that nobody could be persuaded towards a more cautious approach. On balance, *Wisden* is probably closer to the mark. Nevertheless, it was a fine performance by the home side which set them a relatively modest total of 132 with at least a day and a session in which to make the runs required for victory.

There was never any question that Kent might turn the tables on Gloucestershire and bowl them out to atone for their earlier batting indiscretions. The first 50 came up in an hour as "*Mr Barnett and Dipper made a capital start…*

then, after Dipper had left, Mr Sewell helped Mr Barnett put on 41 in just over half an hour for the second wicket".[2]

Fairservice removed the potentially dangerous Jessop and Langdon cheaply, but Nason and "CS" Barnett hit off the remaining 28 runs required without incident to give Gloucestershire their first win over Kent since 1907. Unaccountably, Blythe and Woolley had only bowled ten of the 51 overs in the Gloucestershire second innings. The winning runs were scored, at ten minutes past six, which gave Kent another free day but on this occasion, it wasn't as well deserved as the ones earned at Leicester, Stourbridge and Catford.

Kent's defeat was greeted with great enthusiasm by the counties immediately below them in the table and particularly by the Yorkshire newspapers. The *Hull Daily Mail* printed the piece which is reproduced below.

FROM OUR CRICKET REPRESENTATIVE
SHEFFIELD, Wednesday

Kent has fallen from its proud estate, and great was the shouting of the captains. We were all agog at Lord's on Saturday to see if Warwickshire would seize the opportunity by the locks, but Kent made their dramatic and leviathan effort, saving the match grandly. Now although no one knows what a curse an unbeaten certificate can be – by reason of the strain it imposes – so well as the Yorkshire team – the elder members of it at least – we never expected lowly Gloucestershire to play the part of David and fell Goliath.

It is true that the conjuncture of such stars in the slow bowling world as Dennett, Woolley and Blythe stirred our appetites a little for the western contest at Bristol. But the event eclipsed all anticipations. Dennett who had carried slaughter at Notts and Northants,

bore off all the chaplets of honour, and chiefly due to his grand science, Gloucester possessed a winning chance which the fight of yesterday afternoon only made clearer.

Although Dennett dominates the stage – he took eight wickets for 63 in the Kent second innings and four for 57 in the first – it would be difficult to pick out a single man in the Gloucester side who did not do his devoir nobly. The valiant withstanding of the Kent attack by the Gloucester "tail" first pulled the chances of the game round. Dennett's bowling and Barnett's batting, allied to brilliant keenness in the field and stoutness under fire in the last ordeal of making 132 against a desperate Kent final rally – did the rest. Kent's figures in the championship are now 86 whilst, if we beat Warwick, we shall have 78.33. Verily, Achilles has shown a tender heel.

Sources
1   *The Times* 25th June 1913
2   *Wisden* 1914
3   *The Times* 26th June 1913

Other players from the match. Left – Ted Humphreys, top scorer in the Kent second innings
Centre – Charlie Parker proving that 20 a day keeps a bowler fit
Right – The Gloucestershire captain Mr COH Sewell

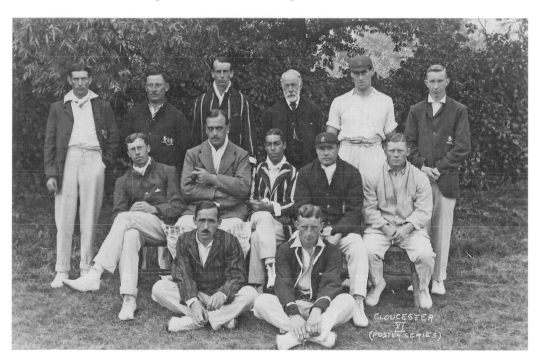

Gloucestershire in 1913
Standing : CWL Parker, T Langdon, FB Roberts, EG Clarke, TH Gange, AE Dipper
Sitting : LD Bownlee, DC Robinson, Mr COH Sewell (Captain), Mr GL Jessop, Mr JWW Nason
On ground : EG Dennett, H Smith

Hampshire 1st Innings

J Stone +	retired hurt	9
HAW Bowell	c Huish b Blythe	35
G Brown	c Seymour b Woolley	71
CP Mead	c Seymour b Woolley	33
Rev WV Jephson	b Fielder	27
Mr EM Sprot *	b Blythe	27
JA Newman	c Huish b Fielder	2
ER Remnant	b Woolley	6
AS Kennedy	b Blythe	18
Mr A Jaques	lbw b Blythe	13
Mr GAC Sandeman	not out	5
Extras	(5 b, 1 lb, 8 nb, 1 w)	15
Total	(all out, 82.4 overs)	**261**

FOW 1st Innings 1-57, 2-135, 3-159, 4-200, 5-212, 6-219, 7-219, 8-244, 9-261

Hampshire 2nd Innings

	absent hurt	
[1]	c Woolley b Blythe	6
[2]	lbw b Woolley	50
	b Fairservice	76
[3]	b Woolley	18
[7]	c Hatfeild b Fairservice	0
[5]	c Huish b Blythe	11
[6]	c Huish b Blythe	12
[8]	c Woolley b Blythe	0
[9]	c Huish b Blythe	2
[10]	not out	0
	(11 b, 2 lb, 3 nb,)	16
	(all out, 63.1 overs)	**191**

FOW 2nd Innings 1-11, 2-60, 3-97, 4-98, 5-155, 6-175, 7-181, 8-191, 9-191

Kent bowling	O	M	R	W
Fielder	31	3	93	2
Blythe	18.4	6	35	4
Fairservice	7	0	34	0
Humphreys	3	0	12	0
Woolley	21	5	64	3
Hatfeild	2	0	8	0

Kent bowling	O	M	R	W
Fielder	13	1	44	0
Blythe	22.1	4	60	5
Fairservice	4	2	3	2
Woolley	24	8	68	2

Kent 1st Innings

E Humphreys	c Bowell b Jaques	2
HTW Hardinge	b Sandeman	168
J Seymour	b Jaques	124
FE Woolley	c Jephson b Jaques	105
JC Hubble	c Sprot b Jaques	4
Mr EW Dillon *	c Newman b Kennedy	48
Mr CE Hatfeild	lbw b Sandeman	8
FH Huish +	c Brown b Kennedy	9
WJ Fairservice	c Sprot b Kennedy	17
C Blythe	st +Jephson b Jaques	6
A Fielder	not out	2
Extras	(19 b, 8 lb, 1 nb, 6 w)	34
Total	(all out, 132.3 overs)	**527**

FOW 1st Innings 1-6, 2-237, 3-404, 4-413, 5-442, 6-459, 7-496, 8-502, 9-509, 10-527

Hampshire bowling	O	M	R	W
Jaques	34	5	101	5
Brown	19	1	96	0
Kennedy	27.3	0	116	3
Newman	17	2	47	0
Remnant	17	2	60	0
Sandeman	18	4	73	2

Hampshire vs Kent

United Services Ground, Portsmouth
Thursday 26th, Friday 27th & Saturday 28th June
Toss: Hampshire
Kent won by an innings and 75 runs
Points: Hampshire 0 Kent 5

KENT ARRIVED IN Portsmouth keen to make amends for their first defeat of the season at Bristol. The weather was fine, the wicket hard and true. When Edward Sprot, the Hampshire captain, won the toss, he told Kent to field, relishing the prospect of what was traditionally a fine batting wicket. Almost immediately, the Hampshire opener and wicketkeeper Jimmy Stone pulled a muscle in his leg and retired hurt, taking no further part in the match.

For some reason, ill feeling crept into this match almost from the start as George Brown, the number three batsman, decided to take on Arthur Fielder. Early in his innings, Fielder bowled a bouncer to Brown, who had a reputation as something of an iron man who could tear a pack of cards in two with his huge hands. *"Dropping his bat to his side, Brown stood up and took the ball full in the chest giving an exultant roar 'He's not fast'."*[1] Many years later, after the War, there was a sequel to this tale. Playing against Lancashire, whose side included the Australian fast bowler Ted MacDonald, Brown attempted the same trick. MacDonald was just about the quickest bowler in the world at this time, and when Brown took the ball full in the chest as he had done to Fielder, he started to roar the same words at the fielders and crowd but managed to deliver only *"He's ...."*[1] before slumping to the ground in a heap.

This incident with Fielder appeared to stiffen Brown's resolve and he went on to make 71 as the only man to pass 50 in the innings. *Wisden* says that *"only Brown and Mead were seen to advantage"*, and the final total of 261 which, given the nature of the wicket and the subsequent Kent total, must have been seen as moderate at

United Services Ground, Portsmouth circa 1905 and 2005

best. With Brown holding the innings together, Hampshire reached 200 for the loss of only three wickets but, from then onwards, the Kent bowlers had matters all their own way. The final seven wickets fell for only 61 runs, and but for some resistance by Alec Kennedy and Arthur Jaques, matters could have been worse.

Kent began unsteadily in the short time they had to bat before the close, losing Humphreys at six to Jaques before Hardinge and Seymour saw them through to stumps on 38-1.

The next day the Kent batsmen took full advantage of a hard, fast batting wicket, and in warm sunshine, they scored 471 runs for the loss of eight wickets. Hundreds were made by Hardinge, Seymour and Woolley and during his innings, the last completed his 1,000 runs for the season.

Hardinge and Seymour put on 231 for the second wicket in just three hours. Seymour played with great freedom and made his 124 in 180 minutes with 17 fours. Hardinge was more circumspect – in all probability because his partners were scoring so freely and his 168 was made in 310 minutes. His partnership with Woolley put on 167 in two hours. He gave one chance in his innings at 140 when he should have been stumped, but as the regular wicketkeeper was off the field it is perhaps understandable that the stand-in missed the opportunity.

Woolley plundered the Hampshire bowling for the remainder of the final session with his hundred taking 140 minutes. Dillon scored a quick 48 and by the

The Hampshire captain, Edward Sprot

'BEST BAT "FORCE" BEST BALL'

G. T. Mead HAMPSHIRE.

Philip Mead:
55,061 runs for Hampshire between 1905 and 1936
17 England caps averaging 49.37

close Kent were 509-9. Despite the severe pummelling they received, the Hampshire side put in *"much persevering work backed up by keen fielding."* [2]

The following morning, Kent continued batting, and after a few hearty blows by Fairservice, Blythe was stumped by the stand-in wicketkeeper, Walter Jephson, to give Jacques his fifth wicket. The innings closed at 527. Jaques, with his leg breaks and googlies had taken 5-101 and Hampshire needed 267 to make Kent bat again.

With Stone unable to bat, the rest moved up one place each and Horace Bowell opened with Brown, who again batted well despite losing his partner for six, caught at slip by Woolley off Blythe. Missed at nine by Hatfeild, Brown made his 50 in only 80 minutes before being trapped lbw by Woolley. Woolley had also bowled Jephson, so that the score at lunch, with Hampshire having batted for an hour and a half, was 108-4. *"After lunch, Mead and Remnant offered such determined opposition for 50 minutes that just after three o'clock Hampshire had 155 on the board with only four wickets down."* [3] At that point, however, Blythe broke the partnership and swiftly followed up with the wickets of Newman and Kennedy, leaving Hampshire 181-7. The last three wickets went down for ten runs with Mead the final batsmen dismissed when *"a ball from Fairservice struck his pad and rolled onto his stumps. This ended the match."* [3] Mead had played admirably and *"looked to possess a capital chance of making*

A cartoon from *The World of Cricket* (Editor AC McLaren) dating from July 1914 by "Chic"

yet another hundred."[4] He had batted for two hours and ten minutes for his 76. Blythe had taken 5-60 and there were two wickets apiece for Woolley and Fairservice.

Kent had shrugged off their defeat at Bristol and now headed north to Trent Bridge to meet Nottinghamshire, who had been held to a draw at Hove and come away with just a single point.

Sources

1   John Arlott – *The Cricketer*: Profile of George Brown
2   *Manchester Courier* 30th June 1913
3   *The Times* 28th June 1913

George Brown: Hampshire and England

The Hampshire side of 1913 at the Bournemouth Cricket Week
Left to right: White, Tennyson, Jaques, McDonnell, Abercrombie, Stone, Brown, Newman, Bowell, Mead
and Kennedy. Amateurs are to the left of the keeper, professionals to the right.

28th June 1913	P	W	L	DWF	DLF	NC	Max	Pts	PtsPC
Kent	11	9	1	1	0	0	55	48	87.27%
Middlesex	8	6	0	0	2	0	40	32	80.00%
Yorkshire	13	8	1	3	1	0	65	50	76.92%
Northamptonshire	10	6	2	0	2	0	50	32	64.00%
Surrey	11	5	2	1	3	0	55	31	56.36%
Lancashire	13	4	4	5	0	0	65	35	53.85%
Nottinghamshire	10	4	2	1	3	0	50	26	52.00%
Sussex	11	4	4	1	2	0	55	25	45.45%
Worcestershire	8	3	4	1	0	0	40	18	45.00%
Warwickshire	11	3	5	2	1	0	55	22	40.00%
Derbyshire	9	3	6	0	0	0	45	15	33.33%
Somerset	5	1	3	1	0	0	25	8	32.00%
Gloucestershire	9	1	5	1	2	0	45	10	22.22%
Leicestershire	10	1	8	1	0	0	50	8	16.00%
Hampshire	11	1	8	0	2	0	55	7	12.73%
Essex	8	0	6	1	1	0	40	4	10.00%

Nottinghamshire 1st Innings

G Gunn	run out	40
GM Lee	c Day b Fielder	0
J Hardstaff	b Fielder	16
JR Gunn	run out	92
WW Whysall	c and b Day	38
J Iremonger	c Humphreys b Fielder	1
Mr GO Gauld *	c Day b Fielder	20
EB Alletson	b Day	9
TW Oates +	c Jennings b Day	0
H Wilson	c Seymour b Day	4
W Riley	not out	7
Extras	(17 b, 14 lb, 8 nb)	39
Total	(all out, 88.5 overs)	**266**

FOW 1st Innings 1-3, 2-40, 3-90, 4-213, 5-214, 6-218, 7-244, 8-244, 9-256, 10-266

Nottinghamshire 2nd Innings

	c Woolley b Fielder	20
	c Mason b Fielder	0
	lbw b Day	17
	c Huish b Mason	55
	b Day	39
	c Hardinge b Mason	8
	b Fielder	0
	b Blythe	18
	c Woolley b Fielder	34
	c and b Fielder	19
	not out	0
	(1 b, 7 lb, 6 nb)	14
	(all out, 71.2 overs)	**224**

FOW 2nd Innings 1-7, 2-38, 3-40, 4-112, 5-125, 6-125, 7-164, 8-174, 9-219, 10-224

Kent bowling	O	M	R	W
Fielder	24.5	1	67	4
Day	21	4	46	4
Blythe	21	3	55	0
Woolley	13	3	26	0
Mason	7	2	27	0
Humphreys	2	0	6	0

Kent bowling	O	M	R	W
Fielder	23.2	3	80	5
Day	19	4	59	2
Blythe	11	4	18	1
Woolley	4	2	9	0
Mason	11	3	34	2
Humphreys	3	1	10	0

Kent 1st Innings

E Humphreys	st Oates b JR Gunn	68
HTW Hardinge	b Iremonger	14
C Blythe	c Gauld b Iremonger	3
FH Huish +	c G Gunn b Gauld	7
J Seymour	b Iremonger	4
FE Woolley	c Hardstaff b Riley	25
Mr JR Mason	b JR Gunn	75
Mr EW Dillon *	b Lee	4
DW Jennings	c Lee b Alletson	48
Mr AP Day	c Oates b Alletson	16
A Fielder	not out	1
Extras	(9 b, 4 lb, 1 nb)	14
Total	(all out, 114.5 overs)	**279**

FOW 1st Innings 1-26, 2-30, 3-44, 4-59, 5-109, 6-141, 7-147, 8-232, 9-274, 10-279

Kent 2nd Innings

	run out	22
	b Wilson	10
	c Alletson b Riley	37
	[9] lbw b Alletson	2
	4 c Oates b Alletson	17
	5 c Iremonger b Riley	16
	[6] b Iremonger	23
	absent hurt	
	[7] c G Gunn b Alletson	0
	[8] c Riley b Alletson	17
	not out	1
	(4 b)	4
	(all out, 60.3 overs)	**149**

FOW 2nd Innings 1-23, 2-45, 3-73, 4-105, 5-113, 6-114, 7-145, 8-146, 9-149

Notts bowling	O	M	R	W
Iremonger	36	19	59	3
Gauld	24	2	85	1
Wilson	11	0	34	0
Riley	20	9	28	1
JR Gunn	15	8	29	2
Lee	7	2	24	1
Alletson	1.5	0	6	2

Notts bowling	O	M	R	W
Iremonger	18	6	38	1
Gauld	4	1	16	0
Wilson	7	1	21	1
Riley	12	2	33	2
JR Gunn	2	2	0	0
Alletson	17.3	2	37	4

Nottinghamshire vs Kent

Trent Bridge, Nottingham
Monday 30th June, Tuesday 1st & Wednesday 2nd July
Toss: Nottinghamshire
Nottinghamshire won by 62 runs
Points: Nottinghamshire 5 Kent 0

KENT MADE THREE changes to the side that had won at Portsmouth. Two amateurs, Mason and Day, came in for Hatfeild and Fairservice, and Jennings replaced Hubble, who had picked up an injury on the south coast. The Nottinghamshire captain, AO Jones, was unwell and so George Ogg Gauld, a 41-year-old Aberdeen-born amateur came in to lead the side in his place. The Kent match was both his first-class and Championship debut. Gauld, who was a doctor, played only 14 first-class matches in his entire career.

This was an excellent example of an amateur being brought into an otherwise good side simply to act as captain, because a professional wasn't deemed suitable to take on the role, when, in reality, the amateur often wasn't worth his place in the side. Whilst it wouldn't be entirely fair to make such a statement of Gauld, one can think of any number of examples where this was the case. Kent were placed in a similar position at the end of the 1913 season when Ted Dillon was obliged to resign the captaincy for business reasons. The choice for captain was probably between Eric Hatfeild and Lionel Troughton. Kent chose Troughton, who had been captain of the 2nd XI since 1911. At the time of his appointment, he was uncapped but, as matters turned out, he did the job well, despite his lack of playing pedigree, in an otherwise strong XI. Troughton captained Kent for six years and handed over to Wykeham Stanley Cornwallis (later, 2nd Baron Cornwallis) in 1924.

There was good news for Frank Woolley in the morning papers when six of the side to tour South Africa during the coming winter were announced. Woolley

A postcard of Trent Bridge showing the pavilion in the centre which dates from 1889

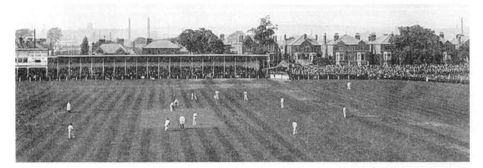

The view from the pavilion at Trent Bridge circa 1910

was to join Wilfred Rhodes, Jack Hobbs, Jack Hearne, William Booth and Sydney Barnes as part of the party to play five Test matches led by Johnny Douglas of Essex. The rest of the touring party was announced a few days later.

Nottinghamshire won the toss and batted on a wicket that offered considerable help for the bowlers with the result that the cricket was pretty dour and attritional. "*At no time during the day were any of the batsmen quite comfortable, the ball getting up off a very fast pitch in a manner most unusual at Trent Bridge.*"[1] Fielder took the first two Nottinghamshire wickets for 40, bringing together the Gunn brothers who put on 50 together, "*batting admirably.*"[2] George Gunn's innings was ended on 40 when Dillon broke the stumps from the long field to run him out. John Gunn and "Dodger" Wysall batted watchfully to produce the major partnership of the Nottinghamshire innings, putting on 123 before Day, whose bowling was "*quite irresistible*",[3] caught Whysall off his own bowling. James Iremonger followed almost immediately, caught by Humphreys off Fielder, and Alletson was bowled by Day so that Nottinghamshire were now 218-6. Gunn and Gauld had managed 26 together when a ball from Woolley was hit towards the boundary. Gunn, who was "*lame from a blow on the leg, failed to make the third run… Dillon, from near the boundary, returning the ball from the long field … threw out John Gunn to terminate the*

John Gunn

Dr George Ogg Gauld

"Dodger" Whysall

George Gunn:	Arthur Fielder:	Jack Mason:
60 runs in the match	10-147	75 & 20

partnership."[1] The rest of the innings was mopped up quickly by Day who finished with 4-46 from 21 overs. Fielder took 4-67. Mr Extras was the third highest scorer with 39 as a result of the "sporting" wicket.

Kent made a reasonable start with Humphreys and Hardinge compiling 26 when Iremonger bowled Hardinge for 14. Kent decided to use a night-watchman and Blythe came in to protect Seymour. When he was caught at slip by Gauld off Iremonger, Huish was promoted to act as the second night-watchman and Kent got through to stumps without further loss at 42-2.

Next morning, the wicket was just as lively and Humphreys continued to bat doggedly while wickets fell at the other end. Huish went after adding just one run to his overnight score and Seymour followed, caught behind by Oates from Ted Alletson's bowling. Woolley hit a quick 25 in a partnership with Humphreys worth 50 runs before falling to the left-arm slows of William Riley.

At lunch, Kent were 151-7, but when play resumed Mason and Jennings put on 85, the best partnership of the innings. Mason's innings of 75 was full of classy shots and lasted for two hours. Jennings gave him excellent support and contributed 40 himself. When Mason played on to John Gunn, Kent needed 35 to pass the Nottinghamshire first innings total. One local newspaper, the *Derby Telegraph*, perhaps a little out of date with their knowledge of the Kent hierarchy, seemed to be under the impression that Mason was still in post as they referred to "*the Kent captain playing on after a splendid display.*"[4]

Jennings and Day took Kent towards a first innings lead in quick time. Day hit Iremonger for six to pass the Nottinghamshire total before Alletson finished off the innings by removing both batsmen in quick succession. The lead was a mere 13 but it might well have secured three points.

Nottinghamshire lost their first wicket at seven when Lee was caught at slip by Mason off Fielder. George Gunn and Joe Hardstaff put on 30, before Fielder had Gunn caught at slip by Woolley and Day trapped Hardstaff lbw to reduce

Nottinghamshire to 40-3, just 27 ahead. John Gunn and Whysall restored the home advantage with a partnership of 72 in 70 minutes, but in the final over of the day, Mason found the edge of Gunn's bat and Huish took the catch to leave the match evenly poised with Nottinghamshire at 112-4, 99 runs ahead.

The third day promised a great deal but turned out to be rather a disappointment, particularly for the Kent supporter. The sun shone and the atmosphere was described as "*very close*".[5] Whysall and Iremonger took the score to 125 when Iremonger was caught at short leg by Hardinge off Mason, and Gauld was bowled by Day for a duck. Alletson struck some typically lusty blows before being bowled by Blythe, having been dropped by Mason at slip before he had scored. The late order substance came from wicketkeeper Tom Oates, whose innings of 34, and partnership with Bert Wilson, allowed Nottinghamshire to reach 224 all out, thereby setting Kent 212 to win. Fielder had bowled with pace but little luck in taking 5-80. Kent suffered some bad luck when Dillon pulled a muscle in his leg and had to be carried from the field. This not only prevented his batting in the fourth innings, but the injury ruled him out of the next two matches.

If Kent were to win this match, one of their top order needed to make 70 or 80 steadily while the "dashers" elsewhere in the order pressed on towards the target. Although most of the batsmen got some sort of start nobody was able to build on it. Blythe was again promoted to bat at three and made the highest score of the innings with some powerful blows, but he was never going to be Kent's match-winner with the bat.

Mason made 23, but wasn't able to stay at the wicket to play the innings Kent needed and, realistically, it couldn't be expected that he would. He was playing his first Championship game since 1911, at the age of 39, and although he was still a class batsman, his lifestyle as a city solicitor and newly married man was not the best

Ted Humphreys

Ted Alletson

Trent Bridge circa 1890

preparation for a three-day cricket match where he was needed to play a second big innings. Jennings couldn't repeat his fine knock of the first innings either, and when he was caught by George Gunn off the bowling of Alletson, and Day was caught by Riley off the same bowler, the innings folded quickly for 149. Nottinghamshire had won by 62 runs. Alletson had been the main wicket-taker with 4-37 from 17.3 overs. The debutant Nottinghamshire captain had made the very best of starts, and he captained the remaining seven matches he played for the county that year, winning four, losing two and drawing two. In fact, he captained every one of his 13 Championship matches and all 14 of his first-class matches – a remarkable record.

Sources

1	*Manchester Courier* 1st July 1913
2	*Wisden* 1914 Nottinghamshire vs Kent p 94
3	*Cricket Magazine* 3rd July 1913
4	*Derby Telegraph* 2nd July 1913
5	*Manchester Courier* 3rd July 1913

2nd July 1913	P	W	L	DWF	DLF	NC	Max	Pts	PtsPC
Kent	12	9	2	1	0	0	60	48	80.00%
Yorkshire	14	9	1	3	1	0	70	55	78.57%
Middlesex	9	6	0	1	2	0	45	35	77.78%
Northamptonshire	11	7	2	0	2	0	55	37	67.27%
Surrey	12	6	2	1	3	0	60	36	60.00%
Nottinghamshire	11	5	2	1	3	0	55	31	56.36%
Lancashire	14	4	5	5	0	0	70	35	50.00%
Worcestershire	8	3	4	1	0	0	40	18	45.00%
Warwickshire	12	4	5	2	1	0	60	27	45.00%
Sussex	12	4	5	1	2	0	60	25	41.67%
Derbyshire	10	3	7	0	0	0	50	15	30.00%
Somerset	6	1	4	1	0	0	30	8	26.67%
Leicestershire	11	2	8	1	0	0	55	13	23.64%
Gloucestershire	10	1	6	1	2	0	50	10	20.00%
Hampshire	11	1	8	0	2	0	55	7	12.73%
Essex	9	0	6	1	2	0	45	5	11.11%

Surrey 1st Innings

TW Hayward	c Huish b Fielder	7
JB Hobbs	b Woolley	17
EG Hayes	c Blythe b Fairservice	62
EG Goatly	c Blythe b Woolley	80
A Sandham	b Fielder	7
HS Harrison	not out	38
Mr MC Bird *	c Humphreys b Woolley	2
H Strudwick +	lbw b Blythe	0
JW Hitch	c and b Woolley	7
Mr EC Kirk	lbw b Woolley	4
T Rushby	b Blythe	3
Extras	(4 b, 5 lb)	9
Total	(all out, 78.2 overs)	**236**

FOW 1st Innings 1-14, 2-38, 3-133, 4-141, 5-203, 6-209, 7-210, 8-221, 9-229, 10-236

Surrey 2nd Innings

	c Huish b Humphreys	41
	c Seymour b Blythe	49
	c and b Blythe	26
	c Humphreys b Blythe	11
	not out	48
	c Humphreys b Fairservice	17
	st Huish b Woolley	7
	c Hubble b Woolley	2
	c Woolley b Blythe	4
	b Blythe	0
	c Day b Blythe	0
	(4 b, 1 lb, 1 nb)	6
	(all out, 80.3 overs)	**211**

FOW 2nd Innings 1-91, 2-94, 3-124, 4-135, 5-187, 6-196, 7-206, 8-211, 9-211, 10-211

Kent bowling	O	M	R	W
Fielder	17	2	56	2
Day	10	4	13	0
Woolley	24	1	70	5
Blythe	20.2	3	73	2
Fairservice	7	2	15	1

Kent bowling	O	M	R	W
Fielder	6	1	12	0
Day	5	0	13	0
Woolley	26	7	72	2
Blythe	26.3	6	74	6
Fairservice	9	1	19	1
Humphreys	8	3	15	1

Kent 1st Innings

E Humphreys	c Hayes b Hitch	31
HTW Hardinge	c Strudwick b Kirk	3
J Seymour	c Hayes b Kirk	8
FE Woolley	c Hobbs b Bird	177
JC Hubble	b Bird	19
Mr AP Day *	b Rushby	0
DW Jennings	b Rushby	40
FH Huish +	st Strudwick b Rushby	21
WJ Fairservice	c Sandham b Rushby	10
C Blythe	st Strudwick b Kirk	1
A Fielder	not out	0
Extras	(11 b, 7 lb, 2 nb, 1 w)	21
Total	(all out, 100.3 overs)	**331**

FOW 1st Innings 1-11, 2-25, 3-93, 4-166, 5-169, 6-247, 7-311, 8-330, 9-331, 10-331

Kent 2nd Innings

	run out	33
	c Harrison b Bird	36
	c Hobbs b Goatly	1
	c and b Bird	12
	not out	13
	not out	17
	did not bat	
	did not bat	
	did not bat	
	did not bat	
	did not bat	
	(4 b, 2 lb)	6
	(4 wickets, 37.3 overs)	**118**

FOW 2nd Innings 1-66, 2-67, 3-82, 4-90

Surrey bowling	O	M	R	W
Hitch	22	2	79	1
Kirk	35	11	95	3
Rushby	25.3	6	71	4
Bird	15	2	53	2
Harrison	3	0	12	0

Surrey bowling	O	M	R	W
Kirk	6	2	12	0
Rushby	12	0	33	0
Bird	9.3	2	35	2
Goatly	10	1	32	1

Kent vs Surrey

The Rectory Field, Blackheath
Thursday 3rd, Friday 4th & Saturday 5th July
Toss: Surrey
Kent won by 6 wickets
Points: Kent 5 Surrey 0

KENT ARRIVED AT Blackheath to face another of the top sides in the Championship, knowing that in order to retain their place at the top of the table, they would probably need to beat third-placed Surrey. Yorkshire, in second place, were to play Leicestershire who, despite their victory of the previous week over Derbyshire, were still rooted firmly to the bottom of the table, having lost eight out of their 11 fixtures to date. Kent, however, would have taken confidence from their excellent recent record at The Rectory Field against Surrey, perhaps their fiercest and strongest rivals. Since the basis of the County Championship had been revised in 1890, Kent had met Surrey at Blackheath on nine occasions – winning six with three drawn matches.

Hubble and Fairservice returned to the side, in place of Dillon and Mason, with the result that Arthur Day, as the only amateur in the side, undertook the captaincy duties.

Surrey won the toss and batted, opening with their two Cambridge-born players, Tom Hayward and Jack Hobbs. Hayward, now approaching his 41st birthday and in the penultimate season of his career, was now overshadowed by Hobbs, aged 30, who was at the peak of his powers. *"Hayward was now heavy on his feet and slow between the wickets but was still a great batsman."*[1] The previous week, in Surrey's match against Lancashire at The Oval, he had completed the 100th first-class century of his career – only the second player ever to do so (the first, of course, being WG Grace).

Fortunately for Kent, this was not to be the Surrey openers' day as Hayward soon got an edge to a lifting ball from Fielder and was caught by Huish. Hobbs had

The Rectory Field, Blackheath

Tom Hayward: 100 hundreds. The Chic cartoon on the right appeared in
Cricket A Weekly Record on Saturday 5th July 1913

reached 17 when Day removed himself from the attack and brought on Woolley, who was immediately successful in bowling "The Master" to reduce the visitors to 38-2.

The third-wicket partnership of 95 between Ernie Hayes and Edward Goatly was the best of the Surrey innings. Goatly was dropped by Hardinge on seven and in its report, the *Kent Messenger* commented grumpily *"Kent have been making rather a name for themselves of late with regard to dropped catches."*[2] The partnership was finally broken when Blythe caught Hayes off Fairservice and ten runs later, Fielder bowled the young Andy Sandham to restore the balance, with Surrey on 141-4. There was another useful partnership of 62 between Goatly and Henry Harrison which caused *The Times* correspondent to say *"it seemed as if at length there was to be a break in the run of failure which has attended Surrey on Kentish ground since 1897, the Surrey score, despite the cheap dismissal of Hayward and Hobbs, reaching 200 with only four men out."*[3] When Goatly was caught by Blythe off Woolley at 203 to end the *"capital partnership"*[3] the remaining wickets were snapped up by Blythe and Woolley for 33 runs with Woolley taking 5-70 and Blythe 2-73. Harrison was left stranded on 38 as the rest of the batting crumbled around him and Surrey were all out for 236.

Kent began badly by losing Hardinge and Seymour, both to Ernest Kirk, by the time the score had reached 25, but Woolley and particularly Humphreys batted patiently to see Kent through to 70-2 at the close, with Humphreys on 19 and Woolley

THE "FORCE" BAT HAS NO EQUAL.

Ernest G. Hayes.

SURREY.

THE "FORCE" BAT IS THE BEST.

J.B. Hobbs. I ALWAYS USE IT.

SURREY.

Ernest Hayes – a thorn in Kent's flesh in 1913, and Jack Hobbs – The Master

on 27. *The Times* commented: *"Kent, as it happened, secured no advantage yesterday."*[3] As matters turned out, they had secured a considerable advantage in having Woolley unbeaten on the Thursday evening and, the following day, he went on to prove why, at that point, he was sitting in fourth place in the national batting averages.

The second day began with Woolley in watchful mood against some good Surrey bowling, but at 93, Humphreys fell to an edge off the bowling of Bill Hitch.[4] Woolley continued in cautious mode, and reached his 50 in an hour and a half, but then scored his second 50 in even time to reach his century before lunch.

After lunch, Kent first lost Hubble to the interestingly named Surrey captain, Morice Carlos Bird, and then Day to Tom Rushby within the space of a few deliveries. The match could well have swung significantly in Surrey's favour had they taken either of the catches offered by Woolley when he was on 108. With the score then on 169-5, Woolley went back into his shell as if knowing instinctively that this was a crucial moment in the passage of play. Together with Jennings, he was able to consolidate Kent's position. They put on 78 before Jennings was bowled by Rushby for a valuable 40, at 247-6. The *Kent Messenger* correspondent was evidently an admirer of Jennings, *"one of the most deserving young cricketers who at present cannot seem to get a permanent place in the Kent eleven... when he does get a show Davy rarely fails"*.[2] Kent secured their first-innings lead and three points in the event that the match would be drawn.

Frank Woolley:
5-70 & 2-72 & and 177 & 12 at Blackheath

Ted Humphreys:
the 1913 Beneficiary

When Jennings departed, Woolley began to attack the bowling with "*great brilliancy*"[5] and, with assistance from Huish and Fairservice, pushed the Kent score to 331 all out to secure a first-innings lead of 95. Woolley's innings lasted 240 minutes and included 28 fours. Surrey had just over an hour and a half to bat during the last session and reached 91 without loss, four runs behind the Kent total, with Hayward on 41 and Hobbs 48.

That night, there was a huge storm over South East London and the wicket and outfield got a thorough drenching. When the players assembled the following morning, the Kent spinners were clearly relishing a bowl on a wicket which they knew would give them assistance.

Hayward went in the first over of the day, caught behind off Humphreys. Hobbs followed after adding just a single to his overnight score when he edged Blythe to Seymour at slip. Hayes and Goatly then attacked the bowling and put on 30 in less than twenty minutes before Goatly was caught by Humphreys off Blythe for 11. Nine runs later, "*Hayes was brilliantly caught and bowled by Blythe, who took the ball with one hand, a few inches from the ground*"[6] and the umpire had to be consulted as to the fairness of the catch. Surrey had lost four wickets during the first half hour of the day and were now struggling at 135-4, only 40 ahead of the Kent total.

Sandham and Harrison put on 52 runs in 45 minutes to give the Surrey innings some hope but at 187, Harrison was out to a fine catch at short leg by

Colin Blythe: 2-73 & 6-74 at Blackheath, which included his 2,250th first-class wicket, and Edward Goatly: top scorer in the Surrey first innings

Humphreys off Fairservice. "*Sandham continued to bat well but received so little support that at luncheon, Surrey were eight down for 211 and after the interval, the last two wickets fell without another run having been scored.*"[7] Blythe had collected 6-74 on the ground where he had first caught the eye of Captain McCanlis in July 1897. Blythe's fifth victim, Kirk, was his 2,250th in first-class cricket.[8]

The final Surrey wicket went down at 20 minutes past two, leaving Kent ample time to score the 117 they needed for victory. This they duly accomplished for the loss of four wickets. Humphreys and Hardinge put on 66 for the first wicket in 70 minutes and had placed Kent within sight of victory when Hobbs, who was probably the last fielder in England to take on for a short single, ran out Humphreys from cover point. In the next over, Seymour was smartly caught by the same fielder. "*With Hardinge out at 82, and Woolley at 90, there were prospects of an interesting finish. The Surrey attack, however, met with no further success. Rain was now falling, and Hubble and Day started hitting hard lest the weather should cheat Kent of victory, Day making the winning hit at twenty-five minutes past four.*"[9]

As the players left the field, the crowd sprinted towards the pavilion to cheer the Kent side for their victory. One spectator bumped into the Surrey captain, perhaps accidentally, perhaps not, but whatever the provocation, Bird retaliated. He was a tall and powerfully built 25-year-old, and having been educated at Harrow, where he was the outstanding sportsman of his year, probably had his own views about being jostled by a Kentish "mob" in SE3. Unwilling to be cowed by a toff like Bird, the crowd besieged the pavilion, booing the Surrey skipper. The *Kent Messenger* observed: *"Nor would the malcontents be appeased until it was announced from the pavilion steps that the Surrey captain had expressed his regret for what had occurred."*[10]

Kent's victory preserved their place at the top of the table as Yorkshire overcame Leicestershire at Aylestone Road by the comfortable margin of 190 runs. Elsewhere, Middlesex lost ground by drawing with Worcestershire at New Road. For Worcestershire, George Simpson-Hayward had one of his occasional outings that season, scoring 69 in the first innings and taking three wickets in the match with his underarm lobs.

Sources

1   Patrick Morrah: *The Golden Age of Cricket*
2   *Kent Messenger* 12th July 1913
3   *The Times* 4th July 1913
4   Bill Hitch was Surrey's main strike bowler and had come to prominence in 1911 taking 151 wickets. He went to Australia as part of Johnny Douglas's 1911/12 Ashes-winning side. He played in three Tests in that series and three more in the 1912 Triangular series. He played one further Test after the War making seven caps in all. In 1912, he took 114 wickets and in 1913 he had his best year with 174 wickets at 18.55 each. He subsequently became a Test match umpire in the 1930s.
5   *Wisden* 1913
6   *The Sportsman* 9th July 1913
7   *The Times* 7th July 1913
8   *Cricket Archive* cc3289
9   *Evening News* 9th July 1913
10   *Kent Messenger* 9th July 1913

5th July 2013	P	W	L	DWF	DLF	NC	Max	Pts	PtsPC
Kent	13	10	2	1	0	0	65	53	81.54%
Yorkshire	15	10	1	3	1	0	75	60	80.00%
Middlesex	10	6	0	2	2	0	50	38	76.00%
Northamptonshire	12	7	2	0	3	0	60	38	63.33%
Nottinghamshire	12	6	2	1	3	0	60	36	60.00%
Surrey	13	6	3	1	3	0	65	36	55.38%
Lancashire	15	4	5	6	0	0	75	38	50.67%
Warwickshire	13	5	5	2	1	0	65	32	49.23%
Worcestershire	9	3	4	1	1	0	45	19	42.22%
Sussex	13	4	6	1	2	0	65	25	38.46%
Derbyshire	10	3	7	0	0	0	50	15	30.00%
Somerset	6	1	4	1	0	0	30	8	26.67%
Leicestershire	12	2	9	1	0	0	60	13	21.67%
Essex	10	1	6	1	2	0	50	10	20.00%
Gloucestershire	11	1	7	1	2	0	55	10	18.18%
Hampshire	11	1	8	0	2	0	55	7	12.73%

Kent County C.C., Rectory Field, Blackheath, July 3rd, 4th and 5th, 1913.

8a

KENT v. SURREY.

SURREY.	First Innings.		Second Innings.	
1 Hayward	c. Huish. b. Fielder.	7	c. Huish. b. Humph's.	101
2 Hobbs	b. Woolley.	17	c. Seymour. b. Blythe	49
3 Hayes	c. Blythe. b. Fairservice	62	c + b. Blythe.	26
4 Goatly	c. Blythe. b. Woolley	80	c. Humph's. b. Blythe	11
5 Sandham	b. Fielder	7	not out	48
6 Harrison	not out	38	c. Humph's. b. Fairservice	17
7 Mr. M. C. Bird	c. Humphr's. b. Woolley	2	St. Huish. b. Woolley	7
8 Strudwick	l.b.w. b. Blythe	0	c. Hubble. b. Woolley	2
9 Hitch	c + b. Woolley.	7	c. Woolley. b. Blythe	40
10 Mr. E. C. Kirk	l.b.w. b. Woolley.	4	b. Blythe.	0
11 Rushby	b. Blythe	3	c. Day. b. Blythe	0
	B 4, l-b 5, w , n-b	9	B 4, l-b 1, w , n-b 1,	6
	Total	236	Total	277

1st Inn. 1-14 | 2-38 | 3-133 | 4-141 | 5-203 | 6-209 | 7-210 | 8-221 | 9-229

2nd Inn. 1-91 | 2-94 | 3-124 | 4-135 | 5-187 | 6-196 | 7-206 | 8-211 | 9-211

Bowling Analysis.

NAME.	First Innings.					Second Innings.				
	O.	M.	R.	W.	Wd. N-b.	O.	M.	R.	W.	Wd. N-b.
Fielder	11	2	56	2	...	6	1	12	0	...
Day	10	4	13	0	...	5	0	13	0	...
Woolley	24	1	70	5	...	26	7	72	2	...
Blythe	20.2	3	73	2	...	26.3	6	74	6	...
Fairservice	7	2	15	1	...	9	1	19	1	...
Humphreys					...	8	3	15	1	...

KENT.	First Innings.		Second Innings.	
1 Mr. A. P. Day	b. Rushby	0	not out	17
2 Humphreys	c. Hayes. b. Hitch	31	run out	33
3 Hardinge	c. Strud. b. Kirk	3	c. Harrison. b. Bird.	36
4 Seymour	c. Hayes. b. Kirk	8	c. Hobbs. b. Goatly.	1
5 Woolley	c. Hobbs. b. Bird	144	c + b. Bird.	12
6 Hubble	b. Bird	19	not out	13
7 Jennings	b. Rushby	40		
8 Huish	St. Strud. b. Rushby	21		
9 Fairservice	c. Sandham. b. Rushby	10		
10 Blythe	St. Strud. b. Kirk	1		
11 Fielder	not out	0		
	B 11, l-b 7, w 1, n-b 2,	21	B 4, l-b 2, w , n-b	6
	Total	337	Total (How)	118

Kent won by 6 wkts

1st Inn. 1-11 | 2-25 | 3-93 | 4-166 | 5-169 | 6-247 | 7-311 | 8-330 | 9-331

2nd Inn. 1-66 | 2-67 | 3-82 | 4-90 | 5- | 6- | 7- | 8- | 9-

Bowling Analysis.

NAME.	First Innings.					Second Innings.				
	O.	M.	R.	W.	Wd. N-b.	O.	M.	R.	W.	Wd. N-b.
Hitch	22	2	79	1	...	...				...
Kirk	35	11	95	3	...	6	2	12	0	...
Rushby	25.3	6	71	4	...	12	0	33	0	...
Bird	16	2	53	2	...	9.3	2	35	2	...
Harrison	3	0	12	0	...					...
Goatly					...	10	1	32	1	...

Umpires—Harrison and Trott.　　　Scorers—W. Hearne and F. Boyington.

LUNCH—1st day, 2 p.m.; 2nd & 3rd days, 1.30 p.m.　　**Stumps drawn 6.30.**

July 14th, 15th, 16th, KENT v. WORCESTERSHIRE } Tunbridge Wells
　,,　17th, 18th, 19th, KENT v. YORKSHIRE 　　　　　} Week.

July 21st, 22nd, 23rd, KENT v. LANCASHIRE } Maidstone Week.
　,,　24th, 25th, 26th, KENT v. MIDDLESEX 　　}

Printed on Ground by C. NORTH, The Blackheath Press, S.E.

An original scorecard for Kent vs Surrey at Blackheath 1913

Warwickshire 1st Innings

EJ Smith +	c Hatfeild b Woolley	28
JH Parsons	b Woolley	31
C Charlesworth	st Huish b Blythe	0
WG Quaife	c Seymour b Blythe	20
Mr FR Foster*	b Woolley	0
CS Baker	not out	35
Mr GW Stephens	c Woolley b Blythe	0
Mr EB Crockford	c Huish b Woolley	16
P Jeeves	b Blythe	3
S Santall	lbw b Blythe	3
A Taylor	c Huish b Woolley	14
Extras	(9 b)	9
Total	(all out, 81.3 overs)	**159**

FOW 1st Innings 1-29, 2-29, 3-80, 4-80, 5-90, 6-90, 7-131, 8-138, 9-142, 10-159
FOW 2nd Innings 1-7, 2-12, 3-65, 4-74, 5-74, 6-95, 7-121, 8-126, 9-132, 10-161

Warwickshire 2nd Innings

	c Hatfeild b Fairservice	11
	c Woolley b Fielder	0
	c Huish b Fielder	43
	b Fielder	8
	b Woolley	7
	c Huish b Woolley	6
	b Fairservice	26
	c Seymour b Fairservice	23
	b Woolley	1
	st Huish b Woolley	12
	not out	14
	(4 b, 1 lb, 5 nb)	10
	(all out, 59.3 overs)	**161**

Kent bowling	O	M	R	W
Blythe	32	13	47	5
Woolley	30.3	8	75	5
Fairservice	12	4	20	0
Humphreys	7	3	8	0

Kent bowling	O	M	R	W
Blythe	7	4	9	0
Woolley	18.3	4	45	4
Fairservice	12	7	27	3
Fielder	22	3	70	3

Kent 1st Innings

E Humphreys	b Jeeves	13
HTW Hardinge	c Charlesworth b Foster	25
J Seymour	c Charlesworth b Santall	106
FE Woolley	lbw b Foster	3
JC Hubble	lbw b Jeeves	75
DW Jennings	c Parsons b Jeeves	72
Mr CE Hatfeild *	b Quaife	33
FH Huish +	c Smith b Santall	4
WJ Fairservice	not out	14
C Blythe	did not bat	
A Fielder	did not bat	
Extras	(14 b, 7 lb, 1 nb, 4 w)	26
Total	(8 wickets dec, 93.2 overs)	**371**

FOW 1st Innings 1-46, 2-46, 3-51, 4-230, 5-267, 6-330, 7-335, 8-371

Warwickshire bowling	O	M	R	W
Foster	27	6	78	2
Santall	18	3	75	2
Jeeves	27.2	4	90	3
Taylor	4	0	25	0
Charlesworth	3	1	12	0
Parsons	2	0	14	0
Quaife	12	0	51	1

Warwickshire vs Kent

Edgbaston, Birmingham
Monday 7th, Tuesday 8th & Wednesday 9th July
Toss: Warwickshire
Kent won by an innings and 51 runs
Points: Warwickshire 0 Kent 5

THE SUMMER OF 1913 was generally dry: there were only six matches in the entire Championship programme (364 matches) where it wasn't possible to complete at least the first innings of the match. Given that the wicket was open to the elements at all times, this is quite remarkable. Nevertheless, the weather became unsettled in the middle of July and Kent's next three matches were significantly affected. The first of these was the return fixture with Warwickshire in Birmingham where the rain over the preceding weekend meant that not a ball could be bowled on Monday.

Kent made one change to the side that played at Blackheath because of the unavailability of Arthur Day. Eric Hatfeild was brought back into the side to act as captain and George Collins was the player left out of the twelve that travelled to Edgbaston.[1]

Frank Foster won the toss for the home side and, on the basis that the wicket was likely to deteriorate over the next two days, elected to bat. Given the ultimate result of the match and the fact that he had significantly misjudged the wicket at Tonbridge three weeks earlier, his decision could be regarded as unfortunate, perhaps even bordering on careless. To begin with, however, it looked as if Warwickshire might prosper as "Tiger" Smith took the long handle to Blythe, and to Woolley in

A postcard of Edgbaston in the early 20th century

Tiger Smith at different stages of his career
Photograph courtesy of Warwickshire CCC

particular. He scored 28 out of the first 29 before he was caught by Hatfeild in the outfield as he mistimed his shot off Woolley. Crowther Charlesworth went in the next over, stumped by Huish off Blythe without addition to the score. Willie Quaife then joined Parsons to put on 51, which turned out to be the highest stand of the innings.

Two more wickets went down with the score at 80, and thereafter the innings fell apart with only Charles Barker with 35 not out able to counter the wiles of Blythe or Woolley. The two left-armers finished with 5-47 and 5-75 respectively. Woolley's figures had suffered as a result of the initial assault by Smith. Warwickshire had been bowled out for 159.

Knowing they needed to force the pace, Kent started poorly, losing Humphreys, Hardinge and Woolley for 51 (*Wisden* describes them as "*crack batsmen*"[2]). Seymour and Hubble came together to restore the innings to 175-3 by the close, a token lead of 16. The next morning, the weather had improved considerably and the playing surface was quite dry. In fact, it was now ideal for batting, again calling into question Foster's decision to bat first. However, what was done was done, and Kent needed to score quickly if there was to be any chance of securing the extra two points that victory would give them.

Seymour and Hubble batted superbly in adding 179 for the fourth wicket in 110 minutes – "*the hitting being of a splendid description.*"[2] Seymour's hundred took him past one thousand runs for the season. When Hubble went, Jennings showed what a fine player he could be for the second consecutive match in making his highest score of the season, 72 in 80 minutes. There was a small cameo of hitting from Hatfeild before the declaration came at 371-8, leaving Warwickshire 212 to avoid an innings defeat.

Frank Woolley (5-74 & 4-45) and Charlie Blythe (5-47)

By now, the wicket was described as *"excellent and Warwickshire should not have experienced much difficulty in staying in for the remainder of the afternoon"*.[2] Wisden describes the batting as feeble *"apart from an admirable innings by Charlesworth and some creditable work by Stephens and Crockford."*[2]

Blythe and Woolley opened the bowling but Hatfeild almost immediately replaced them with Fielder and Fairservice. Fielder induced an edge from Parsons which was caught by Woolley at slip, and a few runs later, Smith holed out to Hatfeild off Fairservice, leaving the home side at 12-2. Once Charlesworth had been caught behind off Fielder, the only real resistance encountered by Kent was from George Stephens and Eric Crockford.

Hatfeild kept Fielder going from one end and rotated Woolley and Fairservice at the other. There was a brief partnership of 29 for the final wicket between Syd Santall and Arthur Taylor before Taylor was stumped by Huish off Woolley to end the Warwickshire innings at 161, giving Kent a fine victory by an innings and 51 runs.

Woolley had taken 4-45 to give him nine wickets in the match, and there were three wickets apiece for Fielder and Fairservice. This was an outstanding performance by Kent to set up a win inside the two days that were available.

The victory enabled Kent to open a larger gap at the top of the Championship table as a result of Yorkshire losing at Headingley to Northamptonshire. The match was a hard-fought affair played on a damp wicket where 22 wickets fell on the first day. John Seymour, the brother of Kent's James Seymour, was one of the major

David Jennings and Jack Hubble: two of the stars of the Kent batting at Birmingham

contributors to his side's victory, top scoring with 75 in Northamptonshire's second innings, and also contributing 32 in the first.

Middlesex were not engaged in this series of matches, having no fixtures between 5th July, after they finished at Worcester, and 19th July, when they were scheduled to meet Surrey at The Oval.

While the matches at Edgbaston and Headingley were being decided, the Varsity Match was being played at Lord's, where Cambridge beat Oxford by four wickets. One of the Oxford side was Mr Freddie Knott, who had made his debut for Kent in 1910. He made little impact at Lord's, scoring 0 and 26.

Sources
1   *Manchester Courier* 8th July 1913
2   *Wisden* 1913 p 209

Jim Seymour: centurion at Edgbaston

9th July 1913	P	W	L	DWF	DLF	NC	Max	Pts	PtsPC
Kent	14	11	2	1	0	0	70	58	82.86%
Middlesex	10	6	0	2	2	0	50	38	76.00%
Yorkshire	16	10	2	3	1	0	80	60	75.00%
Northamptonshire	13	8	2	0	3	0	65	43	66.15%
Nottinghamshire	12	6	2	1	3	0	60	36	60.00%
Surrey	14	7	3	1	3	0	70	41	58.57%
Lancashire	16	4	6	6	0	0	80	38	47.50%
Warwickshire	14	5	6	2	1	0	70	32	45.71%
Worcestershire	9	3	4	1	1	0	45	19	42.22%
Sussex	14	4	6	2	2	0	70	28	40.00%
Derbyshire	11	3	8	0	0	0	55	15	27.27%
Somerset	6	1	4	1	0	0	30	8	26.67%
Leicestershire	13	2	9	1	1	0	65	14	21.54%
Essex	10	1	6	1	2	0	50	10	20.00%
Gloucestershire	11	1	7	1	2	0	55	10	18.18%
Hampshire	11	1	8	0	2	0	55	7	12.73%

Kent 1st Innings

E Humphreys	c Burrows b Nevile	80
HTW Hardinge	c Bale b Burrows	2
J Seymour	b Burrows	1
JC Hubble	b Cuffe	20
Mr AP Day	b Cuffe	5
Mr EW Dillon *	c Burns b Cuffe	38
Mr WA Powell	b Nevile	16
Mr CE Hatfeild	c Bale b Nevile	0
FH Huish +	b Burrows	47
WJ Fairservice	b Cuffe	27
C Blythe	not out	2
Extras	(10 b, 1 lb, 1 nb, 2 w)	14
Total	(all out, 96.3 overs)	252

FOW 1st Innings 1-2, 2-10, 3-70, 4-86, 5-142, 6-172, 7-172, 8-178, 9-242, 10-252

Worcestershire bowling	O	M	R	W
Burrows	25.3	5	67	3
Burns	7	2	15	0
Pearson	5	2	18	0
Cuffe	33	10	64	4
Chester	6	2	15	0
Nevile	8	0	29	3
Hunt	9	2	19	0
Arnold	3	0	11	0

Worcestershire 1st Innings

FA Pearson	b Day	42
FL Bowley	lbw b Fairservice	25
Mr WB Burns *	st Huish b Dillon	34
EG Arnold	b Powell	5
CGA Collier	b Powell	2
JA Cuffe	not out	4
Mr BP Nevile	not out	17
F Chester	did not bat	
F Hunt	did not bat	
RD Burrows	did not bat	
EW Bale +	did not bat	
Extras	(1 lb, 1 w)	2
Total	(5 wickets, 37 overs)	**131**

FOW 1st Innings 1-46, 2-76, 3-107, 4-107, 5-110

Kent bowling	O	M	R	W
Blythe	7	4	11	0
Humphreys	5	0	30	0
Fairservice	4	0	18	1
Day	5	0	13	1
Hatfeild	5	0	18	0
Dillon	7	0	34	1
Powell	2	1	2	2
Seymour	2	0	3	0

Kent vs Worcestershire

Nevill Ground, Tunbridge Wells
Monday 14th, Tuesday 15th & Wednesday 16th July
Toss: Kent
Match Drawn
Points: Kent 0 Worcestershire 0

IN THE EARLY hours of the morning of Friday 11th April 1913, just nine weeks before the start of the county cricket week in the town, a lamp-lighter doing his rounds saw flames coming from the pavilion at the Nevill Ground in Tunbridge Wells. He hared off to summon the still horse-drawn fire carts of the Tunbridge Wells Fire Service but by the time they arrived it was too late to save the building and only the brick walls survived. The value of the damage was stated to be £1,500, and among the items destroyed were the records and archives of both the Tunbridge Wells Club and the Bluemantles Cricket Club that shared the pavilion.

Several valuable and irreplaceable sporting prints also went up in the flames. The following day, *The Times* carried the news in an article headed "Militancy and a Cricket Pavilion". The piece is reproduced below, from which it will be seen that the blame for the conflagration was attributed to the Militant Suffragist movement. *"There seems little doubt that the fire was the work of militant suffragists for not far away were found copies of "Votes for Women" and an electrical torch. One of the copies of the periodical named was spread out on the ground and on the top was placed a photograph of Mrs Pankhurst."* [1]

It was on the basis of this flimsy evidence that the fire has, ever since, been blamed on the Suffragist movement, despite the fact that a police investigation found

MILITANCY AND A CRICKET PAVILION.

Early yesterday the pavilion on the Nevill cricket ground, Tunbridge Wells, was burnt down and damage done to the extent of £1,500. The heaviest loss is the destruction of a collection of valuable sporting prints, photographs of sporting celebrities, and the like, including a very fine print of the first cricket week at Canterbury. The records of the Blue Mantles Cricket Club, which has existed for over 40 years, have also been destroyed. There seems little doubt that the fire was the work of militant suffragists, for not far away were found copies of " Votes for Women " and an electric torch. One of the copies of the periodical named was spread out on the ground, and on the top was placed a photograph of Mrs. Pankhurst.

At Ilford yesterday the fire alarm wires in three

The Nevill Ground, Tunbridge Wells circa 1900 showing the original pavilion on the extreme left-hand edge of the photograph, just above the word "Royal"

no proof of such a connection. As ever, the truth never got in the way of a good story and there was a significant backlash from the good people of Tunbridge Wells. The local branch of the *National League for Opposing Women's Suffrage* reported a boom in membership immediately after the fire. Indeed, one local resident, the celebrated author Sir Arthur Conan Doyle, was sufficiently outraged to take on the role of the original "Disgusted of Tunbridge Wells" to comment *"Female Hooligans!"*, adding that their action had been like *"blowing up a blind man and his dog."* Conan Doyle was a member of the Tunbridge Wells Club and in the early 1900s had played ten first-class matches for MCC, once taking the wicket of WG Grace.[2]

Later research, however, seems convinced of the involvement of the Suffragist movement. Les Scott, in *Bats, Balls & Bails – The Essential Cricket Book*, says the *"pavilion was burned down by Suffragettes who objected to the non-admittance policy towards women, a situation inflamed by a Kent official who reportedly said 'It is not true that women are banned from the pavilion. Who do you think makes the teas?'"*[3] If that was the case, it is hardly surprising the women took their revenge.

Fortunately, it is fairly easy to discount this amusing flight of fancy. An inspection of the Rules & Regulations of Kent County Cricket Club published in the "Blue Book" of the day (the Kent Annual) reveals that "Ladies" were allowed in the pavilion at St Lawrence, and on other grounds where the County played, without the necessity of their knowing how to prepare a cheese and tomato sandwich. While they were restricted to certain seats in the pavilion, they were certainly not excluded.[4]

(Above and below) The ruins of the old pavilion the morning after the fire

If additional proof of the "enlightened" attitude on the part of Kent were needed, there is a note in the 1913 Minute Book which refers to a request received from a Member asking that The Committee make it a Rule of the Club "*that Ladies occupying seats in the pavilion at Canterbury should be requested to remove their hats*"[4] so as to not to restrict the view of the cricket. The ensuing comments make it clear that the gentlemen of the Kent Committee were not prepared to risk the potential consequences of such an edict, because they "*feared that such a request would not be complied with*" – and made no order.[5]

The work of rebuilding the pavilion at the Nevill began immediately, and although a "damned close run thing", it was finished just in time for the cricket which started on Monday 14th July 1913. The "Tunbridge Wells Week" was established in

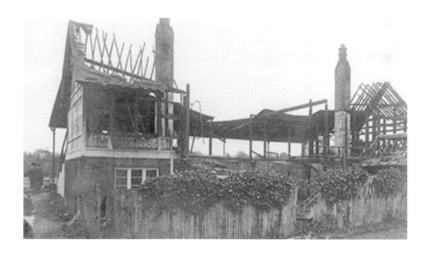

1902, a year after Kent had first played at The Nevill Ground against Lancashire. The initial match, in 1901, was sufficiently well supported that two matches were allocated to the ground the following year.

The first match of 1913 was against Worcestershire and Kent made a number of changes from the side that won at Birmingham. Dillon was now available, as was Arthur Day, who had just played for The Gentlemen against The Players at the Oval. Frank Woolley, who was selected for the second showpiece fixture for The Players at Lord's, was replaced by William Powell. Fielder was left out as he was suffering from a boil on his neck, and the other player to make way for the return of the amateurs was David Jennings.

This was a classic example of a side being picked primarily on the basis of the availability of the gentleman amateurs, who would have made their cricketing arrangements at the very start of the season and notified the County accordingly. Jennings had made his debut for Kent in 1909, but because Kent were so strong at this time, had few opportunities to gain a regular place in the side. Up to the start of the 1913 season, he had played just 13 matches. He had two hundreds to his credit and was generally seen as the likely successor to one of the top five batsmen, but in 1913 they were still performing well enough to command a place above him, and his chances continued to be limited. Having made runs at Trent Bridge, Blackheath and Edgbaston, it must have been exceedingly frustrating for him to be left out.

Kent won the toss and decided to bat. Only 70 minutes' play was possible on the first day. Despite the unsettled weather, and on a wicket which was described as good, the home side *"began badly, Hardinge leaving after only two runs had been scored and Seymour also being sent back by Burrows at 10"*.[6] Despite these early reverses, Humphreys and Hubble scored quickly and 50 came up in just an hour. Fred Pearson, bowling his off-breaks, came in for some severe punishment and a further 20 runs were added in five minutes before the rain arrived and caused play to be abandoned for the day. At the close, Kent had scored 70-2 with Humphreys on 40 and Hubble 20.

No play at all was possible on the Tuesday. This was also the case at Lord's in the Gentleman vs Players fixture, but the other matches in the Championship at Derby, Manchester and Northampton were unaffected.

On the third morning of the match, those who took *The Times*[7] were able to read a letter from the Secretary of Worcestershire CCC setting out details of the parlous state of the county's finances, and appealing for donations to keep the club afloat. The letter is reproduced opposite. The appeal was apparently successful because, nine days later, on 25th July, there was a brief footnote after the cricket scores announcing: *"At a meeting of the committee of the Worcestershire County Club at Dudley yesterday, it was stated that the response to the appeal, which had been made for money, had been so satisfactory that it was to be announced to the general meeting at Worcester on Tuesday that the club would be safe for three years. At the same time further funds are urgently wanted and another appeal will be made for support.*"[8] The position obviously wasn't fully resolved because, a week later, *The Manchester Courier* confirmed that the Worcestershire Committee has met again on Saturday 28th June as "*the financial aspect is again causing grave concern*".[9]

The sum involved was £15,000 – practically loose change today, but a significant sum to have raised in such a short period at the time. To illustrate this sum in a direct, 1913, context, it would have been possible to rebuild the Tunbridge Wells pavilion nine times over for this sum of money.[10]

Worcestershire were by no means the only county club in financial difficulties around this time. Derbyshire in 1910,[11] and Warwickshire, prior to their 1911 Championship, were on their beam end as a result of a rapid decline in their membership numbers. Gloucestershire in 1914 had undertaken not to arrange fixtures for the following season because they could not afford to pay their professional players who had been given permission to seek contracts with other counties.[12] The Ashley Down Ground at Bristol was sold in 1915 to JS Fry & Sons for use as a recreation ground for their employees on the condition that it would be available for any Gloucestershire County fixtures that took place after the war – if the club could be put on a sound financial footing.[12] Northamptonshire were another county who would not have competed in the 1915 season had there been one.[11]

WORCESTERSHIRE CRICKET CLUB—Mr A Wyberg Hon. Secretary of the Worcestershire Cricket Club, writes as follows: "Will you allow me the hospitality of your columns to bring before the notice of Worcestershire men in London the unsatisfactory state of the finances of the county club? Briefly, the club is heavily in debt; and it is vital to its existence that £1500 be raised at once. The Chairman of Farrow's Bank (Limited) has promised £100 provided the liabilities are expunged by the end of the month, and promises aggregating some £500 or £600 have already been received from other sympathisers with the club. I think you will agree that it would be a vast pity that a county that has produced two such fine families of cricketers as the Lytteltons and the Fosters should be the first to drop out of the Championship Table owing to lack of financial support; and I confidently appeal to Worcestershire men in London to come to the rescue of their county. Donations may be sent to me at the County Ground, Worcester, or to the Capital and Counties Bank, Worcester."

Lancashire were also involved in some internal strife between their captain Mr AH Hornby and the Lancashire General Committee. At a Special General Meeting held on 2nd September 1913, Hornby criticised the Committee for their management of the Club and the accrued losses over the previous four seasons which had amounted to £3,500 (2012 equivalent £315,000).[13]

Kent at this time were, however, relatively comfortable. The profit for 1912 was £266. 4s 0d, and in 1913 the figure was £11. 15s 1d after spending £173. 11s 10d on items to commemorate the Championship victory and a donation to Ted Humphreys' benefit of £588. 18s 11d.[14] Given the problems afflicting county cricket a hundred years later, this is definitely a case of *plus ça change, plus c'est la même chose.*

But, to return to the cricket at The Nevill, the position at the start of play presented Kent with something of a dilemma. Unless they could force a win, their position in the Championship Table would suffer, albeit by just over one percentage point (1.33%). Given the margin by which they had "lost" the 1911 competition (0.16%), and with a further 13 matches still to be played, it is possible that the mathematics of the situation had some bearing on how the rest of the match was played out. Were the game played today, and providing both captains agreed, there might have been a declaration, a forfeiture and then an innings to set up a run chase by Worcestershire, but in those days the Laws and Playing Regulations did not permit this.

Kent, therefore, continued to bat, but with the wicket soft and the outfield slow, conditions weren't conducive to quick scoring. Hubble went without adding to his overnight score and Day followed quickly to leave them on 86-4. Dillon and Humphreys took the score on to 142 when Humphreys was caught by Bob Burrows off Bernard Nevile for a well-made 80. At this point, *The Times* suggests: "*with the wicket drying, they might have declared the innings closed, put Worcestershire in, and tried to get them out quickly; then have gone in again, made a few more, declared the second innings closed, and made a second attempt to get Worcestershire out... an unlikely contingency in the absence of Woolley, who is such a valuable bowler on such a wicket.*"[15]

This is a rather curious comment given the other bowling resources Kent had at their disposal, and completely overlooks the presence of one of the two greatest left-arm spinners of all time in the form of Charlie Blythe (the other being Wilfred Rhodes). In addition to Blythe, Kent had three other left-arm spinners – Humphreys, Hatfeild and Hardinge – and although there can be little doubt that Woolley was their superior on a soft wicket, the combination of Blythe and one or more of the others may well have proved sufficient.

The question, however, was academic, as rain again interfered with play for a short time and Dillon chose to bat on with all except Hatfeild contributing runs. Huish had the opportunity to enjoy himself, falling just three short of his half century but, nevertheless, contributed his highest score for the season.

Ted Humphreys

Kent were all out for 252, leaving Worcestershire around an hour and a half to bat. They opened the bowling with two of their regulars in the form of Blythe and Humphreys but, said *The Times*, Blythe "*was taken off just when he appeared to be becoming difficult, and men who do not bowl regularly were put on. It was an unsatisfactory state of affairs.*"[16] Whether this was a correct assessment or not, the Worcestershire batting order showed no sign of collapse. Six other bowlers were used. Pearson[17] and Bowley put on 46 for the first wicket and then Pearson and Burns added 30 together for the second wicket. Three wickets went down in quick succession towards the end with Powell collecting 2-2 from two overs.

The match was, therefore, drawn and Kent's margin at the top of the table was unaffected, because under the points system in place at that time, matches where neither first innings was complete did not count towards the total matches played. This meant that although Kent had completed 16 matches, their points total was only divided by 15 to give the percentage of the maximum available points secured.

Later in the season, it transpired that Kent had lodged a protest with the Secretary of MCC against the inclusion in the Worcestershire side of the amateur Mr BP Nevile, who had previously represented Lincolnshire in 1913. Worcestershire acknowledged the irregularity but, strangely enough, Mr Nevile continued to play for both Worcestershire and Lincolnshire for the remainder of the season.[18]

Fred Huish: season's best at Tunbridge Wells. Seen here at Dover in 1912

Sources

1   *The Times* 12th April 1913

2   Arthur Conan Doyle was a very keen cricketer and played a huge amount of cricket at a very decent level. He played in ten first-class matches for MCC against Derbyshire, Leicestershire, London County and Kent. In 1900 (his first ever first-class match at the age of 41), during a match against London County and with WG Grace 100 plus not out, Conan Doyle was brought on to bowl – presumably to hasten the declaration. From the first ball of his third over, Grace was caught by the former England and Derbyshire player, William Storer. Grace then declared the innings closed. Conan Doyle's figures were 2.1 Overs, 1 Maiden, 4 Runs, 1 Wicket. Conan Doyle commemorated his "great feat" by writing a 17-stanza poem about that one ball. In the poem, he suggests it was a genuine dismissal. The poem tells how Grace got a top edge which was caught by Bill Storer – Doyle says – while he was keeping wicket. The scorecard of the match does not indicate who was keeping wicket for MCC and Storer is also shown as bowling eight overs in the London County innings. Storer was Stoddart's wicketkeeper on the 1897/98 Australia tour, when he was also pressed into service as a bowler in the third and fourth Tests.

3   *Bats, Balls & Bails – The Essential Cricket Book* by Les Scott 2009 Bantam Press p265

4   Page 13 of the Kent County Cricket Club Yearbook says: "Except where the Committee otherwise decides, Ladies and Juvenile Members will not be allowed to occupy seats on the Ground Floor of the Pavilions"

5   KCCC Committee Minute Book 15th May 1913

6   *The Times* 15th July 1913

7   *The Times* 16th July 1913

8   *The Times* 25th July 1913
9   *Manchester Courier* 30th June 1913
10 By applying a simple "then and now" indexation, the £15,000 appealed for by Worcestershire in 1913 works out at £135,000 in today's terms. The better indication would be the cost of rebuilding the Tunbridge Wells pavilion which certainly couldn't be done for a similar sum today.
11 Derek Birley: *A Social History of English Cricket* p202–04
12 *Gloucestershire Road – A History of Gloucestershire CCC* Graham Parker 1983
13 *The Manchester Courier* 3rd September 1913
14 Kent County Cricket Club Annual 1914 "The Blue Book"
15 *The Times* 17th July 1913
16 *The Times* 21st July 1913
17 Fred Pearson, who played for Worcestershire from 1900, trialed for Kent in 1898. Judged "*a good bat, fair bowler, would take an engagement*" in the Kent Trials Book.
18 Kent CC Minute book 1913

Authors vs Artists 1903
Conan-Doyle is in the back row sixth from the left. Also in the photograph are
PG Wodehouse, EW Hornung, Albert Chevallier Tayler and JM Barrie

Arthur Conan Doyle
at 14

16th July 1913	P	W	L	DWF	DLF	NC	Max	Pts	PtsPC
Kent	15	11	2	1	0	1	70	58	82.86%
Middlesex	10	6	0	2	2	0	50	38	76.00%
Yorkshire	16	10	2	3	1	0	80	60	75.00%
Northamptonshire	15	9	2	0	4	0	75	49	65.33%
Nottinghamshire	12	6	2	1	3	0	60	36	60.00%
Surrey	14	7	3	1	3	0	70	41	58.57%
Lancashire	17	5	6	6	0	0	85	43	50.59%
Warwickshire	15	5	7	2	1	0	75	32	42.67%
Sussex	16	4	6	4	2	0	80	34	42.50%
Worcestershire	11	3	5	1	1	1	50	19	38.00%
Somerset	8	2	5	1	0	0	40	13	32.50%
Leicestershire	14	3	9	1	1	0	70	19	27.14%
Derbyshire	13	3	9	0	1	0	65	16	24.62%
Essex	10	1	6	1	2	0	50	10	20.00%
Hampshire	12	2	8	0	2	0	60	12	20.00%
Gloucestershire	12	1	8	1	2	0	60	10	16.67%

Yorkshire 1st Innings

W Rhodes	c Seymour b Woolley	21
BB Wilson	st Huish b Fairservice	5
D Denton	c Powell b Blythe	19
R Kilner	hit wkt b Woolley	27
GH Hirst	c Dillon b Blythe	0
A Drake	c Dillon b Blythe	0
MW Booth	c Seymour b Blythe	12
TJD Birtles	b Blythe	8
S Haigh	c Fairservice b Woolley	0
Sir AW White *	c Blythe b Woolley	4
A Dolphin +	not out	0
Extras	(1 b, 2 lb, 1 nb)	4
Total	(all out, 62.3 overs)	**100**

FOW 1st Innings 1-26, 2-36, 3-61, 4-61, 5-61, 6-85, 7-93, 8-93, 9-99, 10-100

Kent bowling	O	M	R	W
Blythe	24.3	10	30	5
Woolley	27	10	40	4
Fairservice	11	3	26	1

Kent 1st Innings

E Humphreys	c Birtles b Drake	5
HTW Hardinge	st Dolphin b Rhodes	7
J Seymour	b Hirst	75
FE Woolley	c Wilson b Rhodes	12
JC Hubble	c Birtles b Rhodes	6
Mr EW Dillon *	c Dolphin b Drake	8
Mr AP Day	b Drake	0
Mr WA Powell	b Hirst	2
FH Huish +	b Rhodes	10
WJ Fairservice	b Rhodes	3
C Blythe	not out	0
Extras	(3 b, 1 lb, 3 nb)	7
Total	(all out, 49.4 overs)	**135**

FOW 1st Innings 1-8, 2-25, 3-51, 4-62, 5-90, 6-90, 7-99, 8-125, 9-135, 10-135

Yorkshire bowling	O	M	R	W
Hirst	16	6	28	2
Drake	11	5	23	3
Rhodes	13.4	3	42	5
Haigh	5	0	18	0
Kilner	2	0	11	0
Booth	2	0	6	0

Kent vs Yorkshire

The Nevill Ground, Tunbridge Wells
Thursday 17th, Friday 18th & Saturday 19th July
Toss: Yorkshire
Match Drawn
Points: Kent 3 Yorkshire 1

IF THE MATCH against Worcestershire was disappointing because of the weather, then the second match of the week was doubly so as the second and third days were completely lost.

Although the showpiece matches – the Gentlemen and Players, the Varsity Match and Eton vs Harrow – were now over, those whose interest lay mainly with Championship cricket were unable to watch what should have been the match of the season played to a finish. In reality, the match was far more important for Yorkshire than it was for Kent, who sat at the top of the table with a 7.86 per cent lead over the Northern county. Both sides deserved the opportunity to pit their relative strengths against each other. What actually ensued was inconclusive, despite the fact that Kent took the lion's share of the points available.

THE TYKES : " I wonder if I can manage to carry off that bone? "
FARMER'S BOY : " Ah, you've got to get over me before you seize that."

A cartoon that appeared in the *Kent Messenger* of 18th July 1913

Kent made one change to their side with Woolley back from Lord's where the Players beat the Gentlemen by seven wickets. He had had a very ordinary match for the Players, scoring 20 and three and bowling only nine overs without taking a wicket. The Players' matchwinner was Francis Tarrant, the Australian born Middlesex player, who took 7-38 in the second innings. The player omitted from the Kent XI was Eric Hatfeild.

With a crowd of more than 2,000 in the ground, Yorkshire won a toss they would probably rather have lost because the wicket was soft from the rain earlier in the week, and there seemed to be a question as to whether it would dry and get better or worse. As might be expected, the wicket was slow and although the ball turned appreciably, it did so at first without causing the batsmen too many problems. Wilfred Rhodes and Ben Wilson faced Blythe and Woolley with the new ball. Wilson confined himself almost exclusively to defence. *The Times* correspondent found it *"interesting to watch, for he adopted the method of playing forward, loosening his grip of the bat at the last moment and, so to speak, dropping it on the ball."*[1] In today's terminology he "played with soft hands". Whatever his method, he was barracked by the normally genteel Tunbridge Wells crowd.

After a slow first hour in which only 25 runs were scored, Dillon brought Fairservice into the attack from the Railway End. Almost immediately, Wilson lost patience and went down the wicket in an attempt to hit over the infield, missed the ball, and was stumped by Huish. This brought the veteran David Denton to the wicket, and he had obviously decided upon attack. He hit two boundaries off Fairservice (a four past extra cover and a pull to mid wicket). Rhodes was not comfortable, however, and this was compounded when, in scrambling home for a single, he slipped and crashed head first into Woolley's elbow, causing a delay of several minutes while he was treated. This clearly unsettled him for, in the next over, he edged Woolley to slip where Seymour *"who is a very fine slip"*[1] took a good catch to reduce Yorkshire to 36-2.

Denton and the new batsman, Roy Kilner, took the score to 61 without difficulty, but after Blythe had been reintroduced, he bowled an over which turned the game in Kent's favour. From the first ball, Denton mistimed a drive and was caught *"splendidly in front of his face"* by Powell at mid off. The third ball to George Hirst was tossed a little higher but dipped quickly and Hirst gave a simple catch to Dillon at mid on, and from the final ball, the exotically named Alonzo Drake was caught by the captain in the same position. The ball was well struck and was passing over Dillon's head when he managed to arrest its progress and make the catch at the second attempt. Three wickets had gone down without addition to the score and Yorkshire were struggling at 61-5.

Kilner and Booth survived until lunch, which was taken at 70-5. On the resumption, this pair had progressed to 85 when Booth edged Blythe to Seymour at

Yorkshire 1913
Rear : G Hayes : BB Wilson : P Holmes : MW Booth : TDJ Bitles : A Drake : Hodge (Scorer)
Front : A Dolphin : S Haig : D Denton : Sir A White (Capt) : W Rhodes : GH Hirst : R Kilner

slip and then, a few runs later, Blythe bowled Thomas Birtles. Kilner was the eighth wicket to fall when, attempting to pull a ball from Woolley, he swung completely round and his hip removed a bail. *The Times* correspondent commented: "*he is a left handed batsman with a strong defence and he scored nearly all of his runs on the on, though at one time there were seven fieldsmen on that side of the wicket*". He continued: "*the placing of the field is one of the most interesting studies in modern cricket. At one period, Blythe was bowling to left-handed batsmen without a short slip and only two men on the off side while to the right-handed there was the usual array of slips, silly point and others hanging on to the bat.*"[1] The remaining two wickets added only seven runs to see the visitors out for exactly 100. Blythe had taken 5-40 and Woolley 4-40.

Before Kent batted, Dillon made use of the heavy roller in an attempt to deaden and smooth the pitch, but the effect did not last long. Under normal circumstances, Schofield Haig would have partnered Hirst but he was suffering from an injury that prevented his bowling more than five overs in the innings, and so Hirst and Drake opened the bowling. The absence of Haig, however, seemed to matter little as Humphreys was caught in the deep by Birtles trying to force the pace and then, on 25, Hardinge moved out of his ground to hit Rhodes and was stumped. Seymour and Woolley put on 26 with Woolley, as usual, forcing the pace until he was caught right in front of the sight-screen trying to hit Rhodes for a six.

Seymour, "*who was playing fine cricket and neglecting no opportunity to score runs*",[1] and Dillon raised the score to 90 when the captain got a thin edge to

Colin Blythe: 5 for 30, and Wilfred Rhodes: 5 for 42

the wicketkeeper and Day was bowled by a good-length ball. Both fell to Drake. *"Seymour was eventually bowled by a good ball by Hirst. He had played a really fine innings. His defence on slow wickets has improved out of all knowledge. And his great value is that his strokes are so hard and that he can make them to all parts of the field; he is both an offside and an onside player."*[1]

Seymour was assisted by a few blows from Huish towards the end but, by and large, he had played almost a lone hand in his 75 out of Kent's final total of 135 all out. Rhodes had taken 5-42, Drake 3-23 and Hirst 2-28. *The Times* suggested *"that Yorkshire are not the terror to batsmen on sticky wickets that they were in the palmy days when Rhodes and Schofield were at their best."*[1]

The final Kent wicket went down at quarter past six and so there was no time for Yorkshire to begin their second innings before the day ended. The large crowd had enjoyed a fascinating day's cricket which left the match marginally in Kent's favour. The *Kent Messenger* speculated that *"if there is no more rain, then the wicket will probably play more easily and, on a good wicket, Yorkshire may press Kent hard. In Booth they have a fine hard wicket bowler and Kent are without Fielder."*[2] *The Times* was of the opinion that the balance had already shifted: *"after interesting cricket on*

Thursday one may reasonably expect a close fight again today (Saturday) *with the balance now rather in Yorkshire's favour."*[3]

Unfortunately, there was heavy rain during the night and when the players assembled the following morning, the square was covered with puddles. Despite considerable optimism that there would be some cricket, it failed to materialise because the wicket and surrounding areas were still too wet for play, and soon after lunch the match was abandoned. There were a large number of spectators on the ground who had waited patiently in bright and sunny conditions in anticipation of seeing at least a little cricket. *The Times* correspondent comments that despite their disappointment, *"the crowd was admirable"*[3] – what else did he expect in Tunbridge Wells?

Kent took three points from this match which increased their lead over Yorkshire to 9.57 per cent. The two matches at Tunbridge Wells had been a serious disappointment in terms of the weather – just as it would be 100 years later in 2012. In 1759, George Frederick Handel went to see a performance of *The Messiah* given by the Tunbridge Wells Ladies' Music Circle. His well known comment of "God rot Tunbridge Wells" might well have been adapted for use in these two years to read "Wet rot Tunbridge Wells".

Sources

1   *The Times* 18th July 1913
2   *Kent Messenger* 19th July 1913
3   *The Times* 19th July 1913

The original scorecard from the Yorkshire match at Tunbridge Wells
Courtesy of Mr and Mrs Richard Seymour

Lancashire 1st Innings

Mr AH Hornby *	lbw b Fairservice	11
JWH Makepeace	b Blythe	88
JT Tyldesley	b Fairservice	3
J Sharp	b Fairservice	5
GE Tyldesley	run out	9
KG MacLeod	c Hubble b Blythe	9
JS Heap	b Blythe	0
R Whitehead	b Blythe	2
RA Boddington +	c Hubble b Blythe	9
W Huddleston	run out	17
H Dean	not out	1
Extras	(2 lb, 2 nb)	4
Total	(all out, 67.5 overs)	158

FOW 1st Innings 1-23, 2-29, 3-49, 4-81, 5-102, 6-112, 7-116, 8-132, 9-149, 10-158

Lancashire 2nd Innings

	c Woolley b Blythe	3
	not out	39
	b Woolley	13
	c Seymour b Woolley	8
	lbw b Blythe	1
	c sub (Jennings) b Woolley	11
	c Humphreys b Woolley	7
	c Seymour b Woolley	5
	c Hubble b Blythe	1
	c Hardinge b Woolley	0
	c Mason b Blythe	0
		0
	(all out, 34.4 overs)	88

FOW 2nd Innings 1-3, 2-20, 3-38, 4-43, 5-60, 6-69, 7-74, 8-85, 9-88, 10-88

Kent bowling	O	M	R	W
Blythe	24.5	4	60	5
Fairservice	20	8	33	3
Woolley	20	3	48	0
Humphreys	3	1	13	0

Kent bowling	O	M	R	W
Blythe	17.4	4	55	4
Woolley	17	5	33	6

Kent 1st Innings

E Humphreys	c Sharp b Heap	86
HTW Hardinge	b Dean	1
J Seymour	c JT Tyldesley b Dean	19
FE Woolley	b Dean	5
JC Hubble	b Heap	14
Mr EW Dillon *	b Heap	0
Mr JR Mason	lbw b Heap	9
Mr WA Powell	c MacLeod b Dean	8
FH Huish +	b Dean	24
WJ Fairservice	not out	31
C Blythe	b Huddleston	5
Extras	(13 b, 5 lb)	18
Total	(all out, 83.2 overs)	220

FOW 1st Innings 1-3, 2-37, 3-47, 4-64, 5-64, 6-88, 7-120, 8-169, 9-205, 10-220

Kent 2nd Innings

	lbw b Dean	12
	not out	4
	not out	8
	did not bat	
	did not bat	
	did not bat	
	did not bat	
	did not bat	
	did not bat	
	did not bat	
	did not bat	
	(2 b, 1 lb)	3
	(1 wicket, 12.5 overs)	27

FOW 2nd Innings 1-?

Lancashire bowling	O	M	R	W
Dean	36	6	108	5
Whitehead	6	3	7	0
Huddleston	22.2	6	45	1
Heap	19	6	42	4

Lancashire bowling	O	M	R	W
Dean	6.5	3	7	1
Huddleston	6	0	17	0

Kent vs Lancashire

Mote Park, Maidstone
Monday 21st & Tuesday 22nd July
Toss: Lancashire
Kent won by 9 wickets
Points: Kent 5 Lancashire 0

AFTER A WEEK at Tunbridge Wells decimated by rain Kent hoped for better weather for the Maidstone Festival which followed immediately afterwards. The side was unchanged with the exception of the return of Jack Mason for only his second match of the season. Arthur Day, who had scored just five runs in two innings at the Nevill Ground, made way for the former captain. According to the *Kent Messenger*, the *"general opinion on the ground"*[1] was that David Jennings, after scores of 48, 40 and 72 in his last three matches, should have been selected on his home ground.

Dark clouds and a few spots of rain did not deter the Maidstone crowd from gathering in force on Monday for the start of play. They were well rewarded as the poor light in which the game started gave way to dazzling sunshine during the afternoon, by which time it was estimated that there were 3,000 on the ground.

Lancashire won the toss for the 15th time in 19 games this season, and decided to bat, a little surprisingly given that the recent heavy rain had left the pitch soft and the outfield sluggish.

The testing, if not difficult, batting conditions were confirmed immediately as the captain, Albert Hornby, edged Blythe's first ball through the slips for four. Runs came slowly thereafter, largely due to Fairservice's miserly bowling. Harry Makepeace broke the stranglehold by lifting Blythe to the leg boundary and driving Fairservice *"to the tents"*, which probably meant straight back past the bowler to the marquees located at the bottom of the ground. Fairservice responded by trapping Hornby in front and followed up by bowling Johnny Tyldesley, leaving Lancashire 29-2.

The Mote circa 1900

The defence of the Pavilion.

At the Annual Meeting of the Mote Park Cricket Club thanks were accorded the Chairman, who, in reply, expressed his sympathy with the Tunbridge Wells C.C. in the loss they had sustained as the result of the suffragist outrage. As far as the Mote Pavilion was concerned, he added, they were taking every precaution, and he thought he might say that if the ladies went there they would have a very warm reception.

Our Artist has tried to imagine some of the Vice-Presidents, viz., Lord Castlereagh, Colonel Warde, M.P., and Sir Marcus Samuel, Bart., prepared to receive suffragettes within the hastily barricaded Pavilion.

A cartoon that appeared in the *Kent Messenger* the week prior to the Maidstone Cricket Week. It seems that the Mote CC Committee was determined there would be no repeat of the "enemy action" that so nearly disrupted the Tunbridge Wells Week.

The new pairing of John "Jack" Sharp and Makepeace, both fine footballers as well as Lancashire team-mates, survived lucky snicks to leg off Blythe before the former, playing a "*wretched stroke with a crooked bat*", had his stumps shattered by Fairservice after scoring just five runs in 35 minutes. Continued slow progress owed much to Kent's excellent bowling and keen fielding by Woolley, Humphreys and Hardinge in particular. Shortly before lunch, with Makepeace and Ernest Tyldesley starting to rebuild the innings, Humphreys threw down the stumps at the bowler's end, beating Tyldesley's attempt to get home. At lunch, Lancashire were 86-4 with Makepeace on 54, accompanied by the new batsman Kenneth MacLeod. During the course of his innings, Tyldesley had become the third Lancashire batsman to pass 1,000 runs for the season – Hornby and Makepeace having done so before him.

The Times praised the "*really fine bowling*" of Fairservice, who "*varied his pace and break with excellent judgement, and was bowling as well at the end of his long spell as when he started*".[2]

After lunch, MacLeod brought up the Lancashire hundred with a magnificent drive for six off Woolley, but shortly afterwards he played lazily at Blythe and popped up a simple catch to Hubble at silly point. Makepeace took this as a call for aggression, hitting Woolley for ten in one over. James Heap was then bowled by Blythe, who by now was turning the ball considerably, and Whitehead followed immediately, changing his mind mid shot and succeeding only in playing the ball into his stumps. At 116-7, following these quick reverses, Makepeace retreated into his shell, but when Fairservice replaced Woolley in the attack, he gratefully accepted two full tosses which were dispatched to the boundary. This surge of activity encouraged him to further aggression and at 132 he attempted "*a mighty swipe*" off Blythe and lost his off stump. His innings had lasted three hours and included eight fours. At 149, Bill Huddleston ran himself out calling Robert Boddington for a suicidal run to cover point and, nine runs later, Blythe took his 100th wicket of the season by luring Boddington into presenting Hubble with another catch at slip. The general opinion on the ground was that Lancashire's total of 158 would take some matching, and for a large part of the innings, that judgement was borne out.

The Kent openers began at exactly four o'clock, but Hardinge was back in the pavilion with the score at three when Harry Dean uprooted his stumps. The same bowler then missed a sharp caught and bowled chance offered by Humphreys at 14. Seymour made a promising start but was unluckily caught off the back of his bat at second slip by Johnny Tyldesley. After receiving a rousing ovation on his way to the wicket, Woolley, for once, disappointed, being bowled by Dean for five. Kent were now struggling at 49-3 and *The Times* claimed that the Kent batting "*was, so to speak, too correct for the conditions*" and suggested "*a really quick-footed enterprising hitter would have been of estimable value; some one was wanted who would 'go for' the bowling*".[1]

Ted Humphreys 86 in Kent's first innings

Heap replaced Huddleston and bowled Hubble with his first ball and then removed Dillon with the final ball of the same over. Half the Kent side were out for 64, a hefty 94 adrift of the Lancashire total.

Humphreys was at this stage playing something of a lone hand as his partners concentrated on simple survival. Eventually, the Kent hundred was brought up with a fine on drive by the opener. The biggest cheer of the afternoon, however, had been reserved for the arrival at the wicket of the former captain Mason, who became Heap's third wicket in this fine spell with the score at 88-6. Batting in indifferent light, Humphreys (56) and Powell (8) saw Kent through to the close at 116-6.

Rain delayed the start on Tuesday until half past twelve. Humphreys had no sleep the night before due to a bad attack of neuralgia, which made his performance on the first day all the more impressive. Powell failed to add to his overnight score and when Huish joined Humphreys Kent were still 38 short of the Lancashire first innings total. The wicketkeeper's stubborn defence complemented the fine stroke play of the opener to the delight of a crowd of around a thousand. The *Kent Messenger* reported that one lovely off drive by Humphreys *"brought forth loud yells of 'Well played, Teddy'."*

Humphreys' hopes of his first century of the season were first raised by four overthrows as he stole a quick single, and then dashed when, at 86, after three hours at the crease, he was caught by Sharp to give Heap his fourth wicket. Huish then stayed with the new arrival, Fairservice, who gave *"the brightest display of the whole match."*[1] Together, they put on 36 for the ninth wicket by dealing effectively with a series of long hops and half volleys served up to them by the Lancashire attack. Huish fell to Dean at 205, having given great support to both Humphreys and Fairservice for 70 minutes. Fairservice continued to attack but at 220, the innings was brought to a close when Huddleston bowled Blythe. The innings had turned out much better than most envisaged when the score was 64-5 and Kent had secured a valuable 62-run lead. Dean with 5-108 was the most successful bowler but he had been well supported by Heap, whose three wickets in his morning spell had left the home side in serious trouble.

Lancashire began their second innings at five minutes to three, by which time the weather had improved and the crowd was bathing in hot sunshine and enjoying the pipes and drums of the Black Watch Band that played throughout the afternoon. It was that same brilliant sunshine which probably accounted for what seemed to be a significant change in the character of the wicket because Lancashire were soon in trouble, with only Makepeace holding the Kent attack at bay. Whatever the reason, the ball started doing things for Blythe and Woolley that it hadn't done for the Lancashire bowlers. Hornby was the first to go for three, caught by Woolley at slip off Blythe. Seventeen runs later, Johnny Tyldesley, attempting an expansive pull, was bowled by Woolley, who then had Sharp caught by Seymour at slip. Thirty-eight for three became 43-4 when Blythe trapped the other Tyldesley brother lbw.

Blythe and Woolley bowled unchanged in Lancashire's second innings; Blythe 4-55, Woolley 6-33

Harry Makepeace in real life and cartoon form

The fifth wicket fell at 60, courtesy of a "*magnificent*" catch on the boundary by Jennings, fielding as substitute for Powell, who was unwell, to dismiss MacLeod. Another great running catch was taken nine runs later by Humphreys at long leg to dispose of Heap. Ralph Whitehead mishit Woolley to gift Seymour a catch and Boddington edged Blythe to Hubble at slip. Kent wrapped up the innings at 20 minutes to five for 88. Blythe, making the ball turn prodigiously, and Woolley, relying on a perfect length, had bowled "*irresistibly*" in the opinion of the *Times* correspondent. Woolley had taken 6-55 and Blythe 4-55 and they had bowled unchanged throughout the afternoon.

After his heroics of the first innings, Makepeace again defied Kent with a mixture of caution and apt dispatch of the rare bad ball, carrying his bat for 39, and "*was heartily applauded on his way to the pavilion*".[1] The *Times* said that he "*seemed to have plenty of time to make his stroke when playing back, a sure sign of a great batsman, and he frequently smothered the break-backs of the left-handed bowlers by playing right out to the pitch*".[2] Kent scored the 27 required for victory without difficulty apart from losing the hero of the first innings, Humphreys, for 12.

One of the curious aspects of the match was that neither wicketkeeper claimed a single victim, which is surprising given the help extracted from the pitch by the array of left-arm bowlers on show. And there were opportunities – the Lancashire stumper, Boddington, missed four chances.

The 4,000-strong crowd got even more than they bargained for towards the end of the Lancashire innings. An aeroplane circled the field of play "*two or three times before it gracefully planed down just above the refreshment tent*". The *Kent Messenger* reported that one old cricketer, appalled at such impertinence, spluttered that it was "*like having a caterpillar land on a dinner plate.*"[1]

Another cartoon based on the Maidstone and Tunbridge Wells Weeks, published in the *Kent Messenger*

The biplane that arrived at The Mote on Tuesday 22nd July 1913

Spectators enjoying the opportunity to walk on the outfield at The Mote during an interval

The biplane contained Captain G Wildman-Lushington[3] of the Royal Marine Artillery (the pilot) and his navigator, Captain AC Barnby, of the Royal Marines Light Infantry, based the Army Aviation School at Eastchurch. *"They had telegraphed that they would arrive by airship at one o'clock, and they did so almost to the minute, having come across in twenty minutes. During the luncheon interval hundreds of sightseers took the opportunity of scrawling their autographs on the canvas wings for the aviators remained to see Blythe and Woolley fire out the Lancashire men in their second innings and to see Kent's victory – the twelfth this season – assured. Then the visitors, cheered by the crowd, soared upwards on their return journey"*.[1]

It seems it wasn't only Kent who were flying high on that final afternoon.

Another photograph of the biplane that arrived at The Mote during the Lancashire match

Sources

1   *Kent Messenger* 26th July 1913

2   *The Times* 23rd July 1913

3   There was a sad postscript to this event in that Wildman-Lushington was the first officer of the Naval Wing to lose his life while flying a naval machine on duty. He had been for a flight over Sheerness with Captain Henry Fawcett RMLI as passenger, on a Henry Farman biplane No. 23, when, on returning to Eastchurch, the plane fell into a side-slip and hit the ground from about 50 feet. The plane was completely wrecked and the body of the pilot was found under the fuel tank with a broken neck. Captain Fawcett was dazed but suffered only slight injuries.

19th July 1913	P	W	L	DWF	DLF	NC	Max	Pts	PtsPC
Kent	17	12	2	2	0	1	80	66	82.50%
Middlesex	11	6	0	3	2	0	55	41	74.55%
Yorkshire	18	10	3	3	2	0	90	61	67.78%
Northamptonshire	16	10	2	0	4	0	80	54	67.50%
Nottinghamshire	13	7	2	1	3	0	65	41	63.08%
Surrey	15	7	3	1	4	0	75	42	56.00%
Lancashire	19	5	8	6	0	0	95	43	45.26%
Warwickshire	17	6	8	2	1	0	85	37	43.53%
Sussex	18	5	7	4	2	0	90	39	43.33%
Worcestershire	11	3	5	1	1	1	50	19	38.00%
Somerset	8	2	5	1	0	0	40	13	32.50%
Hampshire	14	3	8	1	2	0	70	20	28.57%
Leicestershire	14	3	9	1	1	0	70	19	27.14%
Derbyshire	14	3	10	0	1	0	70	16	22.86%
Gloucestershire	14	2	9	1	2	0	70	15	21.43%
Essex	11	1	6	1	3	0	55	11	20.00%

Middlesex 1st Innings

Mr SH Saville	c Seymour b Blythe	17
FA Tarrant	c Hatfeild by Woolley	7
JW Hearne	c Dillon b Blythe	7
Mr PF Warner *	c Hatfeild b Woolley	8
Mr EL Kidd	c Hardinge b Blythe	4
EH Hendren	c Woolley b Blythe	8
Mr FT Mann	b Blythe	0
Mr NE Haig	st Huish b Woolley	2
HR Murrell +	run out	0
JT Hearne	not out	1
E Mignon	run out	0
Extras	(1 b, 1lb)	2
Total	(all out, 27 overs)	56

FOW 1st Innings 1-11, 2-33, 3-34, 4-42, 5-49, 6-53, 7-54, 8-55, 9-56, 10-56

Middlesex 2nd Innings

b Blythe		0
c Dillon b Blythe		12
c Dillon b Blythe		2
c & b Woolley		4
lbw b Blythe		22
b Woolley		9
c Huish b Woolley		26
[9]b Blythe		3
[8]b Woolley		1
not out		0
b Blythe		0
(1 b, 6 lb)		7
(all out, 33 overs)		86

FOW 2nd Innings 1-1, 2-3, 3-12, 4-38, 5-49, 6-61, 7-62, 8-85, 9-85, 10-86

Kent bowling	O	M	R	W
Fairservice	3	0	6	0
Woolley	13	3	31	3
Blythe	11	4	17	5

Kent bowling	O	M	R	W
Woolley	16	8	31	4
Blythe	17	3	48	6

Kent 1st Innings

E Humphreys	lbw b JT Hearne	5
HTW Hardinge	lbw b Tarrant	6
J Seymour	b Tarrant	1
FE Woolley	not out	33
JC Hubble	b JT Hearne	0
DW Jennings	st Murrell b Tarrant	9
Mr EW Dillon *	c Haig b Tarrant	4
Mr CE Hatfeild	b JT Hearne	4
FH Huish+	b JT Hearne	0
WJ Fairservice	b JT Hearne	9
C Blythe	b JT Hearne	4
Extras	(4 lb)	4
Total	(all out, 29.5 overs)	79

FOW 1st Innings 1-6, 2-8, 3-12, 4-12, 5-29, 6-35, 7-41, 8-49, 9-71, 10-79

Kent 2nd Innings

[4] c & b JT Hearne		5
not out		25
[5] not out		29
did not bat		
did not bat		
did not bat		
[1] lbw b JT Hearne		2
did not bat		
[3] c Warner b Tarrant		3
did not bat		
did not bat		
		0
(for 3 wickets, 35.1 overs)		64

FOW 2nd Innings 1-3, 2-6, 3-23

Middlesex bowling	O	M	R	W
Tarrant	15	1	54	4
JT Hearne	14.5	6	21	6

Middlesex bowling	O	M	R	W
Tarrant	15	5	27	1
JT Hearne	17.1	6	21	2
Mignon	1	0	8	0
JW Hearne	2	1	8	0

Kent vs Middlesex

Mote Park, Maidstone
Thursday 24th & Friday 25th July
Toss: Middlesex
Kent won by 7 wickets
Points: Kent 5 Middlesex 0

THE SECOND VISITORS to Maidstone, Middlesex, were expected to provide a stern test for Kent's title credentials, having beaten Yorkshire two days previously. Despite their eventual victory over Lancashire, Kent made two changes to the side, with Jennings and Hatfeild coming into the side for Powell and Mason, who had to return to his legal practice in Cheapside. By this stage of the season, Kent supporters were becoming increasingly confident that the Championship was theirs. This was reflected in a cartoon that appeared in the *Kent Messenger* depicting the dismissal of the visiting side for 56 with a laurel wreath at the top of the page which had a "Championship" label attached.

With Kent having beaten Lancashire in two days, there was no play on the Wednesday of the Week, which was just as well as heavy rain fell for the best part of the day. Thursday morning, however, was dry and there were around 2,000 spectators on the ground at the start of the match, a number that swelled significantly as the day progressed and news spread about the extraordinary events taking place. The *Kent Messenger* reported that *"the rank and fashion of the county were well represented and it is estimated that the Mote never presented a prettier sight"*.[1]

The Members' Pavilion on the first day of the Middlesex match

Despite the bright sunshine, it was likely that the wicket would be treacherous. This certainly proved to be the case as an incredible first day's play saw 226 runs scored for the loss of 32 wickets. At the close of play, the match was almost decided with Kent needing 58 runs to win with eight wickets in hand. In fact, at ten minutes to five, with Middlesex only 26 runs ahead and half the side out, there seemed a distinct possibility that the game might finish in a single day.

The former England captain, PF "Plum" Warner, must have dreaded the drop of the coin as he and Dillon met for the toss. It is not unreasonable to suggest that his first mistake was to win it and his second to elect to bat, though *The Times* said that *"there can have been very little to choose, and no one could have foreseen that the wicket would be quite as bad as it was. Moreover, Middlesex proceeded to bat with an amazing recklessness. Most of the men hit out at anything and everything in the wildest fashion, and, to make things even worse than they might have been, the last two wickets were thrown away by bad judgement in running."*[2]

Through their cavalier approach, Middlesex were dismissed by Blythe and Woolley for a mere 56 in 27 overs with only Stanley Saville reaching double figures. *Wisden* endorsed *The Times'* judgement and stated that Middlesex had batted *"wildly"*. The innings had lasted less than 90 minutes and once again, on a wicket very much to his liking, Blythe was the main destroyer with 5-17, backed up by Woolley with 3-31.

Fairservice opened the attack with Woolley, though he soon made way for Blythe. Saville's two pulls to the boundary off Woolley were the only strokes

I ALWAYS USE A "FORCE" BAT.

MIDDLESEX

Frank Tarrant: early marketing

A cartoon from the *Kent Messenger* of 2nd August 1913

of note in a slow start by the visitors. Middlesex were at one point 33-1 with the only wicket to fall being that of the Australian Frank Tarrant to a *"well judged"* catch by Hatfeild in the outfield. But the remaining nine went down for just 23 runs.

The first wicket to fall was that of JW "Young Jack" Hearne, who, after lofting Blythe into the grandstand, played the left-armer "tamely" into Dillon's hands at mid off. Warner was warmly greeted by the crowd but he was condemned to be a helpless onlooker as Saville and Leslie Kidd, bamboozled by Blythe, gave catches to Seymour and Hardinge respectively to leave Middlesex 42-4.

Not for the first time in this season, the Kent fielding was *"brilliant"*, backed up by smart work behind the stumps by the 43-year-old Huish. The *Kent Messenger* reporter marvelled at how he had the bails *"nipped off in a twinkling"* in attempting to outwit Warner on two occasions. The Middlesex captain's downfall, however, was to another great catch by Hatfeild in front of the large scoreboard. Half the side were out for 49. Mann was bowled first ball by Blythe, who also induced Hendren to pop a catch to Woolley. In the sparkling form he was in, Huish was not prepared to allow the innings to subside without his name on the scorecard, and made a slick stumping to take care of Jo Murrell. The Middlesex side were in such a state of panic by this point that the final two wickets were both run outs, one to a brilliant piece of fielding by Blythe. The last six batsmen had departed for seven runs. The visitors were 56 all out in just an hour and a half.

Kent had 20 minutes to restore some sanity to the proceedings before the lunch interval, but they made a poor job of it. Hardinge was out to the third lbw appeal made by Tarrant against him in his first two overs. Seymour played on, and after Humphreys had played one fine on drive, he too was adjudged leg before. With the score at 12-3, it seemed that even a first-innings lead could not be guaranteed. The fourth wicket fell without addition to the score immediately on the resumption of play, with Hubble being bowled by JT "Old Jack" Hearne. Jennings (17 for the fifth) and Fairservice (22 for the ninth) kept Woolley company as he produced a 70-minute masterclass on how to play on a turning wicket. His 33, which included *"one glorious hit for 6"*, proved to be the highest score of the match and its majesty caused *The Times* to exclaim that *"in the circumstances his innings was better than many a one of a hundred or more."*[2]

Middlesex used only two bowlers in the Kent innings – Tarrant (4-54) and "Old Jack" Hearne, who took 6-21 from 14.5 overs in an innings that had lasted just 29.5 overs. And so, well before tea on the first day, Kent were in the field again for the Middlesex second innings.

When the visitors started their second innings, the deficit of 23 seemed, in the context of the day, a daunting one. And they too found themselves 12-3 in no time before Tarrant and Kidd produced what at that point was the highest partnership of the match – 26 for the fourth wicket. At 38-3, 15 runs ahead with two batsmen relatively well set, there might have been a glimmer of hope. But when that fourth wicket fell, followed 11 runs later by Hendren's, handing Blythe his 2,000th scalp for the county, five wickets were down for 49, and the lead was just 26.

The Times reports that Kidd then "*batted with really admirable skill and judgement for over half an hour*". Mann endured for three quarters of an hour and even managed to strike some "*very hard*" blows against the Kent left-armers. He was ably supported by Nigel Haig in adding 23 for the eighth wicket. But for these two, Kent would have been set an easy target. Blythe was the scourge of the batsmen but, with the wicket as it was, Woolley was scarcely any less formidable. Blythe's tally in the second innings was 6-48 from 17 overs to give him 11-65 in the match. Woolley had taken 4-31 and 7-62 in the match. For the second time in the week, they had bowled unchanged throughout the afternoon.

There was much speculation on the ground as to whether Kent could actually make the 64 required for their second victory of the week. Not wishing to sacrifice top order batsmen in the 15 minutes remaining in the day's play, Dillon himself opened the batting, and when he was out leg before to "Old Jack" Hearne, he sent in Huish in a further effort to protect his main batsmen. The plan, however, backfired when he fell to a fine rolling catch at point by Warner to give Tarrant his 100th wicket of the season.

Kent ended an astonishing day at 6-2, still 58 short of their target. The consolation was that Hardinge was still at the crease and the wickets of the remaining front-line batsmen were all intact.

Mr Leslie Kidd and Mr Frank Mann: top scorers in the Middlesex second innings

Seymour and Hardinge – the run makers in the Kent second innings

There was a heavy dew early on the next morning, but a drying wind and intermittent bright sunshine soon lessened the spite in the wicket. At 15, Hardinge was almost run out when he was sent back by his partner, Humphreys, only for Saville, regarded as one of the best cover fieldsmen in the country, to gift Kent four overthrows in narrowly missing the stumps with his throw. The third wicket was not long in arriving, however, as Humphreys succumbed to an excellent return catch by "Old Jack" Hearne. Kent were 23-3, with 41 still required.

After three quarters of an hour's play, Kent had added 26 to their overnight score for the loss of that one wicket. With Seymour living a charmed life, including being "missed" by Edward Mignon at long on off a full toss, the situation remained precarious. But suddenly, Seymour hit Tarrant for ten runs in one over to ease the tension. Hardinge was playing a watchful, professional innings at the other end until "Old Jack's" removal from the attack proved to his liking as he scored seven runs in two balls off the replacement bowler, Mignon.

Seymour then took eight off "Young Jack" to level the scores, leaving Hardinge, who had batted expertly for 85 minutes, to make the winning runs "*amidst ringing cheers*" from the crowd of 2,600. The crucial unbroken partnership of 41 had been scored at a run a minute. *Wisden* speculated that "*Could the game have been played out on Thursday, Kent would probably have experienced some difficulty in winning.*"[3]

There had barely been more than three days' play over the two games of Maidstone Week; long enough, however, to strengthen Kent's hold on the leadership of the County Championship with an increased average of 83.52 per cent.

The *Kent Messenger* summed up the week thus: *"Maidstone Cricket Week for 1913 will not be readily forgotten by those who had the good fortune to witness the play. It was full of incidents from commencement to finish, incidents that will doubtless find their way into the record books of enthusiasts of the game. With two such powerful teams as Lancashire and Middlesex pitted one after the other against Kent, one might naturally be excused for expecting to see cricket at the Mote on almost every day of the week. But the rain of the previous week and the downpour of Wednesday affected it in an unlooked for degree. Yet, even with the rain thrown in, could there have been anyone found on Monday morning daring enough to prophesy that the two matches would be brought to a conclusion in, practically, three days?*

"One can readily assume from this that the ball held high revel, and that the bowlers reaped a veritable harvest… 64 wickets fell for 778 runs, giving an average of only just over 12 runs per wicket. On Thursday 30 batsmen could only score 103 runs between them, and this was the day that furnished the most sensational cricket, when the match nearly became numbered among those commenced and finished in a single day."[1] It would be 47 years, during another of the county's traditional cricket weeks, before Kent would add another to that particular list.[4]

One other comment in the *Kent Messenger*'s summary of the week has a more poignant note. On the occasion of Blythe's 2,000th wicket for Kent, the paper

Charlie Blythe: 5-17 & 6-48 against Middlesex   "Old Jack" Hearne: 8-42

speculates that: *"Given health and strength, 'Charlie' should continue to cause trouble in the enemy's camp for years to come, seeing that he is only 34 years of age".*[1]

Before the 1914 season was done, however, Blythe is reported to have made up his mind to retire. It is often said that he had become convinced he had lost the ability to spin the ball to the same extent as in previous years. This is most unlikely to have been the case in 1914 and Chris Scoble in his excellent book, *Colin Blythe – lament for a legend*, says: *"A similar distortion by hindsight has been applied to the career of Colin Blythe at this time. In a few very patchy accounts in cricket histories, he is often supposed to have announced his retirement at the end of the season, as if he himself knew there would be no more first-class cricket for five years to come. But the reality was somewhat different."*[5]

The Kent records show that Blythe remained on the payroll up to the time of his death in November 1917. He played in various services and charity matches, and it was not until that year, at the age of 38, that he began to have his doubts and spoke of his misgivings to Lord Harris. Even by this stage, his decision would have been unusual, for at that time, many cricketers, and particularly slow bowlers, played on well into their forties and sometimes even into their fifties. However, in *A Few Short Runs*, Lord Harris says, *"One of the last things Charley Blythe said to me, before he left for the Front never to return, was that he would not be fit for the County Eleven when the war was over; he knew what there was of spin left in his bowling, and that without that he would not be good enough."*[6] The key words here are *"before he left for the Front"*, which was not until the end of September 1917. His retirement was

Colin Blythe in uniform before being promoted to Sergeant in the Kent Fortress Engineers

announced to the press in the middle of September and he had agreed to take up a coaching position at Eton after the war. Less than two months later, however, the great left-arm spinner was killed by splinters from a German shell in field near the Belgian village of Passchendaele.

Sources

1   *Kent Messenger* 26th July 1913
2   *The Times* 25th July 1913
3   *Wisden* 1914
4   Kent vs Worcestershire at Tunbridge Wells – 15th June 1960. This match was concluded in a single day. Kent batted first and scored 187 with Peter Jones top scoring with 73. Worcestershire were then bowled out for 25 by David Halfyard (4-7) and Alan Brown (6-12). Asked to follow on, the visitors did significantly better, scoring 61. Halfyard took 5-20, Brown 3-22 and Peter Shenton 2-12. Kent won by an innings and 101 runs.
5   *Colin Blythe – lament for a legend* : Christopher Scoble April 2005 p171
6   *A Few Short Runs* – Lord Harris p160

25th July 1913	P	W	L	DWF	DLF	NC	Max	Pts	PtsPC
Kent	18	13	2	2	0	1	85	71	83.53%
Yorkshire	19	11	3	3	2	0	95	66	69.47%
Middlesex	12	6	1	3	2	0	60	41	68.33%
Northamptonshire	16	10	2	0	4	0	80	54	67.50%
Nottinghamshire	14	7	3	1	3	0	70	41	58.57%
Surrey	16	7	3	2	4	0	80	45	56.25%
Sussex	19	6	7	4	2	0	95	44	46.32%
Warwickshire	17	6	8	2	1	0	85	37	43.53%
Lancashire	20	5	9	6	0	0	100	43	43.00%
Worcestershire	12	3	5	1	2	1	55	20	36.36%
Somerset	8	2	5	1	0	0	40	13	32.50%
Hampshire	15	3	8	1	3	0	75	21	28.00%
Leicestershire	15	3	9	1	2	0	75	20	26.67%
Essex	12	1	6	2	3	0	60	14	23.33%
Derbyshire	14	3	10	0	1	0	70	16	22.86%
Gloucestershire	14	2	9	1	2	0	70	15	21.43%

Gloucestershire 1st Innings

Mr CS Barnett	b Fielder	3
AE Dipper	c and b Fielder	5
T Langdon	lbw b Carr	19
Mr JWW Nason	c Dillon b Fielder	0
Mr GL Jessop	c Humphreys b Carr	87
JH Board +	b Carr	0
Mr COH Sewell *	b Carr	0
LL Cranfield	b Carr	0
TH Gange	c Dillon b Fielder	20
CWL Parker	c Hubble b Fielder	3
EG Dennett	not out	0
Extras	(5 b, 1 lb, 1 nb)	7
Total	(all out, 24.3 overs)	**144**

FOW 1st Innings 1-6, 2-15, 3-15, 4-84, 5-84, 6-110, 7-110, 8-121, 9-139, 10-144

Gloucestershire 2nd innings

	b Fielder	3
	c and b Blythe	14
	[6] st Huish b Carr	13
	c Seymour b Blythe	9
	st Huish b Carr	3
	[7] c Huish b Carr	14
	[3] st Huish b Carr	58
	b Fielder	1
	c Hubble b Fielder	4
	not out	17
	c Fielder b Carr	26
	(5 b, 4 lb, 4 nb, 1 w)	14
	(all out, 44.5 overs)	**176**

FOW 2nd Innings 1-6, 2-65, 3-83, 4-93, 5-98, 6-120, 7-122, 8-126, 9-130, 10-176

Kent bowling	O	M	R	W
Fielder	7.3	0	55	5
Blythe	6	1	29	0
Woolley	5	0	27	0
Carr	6	1	26	5

Kent bowling	O	M	R	W
Fielder	12	2	47	3
Blythe	17	4	41	2
Carr	15.5	0	74	5

Kent 1st Innings

E Humphreys	b Dipper	59
HTW Hardinge	b Parker	50
J Seymour	c and b Dennett	29
FE Woolley	c Board b Gange	0
JC Hubble	run out	38
Mr EW Dillon *	c Dennett b Gange	33
Mr CE Hatfeild	c Gange b Cranfield	18
FH Huish +	b Cranfield	0
Mr DW Carr	c Board b Cranfield	0
C Blythe	c Jessop b Gange	0
A Fielder	not out	6
Extras	(13 b, 1 lb, 2 nb)	16
Total	(all out, 80.5 overs)	**249**

FOW 1st Innings 1-112, 2-125, 3-126, 4-171, 5-215, 6-234, 7-235, 8-235, 9-236, 10-249

Kent 2nd Innings

c Dipper b Cranfield	21
b Cranfield	15
not out	20
not out	10
did not bat	
did not bat	
did not bat	
did not bat	
did not bat	
did not bat	
did not bat	
(1 b, 3 lb, 1 nb, 1 w)	6
(2 wickets, 19 overs)	**72**

FOW 2nd Innings 1-39, 2-48

Gloucester bowling	O	M	R	W
Gange	26.5	4	70	3
Parker	14	6	28	1
Dennett	20	4	82	1
Dipper	11	4	22	1
Cranfield	9	3	31	3

Gloucester bowling	O	M	R	W
Gange	5	1	16	0
Dennett	9	2	33	0
Cranfield	5	2	17	2

Kent vs Gloucestershire

Bat & Ball Ground, Gravesend
Monday 28th & Tuesday 29th July 1913
Toss: Gloucestershire
Kent won by 8 wickets
Points: Kent 5 Gloucestershire 0

HAVING ENJOYED THE entire weekend off, the players arrived at the Bat & Ball to meet Gloucestershire, who had inflicted one of their only two defeats so far in this splendid season. Kent made two changes, leaving out Fairservice and Jennings to bring back Fielder, now recovered from the boil on his neck that had kept him out of the side since Birmingham, and Douglas Carr who, now that the summer holidays had arrived, was available for most matches.

Winning the toss, Gloucestershire chose to bat first on what was usually a good batting wicket with a fast outfield that was also one of the smallest used for first-class cricket in the country. *The Times* says that "*the finest cricket was seen before lunch*"[1] and it is certainly true that it was eventful. Fielder picked up the first three wickets (Charles Barnett, Alf Dipper and Mr John Nason) with only 15 on the board, bringing Gilbert Jessop in at number five to bat with Sussex-born Tom Langdon. Jessop had played at Gravesend twice before[2] but had never met with any success at a ground which might have been made for his sparkling brand of batsmanship. He started to attack immediately, scoring 45 out of 55 in 23 minutes. "*His first four was sent to the canvas screen where, amid laughter, the ball was fielded by a friendly policeman.*"[3] Dropped by Seymour at long on from Woolley's bowling at 46,[4] he then took 13 off an over from Fielder, followed by 17 from one bowled by Blythe. He reached his fifty in only half an hour. Having tried Fielder, Blythe and Woolley, Dillon then turned to Carr.

The move was immediately successful as he removed Langdon and Jack Board with successive deliveries to reduce the visitors to 84-5. Jessop continued his assault on the bowling and Carr was the only bowler to whom he showed the slightest respect. Soon, however, Jessop ran out of luck and was caught at mid on by Humphreys off Carr. He had scored 87 in 55 minutes including three sixes (one into the workhouse and two over the pavilion). His innings included nine fours and two threes. "*The value of his innings was enhanced by reason of the complete failure of the others to successfully defend their wickets ... on retiring, Jessop received an ovation.*"[5]

As the *Evening News* rather dismissively suggests, the rest of the batting, with the exception of Tommy Gange, produced little, and Gloucestershire were bowled out for 144 in 24.3 overs before the lunch interval. Carr had taken 5-26 from six

The Kent XI that played at Gravesend against Gloucestershire
Back Row: FH Huish, W Fairservice (12th Man), JC Hubble, A Fielder, E Humphreys, HTW Hardinge, FE Woolley. Front Row: C Blythe, Mr DW Carr, Mr EW Dillon, Mr CE Hatfeild, J Seymour

overs and Fielder 5-55 from 7.3 overs. Those who turned up after lunch to find the second innings already in progress had to be convinced that Kent had not batted first and that the match had started at the advertised time.[3]

Kent's batting was less spectacular than that of their opponents but infinitely more effective. Humphreys and Hardinge began steadily on what was now a very good batting surface, putting on 102 for the first wicket (their first century opening stand of the year), with some strong driving in 80 minutes during which Humphreys completed his thousand runs for the season. The partnership was ended when he played on to Dipper for 59, having hit nine fours. Shortly after reaching his 50, Hardinge too was bowled (by Parker) after occupying the crease for an hour and 35 minutes.

The Gloucestershire total was passed for the loss of only three wickets. The crowd was disappointed, however, that Woolley departed without scoring, but Hubble and Dillon batted brightly to take the score to 215-5. A few blows from Hatfeild (including 12 from five balls) aside, the remaining five wickets fell for only 34 runs (the last four for 15) and Kent were all out for 249. Hubble, having gone in at six, was run out to end the innings. Gange and Lionel Cranfield were the beneficiaries of the largesse of the Kent lower order, collecting three wickets each.

Douglas Carr: 5-26 & 5-74, and Arthur Fielder: 5-56 & 3-47, at Gravesend

The following morning, Gloucestershire received a visit from Dr Grace. WG was revisiting the scene of a former triumph where, against Gloucestershire in Kent's first championship match in 1895, Grace's *annus mirabilis,* he reached his one thousand run in the month of May. In that match, he spent every ball on the field of play – a remarkable feat of endurance for a man in his 48th year. Kent batted first scoring 470, during which Grace bowled 43 overs. He then opened the batting, and was last out for 257. Kent were bowled out cheaply and Gloucestershire had to make 106 for victory. Grace again opened the batting, and when the winning runs were scored, was not out 73.

The presence of the "Grand Old Man" should have been an inspiration, and Gloucestershire were expected to make the most of what was still a very good wicket. But, although they fared better in the second innings, they were far from convincing. Losing "CS" Barnett to Fielder in the first over, Dipper and the captain, Cyril Sewell, put on 59 runs for the second wicket largely due to *"Mr Sewell … who hit up 58 runs out of 77 in 40 minutes. His brilliant innings included three 6's – one off Fielder and two off Mr Carr – and seven 4's."*[6] With the score at 83, however, Sewell attempted to repeat his harsh treatment of Carr and gave a chance to Woolley at mid off which was dropped but, off the very next ball, he was stumped by Huish. Langdon was then stumped off Carr so that Gloucestershire were five down for 98 with their best batsmen back in the pavilion, and their combined score still seven runs behind the Kent first innings total.

The rest of the innings fell away until Parker and Dennett came together with nine wickets down at 130 and provided some fun for the crowd. They *"hit*

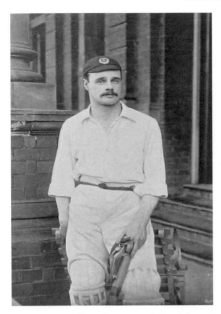

Gilbert Jessop and Cyril Sewell, the former and current Gloucestershire captains

vigorously and put on 46 together for the last wicket in 25 minutes, the innings closed on 176."[7] Carr had taken his second five-wicket haul in the match to give him figures of 10-100. Fielder enjoyed his return to the side with 8-102 and Huish had four victims in the second innings, three of them stumped. Kent needed 72 to win, which they accomplished easily for the loss of two wickets in 45 minutes with the last 24 coming in ten minutes. The game ended at half past three on the second day.

The match had been blessed with some of the best weather of the season and the local press hailed the event as a success. *"Gravesend does not outwardly enthuse so much on these county cricket days as some towns, but a festive touch was given to the ground by the prettily arranged Tents of The Mayor (Councillor F Goldsmith) and Corporation, and the North Kent Club, where hospitality was dispensed."*[6]

Delight at Kent's victory would have been tempered by the absence of a third day's takings for the county club – for the third match in succession. With crowds of 5,000 for each day, the gate receipts were a record £208 10s 3d, a healthy £30 more than the previous best and double the average at other Kent grounds – and that all in less than two days. The county, sensing they might have made a mistake in reducing Gravesend's quota of matches from two in 1912 to just the single match in 1913, restored two matches for 1914 when they played one game against Somerset in the middle of July (winning by nine wickets) and one against Warwickshire in late August (after the outbreak of war), which was won by 99 runs. This may not have been the most cost-effective way of staging two matches at a single venue but, in those days, the Bat & Ball was literally a happy hunting ground for Kent as by the end of 1914, they had won 12 consecutive matches at the venue.[8]

Their earlier defeat at Bristol thus avenged, and, with Surrey having beaten Yorkshire at Hull, Kent had opened up a comfortable 18.44% gap at the top of the Championship table. Northamptonshire had moved into third place as a result of good wins in their last two matches.

Sources

1   *The Times* 29th July 1913
2   1896 24, 1901 1 & 4.
3   *The Sportsman* 29th July 1913
4   *Manchester Courier* 29th July 1913
5   *Evening News* 28th July 1913
6   *Kent Messenger* 2nd August 1913
7   *The Times* 30th July 1913
8   *The Bat & Ball Gravesend: A First Class Cricket History* – Howard Milton 1999 p41

29th July 1913	P	W	L	DWF	DLF	NC	Max	Pts	PtsPC
Kent	19	14	2	2	0	1	90	76	84.44%
Northamptonshire	17	11	2	0	4	0	85	59	69.41%
Middlesex	12	6	1	3	2	0	60	41	68.33%
Yorkshire	20	11	4	3	2	0	100	66	66.00%
Surrey	17	8	3	2	4	0	85	50	58.82%
Nottinghamshire	15	7	3	1	4	0	75	42	56.00%
Lancashire	21	6	9	6	0	0	105	48	45.71%
Sussex	20	6	8	4	2	0	100	44	44.00%
Warwickshire	18	6	9	2	1	0	90	37	41.11%
Worcestershire	12	3	5	1	2	1	55	20	36.36%
Hampshire	16	3	8	2	3	0	80	24	30.00%
Essex	13	2	6	2	3	0	65	19	29.23%
Somerset	9	2	6	1	0	0	45	13	28.89%
Leicestershire	15	3	9	1	2	0	75	20	26.67%
Derbyshire	15	3	10	1	1	0	75	19	25.33%
Gloucestershire	15	2	10	1	2	0	75	15	20.00%

Humphreys and Hardinge batting in the first innings, taken from the steps outside the home dressing room

Kent 1st Innings

HTW Hardinge	b Douglas	13
E Humphreys	c Russell b Buckenham	131
J Seymour	c Russell b Elliott	48
FE Woolley	b Buckenham	48
JC Hubble	b Buckenham	23
DW Jennings	b Buckenham	17
Mr EW Dillon *	c McIver b Tremlin	23
FH Huish +	c Freeman b Douglas	21
Mr DW Carr	b Douglas	23
C Blythe	st McIver b Davies	2
A Fielder	not out	0
Extras	(24 b, 9 lb, 2 w)	35
Total	(all out, 85.1 overs)	384

FOW 1st Innings 1-42, 2-112, 3-228, 4-264, 5-290, 6-327, 7-335, 8-376, 9-383, 10-384

Kent 2nd Innings

	b Buckenham	17
	c McIver b Douglas	19
	c Fane b Davies	36
	[7] not out	18
	[4] st McIver b Davies	19
	[5]c Gillingham b Buckenham	11
	[6] c Elliott b Davies	15
	b Buckenham	11
	c Douglas b Davies	4
	b Buckenham	0
	c Davies b Buckenham	5
	(10 b, 2 lb, 1 w)	13
	(all out, 41.3 overs)	168

FOW 2nd Innings 1-35, 2-45, 3-92, 4-94, 5-125, 6-135, 7-137, 8-156, 9-156, 10-168

Essex bowling	O	M	R	W
Douglas	19.1	2	60	3
Buckenham	33	2	122	4
Tremlin	11	2	50	1
Elliott	11	0	67	1
Davies	10	0	44	1
Mead	1	0	6	0

Essex bowling	O	M	R	W
Douglas	9	2	27	1
Buckenham	16.3	3	58	5
Elliott	5	0	22	0
Tremlin	2	0	14	0
Davies	9	0	34	4

Essex 1st Innings

Mr CD McIver +	b Blythe	80
CAG Russell	b Blythe	2
JR Freeman	c Dillon b Carr	23
The Rev FH Gillingham	run out	6
Mr FL Fane	b Carr	2
Mr JWHT Douglas *	c Hubble b Carr	45
Mr GB Davies	b Fielder	17
CP Buckenham	b Blythe	1
Mr HDE Elliott	b Carr	0
B Tremlin	b Fielder	13
W Mead	not out	0
Extras	(7 b, 2 lb, 7 nb, 1 w)	17
Total	(all out, 76.3 overs)	206

FOW 1st Innings 1-7, 2-69, 3-83, 4-88, 5-173, 6-175, 7-176, 8-179, 9-205, 10-206

Essex 2nd Innings

	c Huish b Humphreys	53
	c Seymour b Fielder	51
	c Blythe b Fielder	69
	b Carr	7
	b Carr	0
	b Humphreys	7
	run out	27
	b Carr	7
	b Fielder	3
	b Blythe	24
	not out	21
	(3 b, 2 lb, 11 nb, 1 w)	17
	(all out, 102.4 overs)	286

FOW 2nd Innings 1-96, 2-143, 3-158, 4-158, 5-184, 6-224, 7-233, 8-239, 9-250, 10-286

Kent bowling	O	M	R	W
Fielder	17.3	3	66	2
Blythe	29	10	44	3
Carr	26	4	71	4
Humphreys	4	0	8	0

Kent bowling	O	M	R	W
Fielder	25	4	100	3
Blythe	31.4	12	56	1
Carr	32	9	84	3
Humphreys	14	2	29	2

Essex vs Kent

The County Ground, Leyton
Thursday 31st July, Friday 1st & Saturday 2nd August
Toss: Kent
Kent won by 50 runs
Points: Essex 0 Kent 5

KENT MADE THE relatively short trip from Gravesend to Leyton to play their local rivals, who had just managed to prise themselves off the bottom of the table with a good win over Sussex at Hove. Set to chase 213 in the fourth innings, they did so for the loss of only four wickets. Their most successful batsman in that match had been Peter Perrin, who scored 49 and 55, but he wasn't available. Kent made one change to their side in restoring Jennings to the team in place of Hatfeild. The Essex side included JR Freeman, the brother of "Tich" Freeman,[1] who was on the Kent Nursery Staff at Tonbridge, and CAG "Jack" Russell, who was a cousin.

Kent won the toss and, batting on a good wicket, made 384 in front of a crowd of 6,000. *The Times* reports that the Kent batting *"was not up to its usual standard and the total was largely due to some very indifferent fielding of the Essex side."*[2] If the "extras" column is anything to go by, this was certainly the case as they were fourth highest scorer at 35 (24 byes, nine leg byes and a wide).

Humphreys was the mainstay of the Kent innings with 131 in 220 minutes with 16 fours and a six. He was, however, dropped at six, 49 and 107 and apparently used the edge to very good effect throughout his innings. Having listed his shortcomings in great detail, *The Times* concedes *"he brought off some good hits which included a straight drive into the pavilion for 6 and sixteen 4's"*. Humphreys wasn't the only beneficiary of the fielders' generosity as Hardinge, Jennings and Carr were also given at least one life each. *Wisden* says that *"Woolley and Seymour*

The County Ground, Leyton circa 1906

A cartoon that appeared in one of the newspapers reporting the first day's play at Leyton – possibly *The Sportsman*. It was discovered in a scrapbook kindly loaned to the authors by Paul Lewis for the purposes of research. Unfortunately, the cartoon had been damaged prior to its inclusion in the scrapbook. The majority of the contents are reports from *The Sportsman*, which ran from 1864 until 1924.

hit freely"[3] for their 48 runs each but otherwise, like *The Times*, concentrates on the deficiencies of the Essex fielding. Kent were bowled out just before six o'clock and, in the half hour before the close, Essex reached 38-1, losing Russell bowled by Blythe for just two.

Ted Humphreys: 131 in 220 minutes. Seen here in 1905

On Friday, the Essex innings was held together by Colin McIver, the only batsman apart from the skipper Johnny Douglas to come to terms with the Kent bowling. "*So long as Mr McIver stayed there was every prospect of a fight. He was a little lucky and rather unequal, but he played a most creditable innings without which his side would have been in a hopeless plight. He made a very shaky start. When he was 30 he cut a ball to short third man where Hardinge dropped a sharp but apparently not difficult catch, and in the same over he put up a ball to mid-on – a very weak stroke.*"[4] Woolley was unable to bowl due to an injury to the middle finger of his left hand sustained while batting and the main burden fell on Blythe, Carr and Fielder.

Essex had two pieces of bad luck in their first innings. Frank Gillingham was run out from a smart piece of fielding by Huish when McIver popped up the ball short on the leg side towards mid on, and set off for the run that would have brought up his fifty. Humphreys, running in from mid on, could not quite reach the catch and knocked the ball back towards short leg. Huish rushed out from behind the wicket, gathered the ball, spun round and threw down the stumps with Gillingham still short of his ground. This was an excellent effort from two men with a combined age of 74. Shortly after, Fred Fane played on to Carr to leave Essex 88-4.

Douglas then joined McIver to produce the best stand of the innings. "*McIver altered his style of play completely and scored only 8 out of 47 before luncheon. He was more himself afterwards.*" McIver restored to "himself" by lunch, the pair took the score to 173 when Dillon reintroduced Blythe, who immediately deceived and bowled McIver. Douglas made 45 before being caught by Hubble off Carr. The Times said "*he had played the best cricket on the side.*" The last five wickets went

Three of the Essex players in the match at Leyton:
Jack Russell, Walter Mead and Fred Fane

down for 33 runs and Essex were all out for 206. Blythe had bowled very accurately, conceding 44 from 29 overs and taking three wickets. Carr, however, had the best analysis with 4-71.

The Essex innings closed at 25 minutes to four, leaving Kent two and three quarter hours' batting before the close, during which time they were bowled out for 168. Seymour top scored with 36 – he was rather unlucky to be out to a brilliant catch by Fane. He drove the ball strongly *which looked perfectly safe. Mr Fane ran across the ball and, stooping down, just reached it with both hands.* The last five wickets fell for 43 runs – *"Kent no doubt wanted to score rapidly irrespective of wickets falling, but they seemed too anxious to force the game and, moreover, did not succeed in doing so to much purpose."*[4]

The Olympic association football gold medallist Claude Buckenham[5] *"again bowled chiefly on the leg stump with four fieldsmen close in on the on side and he had a splendid analysis"* – 5-58 – and Geoffrey Davies returned his best bowling analysis in Championship cricket with 4-34. Kent's rather lacklustre performance with the bat had, nevertheless, set their hosts the stiff target of 347 to win on the following day.

Essex made a spirited start on Saturday with McIver and Russell putting on 96 for the first wicket. McIver, although benefitting from a significant element of luck (a close run out, a missed stumping and a further chance off Carr's bowling), *"played sound cricket and put plenty of power into the strokes. Some of his late cuts were exceptionally good."*[6] When he fell to an edge off Humphreys, Freeman and Russell batted carefully up to the lunch interval.

After lunch, Russell fell to a fine stooping catch by Seymour at slip for 51 with the score on 143. Carr then snapped up Gillingham and Fane, both with the

Johnny Douglas, the Essex captain, bowling in the nets

googly, and Douglas was bowled by Humphreys to swing the game back in Kent's favour. Davies helped Freeman to take the total to 201 at tea, which meant Essex needed a further 146 for victory with half their wickets remaining and two hours in which to get the runs.

After tea, the batsmen tried to raise the tempo and Davies struck three fours in one over from Fielder, but was then dismissed in the unluckiest manner – run out while backing up. Freeman drove the ball back hard at Fielder who, in his attempt to stop the ball, succeeded in turning it on to the stumps with Davies out of his ground. Buckenham hit one boundary and was then dropped in the slips by Hubble. Dillon replaced Blythe with Carr, who at once bowled Buckenham to reduce Essex to 233-7. Freeman then drove in the air to Seymour at cover point to bring an end to *"a fine innings which had lasted for nearly three hours… his cuts and off drives were particularly good."*[6]

In the next over, Fielder bowled Elliott – 250-9 and victory seemingly close, but Bert Tremlin and Walter Mead, dropped at three by Jennings at slip, hit strongly for a while to put on 36 for the last wicket. Blythe was reintroduced and immediately bowled Tremlin with a ball that went on with the arm and grazed his leg stump. It was Blythe's only wicket of the innings. Fielder and Carr both took three wickets and Humphreys two. Kent had won by 60 runs at half past five which, considering their position in the early afternoon, was perhaps a flattering margin. Rather as Essex had done in the first innings, Kent had missed plenty of chances which, against a stronger side, might have proved critical.

It had been an interesting game throughout and a financial success for the home county with an enthusiastic crowd reaching 5,000 on the final day. After

The Kent side at Leyton
J Seymour, FE Woolley, C Blythe, E Humphreys, JC Hubble, DW Jennings, A Fielder, FH Huish
Mr DW Carr, Mr EW Dillon, HTW Hardinge
Photograph courtesy of Mr & Mrs R Seymour

mornings that were overcast, the cricket had been played out in warm sunshine in the afternoons. Kent had been pushed harder than they might have expected by their struggling neighbours; *"one of the hardest struggles they have had this season."*[7]

Despite their victory, Kent lost a little ground to Yorkshire in the Championship table. Having been 18.44 per cent ahead after Gravesend, this had now fallen to 17.62 per cent because Yorkshire won their game against Hampshire at Harrogate by 182 runs.

Sources

1   Tich Freeman joined the Kent staff in 1912, and during that season and 1913, played for Kent in the Minor Counties Championship. He made his first-class debut in May 1914 against Oxford University, and in August his Championship debut against Surrey at Lord's because The Oval had been requisitioned by the War Office for military use.

2   *The Times* 1st August 1913

3   *Wisden* 1914

4   *The Times* 2nd August 1913

5   Claude Buckenham – see page 71 Kent vs Essex at Tonbridge.

6   *The Times* 4th August 1913

7   *Cricket Magazine* 9th August 1913

John Freeman

3rd August 1913	P	W	L	DWF	DLF	NC	Max	Pts	PtsPC
Kent	20	15	2	2	0	1	95	81	85.26%
Northamptonshire	17	11	2	0	4	0	85	59	69.41%
Middlesex	12	6	1	3	2	0	60	41	68.33%
Yorkshire	21	12	4	3	2	0	105	71	67.62%
Surrey	17	8	3	2	4	0	85	50	58.82%
Nottinghamshire	15	7	3	1	4	0	75	42	56.00%
Lancashire	21	6	9	6	0	0	105	48	45.71%
Sussex	21	6	8	4	3	0	105	45	42.86%
Warwickshire	18	6	9	2	1	0	90	37	41.11%
Worcestershire	12	3	5	1	2	1	55	20	36.36%
Somerset	10	2	6	2	0	0	50	16	32.00%
Leicestershire	14	3	8	1	2	0	70	20	28.57%
Hampshire	17	3	9	2	3	0	85	24	28.24%
Essex	14	2	7	2	3	0	70	19	27.14%
Derbyshire	15	3	10	1	1	0	75	19	25.33%
Gloucestershire	15	2	10	1	2	0	75	15	20.00%

Kent 1st Innings

E Humphreys	c RR Relf b AE Relf	9
HTW Hardinge	b Vincett	47
J Seymour	b Holloway	12
FE Woolley	c Street b Vincett	16
JC Hubble	b RR Relf	8
Mr EW Dillon *	not out	63
FH Huish +	b Vincett	1
WJ Fairservice	c Fender b RR Relf	4
Mr DW Carr	c Street b RR Relf	1
C Blythe	c Jupp b RR Relf	25
A Fielder	c Street b RR Relf	6
Extras	(19 b, 4 lb)	23
Total	(all out, 71.2 overs)	**215**

FOW 1st Innings 1-27, 2-64, 3-91, 4-100, 5-116, 6-120, 7-131, 8-155, 9-205, 10-215

Kent 2nd Innings

	c Chaplin b AE Relf	23
	c RR Relf b Holloway	71
	b Jupp	33
	lbw b RR Relf	41
	c Street b Holloway	1
	b Jupp	62
	b Vine	42
	b Holloway	48
	c Wilson b Vine	14
	not out	8
	c Harrison b Vine	1
	(5 b, 3 lb, 6 nb, 1 w)	15
	(all out, 99.3 overs)	**359**

FOW 2nd Innings 1-40, 2-99, 3-173, 4-174, 5-187, 6-267, 7-288, 8-335, 9-357, 10-359

Sussex bowling	O	M	R	W
AE Relf	22	5	54	1
Jupp	6	0	26	0
Holloway	8	2	28	1
RR Relf	21.2	3	47	5
Vincett	14	6	37	3

Sussex bowling	O	M	R	W
AE Relf	18	6	48	1
Jupp	13	0	53	2
Holloway	24	3	76	3
RR Relf	20	0	76	1
Vincett	14	3	41	0
Vine	10.3	1	50	3

Sussex 1st Innings

Mr HL Wilson	c Seymour b Fielder	10
J Vine	c Huish b Fielder	6
VWC Jupp	c Woolley b Carr	17
AE Relf	c Fielder b Blythe	89
Mr HP Chaplin *	c Huish b Fielder	11
RR Relf	c Seymour b Fielder	1
Mr PGH Fender	b Fielder	4
AM Harrison	c Humphreys b Carr	7
JH Vincett	b Fielder	1
GB Street +	not out	21
NJ Holloway	c Seymour b Fielder	24
Extras	(5 lb, 15 nb, 1 w)	21
Total	(all out, 72.2 overs)	**212**

FOW 1st Innings 1-16, 2-23, 3-50, 4-70, 5-85, 6-90, 7-103, 8-104, 9-180, 10-212

Sussex 2nd Innings

	b Fielder	19
	c Woolley b Carr	46
	c Seymour b Fielder	12
	b Fairservice	6
	b Carr	5
	c and b Fairservice	11
	b Carr	0
	b Carr	6
	b Carr	10
	c Dillon b Fielder	0
	not out	0
	(2 b, 2 lb, 3 nb)	7
	(all out, 51 overs)	**122**

FOW 2nd Innings 1-39, 2-57, 3-76, 4-93, 5-93, 6-94, 7-112, 8-118, 9-118, 10-122

Kent bowling	O	M	R	W
Fielder	23.2	5	41	7
Blythe	19	7	51	1
Carr	24	6	67	2
Fairservice	4	0	23	0
Humphreys	2	0	9	0

Kent bowling	O	M	R	W
Fielder	13	2	38	3
Blythe	1	0	4	0
Carr	10	2	28	5
Fairservice	19	7	28	2
Woolley	8	1	17	0

Kent vs Sussex

St Lawrence Ground, Canterbury
Monday 4th, Tuesday 5th & Wednesday 6th August
Toss : Kent
Kent won by 240 runs
Points : Kent 5 Sussex 0

KENT OPENED CANTERBURY WEEK on Bank Holiday Monday against neighbours Sussex. The only change to the team was the omission of Jennings for Fairservice, the latter bolstering an attack which was missing Woolley, who had an injured left hand. This meant that the side, unusually, only contained two amateurs. Canterbury Week traditionally saw the reappearance of several amateurs in favour of otherwise ever-present professionals such as Fairservice. This was indicative of the shift that had taken place in both the composition and approach of the county side since the first Championship seven years before.

Sunny intervals and a cool northeasterly wind greeted the captains at the toss, which Dillon won and elected to bat. Within 20 minutes of the start, however,

Albert Relf: 89 in the Sussex first innings

threatening clouds emitting a steady rain caused a stoppage. The interruption dismayed the very large crowd of 11,258 (of which 8,228 had paid, and which was a significant increase on the previous year's numbers). *The Kentish Gazettee & Canterbury Press* captured the mood of those present: *"Large numbers of excursionists who had started out from their respective towns with every likelihood of a bright and pleasurable day – and for many of them be it remembered this was their one day's cricket in the year – obviously became very depressed as solid banks of cloud cast a deep gloom over the ground, and visions of last year's disastrous Week were recalled. Like all holiday crowds, they were ready to catch at the proverbial straw, and as the rain began to cease, a section of the spectators raised impatient calls for a resumption".*[1]

Almost as suddenly as the rain had arrived, it stopped. The same local reporter congratulates *"Mr. Pawley's appliance for covering the creases and the bowlers' footholds"* for enabling a restart *"at the earliest possible moment, the appearances of the umpires evoking something in the nature of an ovation".*[1]

The delay had only been 25 minutes and the vast crowd now settled back on their benches and carriages to watch an *"interesting"* if *"by no means inspiriting"* day's cricket, initially in dull, miserable conditions before a warming sun made a welcome appearance in mid-afternoon.

On a quick, lively pitch Kent, largely through the efforts of Hardinge and Dillon, made a modest 215, around a hundred short of expectations. The local correspondent found this *"inexplicable"* as the groundsman, Murrin, had prepared a *"beautiful"* wicket that provided the bowlers with *"little or no help"*, though he

Ted Dillon

St Lawrence in 1901: the view from the top of the Pavilion

concedes that the heavy dew might have made the "*ball pop a little*". Nonetheless, he complained that Humphreys, Seymour and Woolley in particular got out to "*rank bad shots*".[1]

Hardinge played some fine cuts early on, but after losing Humphreys and Seymour, he took a more cautious approach, guiding Kent to 100-4 at lunch. Fifth out at 116, he batted for an hour and three quarters and hit five fours. Dillon was dropped at 19 by the short leg, Herbert Chaplin, whose hand was bandaged after sustaining a blow at Bath, and then by Albert Relf when on 40. Nevertheless, he held the innings together, hitting five boundaries in his vital, unbeaten 63 made in an hour and 50 minutes. Blythe provided the staunchest support, contributing exactly half of their ninth-wicket partnership of 50, demonstrating that there were few demons in the wicket. The general feeling around the ground was that the home side's total was a little under par. Sussex had an hour and a quarter's batting before the close, losing three wickets, two to Fielder, while reducing the deficit to 165.

The visitors resumed their innings on Tuesday in sunnier conditions after a sharp shower in the early hours of the morning. The crowd was 7,121, of which 3,990 had paid, a much lower proportion than at other Kent grounds during the season, indicative presumably of the number of both members and "guests" present.

The game quickly turned in Kent's favour as Fielder, despite overstepping 17 times, bowled "*magnificently*" – making the ball swing and rise nastily. While Albert Relf batted steadily, and dealt effectively with the occasional loose ball, he could only watch as his team slumped to 104-8. Chaplin was taken by Huish, Robert Relf brilliantly caught by Seymour at slip and Percy Fender was clean bowled. Aelfric Harrison was caught cleverly, left-handed, by a rolling Humphreys at mid on, and John Vincett had his off stump uprooted.

This prompted Albert Relf to take more chances, and after spending 135 minutes over his 50, he added a further 39 in as many minutes, including 12 off one over from Fairservice. He was also severe on Blythe in his innings of 89, which contained 13 fours. The last three Sussex batsmen offered excellent support to Relf in his attempt to overhaul the Kent total. With George Street, Relf put on 76 for the ninth wicket before he was out to a fine running catch at mid off by Fielder. Norman Holloway struck several mighty blows, and the score gradually crept nearer the Kent total.

The crowd, aware that Kent might, after all, concede a first innings advantage, became further engrossed and the tension increased as the score rose. The matter was finally resolved when Fielder took his seventh wicket of the innings with the third ball of a new spell which was, in fact, the first legal ball – the first two were no balls. Holloway played at that third ball and, having got a thick edge, saw Seymour take his second great slip catch of the innings. With Blythe uncharacteristically ineffective, and Woolley unable to bowl, it was a timely return to form for the quick bowler.

With a lead of just three, Kent's second innings commenced at three o'clock. The openers batted steadily, adding 40 runs in 45 minutes, before Humphreys fell to a smart slip catch. Hardinge and Seymour took the score to 99 with some fine stroke play, but Vallance Jupp's introduction to the attack saw the downfall of Seymour. Woolley helped Hardinge add a further 74 in 55 minutes, but from the promising position of 173-2 Kent slipped to 187-5 shortly before the close. Woolley went leg before to Robert Relf, Hubble to an indifferent stroke off Holloway, and Hardinge was caught by Robert Relf, also off the same bowler. Hardinge's 71 was his highest score at the St Lawrence and presaged his glorious end-of-season form. Dillon and Huish saw the home side through the last couple of overs of the day without further problems. At the close Kent were 193-5, a lead of 196. An exciting final day lay ahead.

St Lawrence Cricket Ground

It was all the more disappointing, therefore, that the final day's action was witnessed by the much smaller crowd of only 2,155. Perhaps many prospective spectators were saving themselves for Ladies' Day on Thursday, the opening day of the Nottinghamshire game. Nevertheless, this was a shame as those who did not attend missed yet another outstanding all-round performance on the day by Kent.

In the morning, Dillon was clearly eyeing quick runs and a declaration as he took two rasping boundaries off Holloway. His progress, however, was temporarily halted when he suffered an injury in fending off Robert Relf's second ball of the day. Huish joined in the entertainment, hitting three boundaries and a single from one Albert Relf over. The captain followed by *"delivering the ball to the Conservative Club tent abuzz with preparations for luncheon."*[1] The 50 partnership came up in just 30 minutes, but at 267, with the stand at 80, Huish's 65-minute innings came to an end when he was bowled round his legs by Joe Vine. Dillon followed 21 runs later, bowled when trying to clip Jupp to leg. He had batted for nearly two hours and hit seven fours. Most importantly, he had put his side in a strong position to push on for a win.

Fairservice made a slow start, but eventually found his form and hit four boundaries in quick succession but, when he was on 28, was dropped by Vine off his own bowling. Relishing his escape, Fairservice hit two more fours which encouraged Carr to join in the fun, and he too hit two good fours. But in attempting the third, he was caught at short square leg from a mishit. Their stand was worth 47 runs and had taken only 25 minutes. Fairservice's *"very merry"* innings was ended by Holloway rearranging his stumps, and as the innings reached five hours' duration, Fielder was last man out to a *"good catch in the country"*.[1]

Sussex went in to bat again at ten minutes past two, needing an improbable 363 runs to win in three and three quarter hours. The important question however, was could Kent capture ten wickets to secure the additional two points that would

Douglas Carr: 5 for 28

cement their Championship title aspirations? Wilson and Vine made a brisk start, and although Fairservice, replacing Blythe after just one over, missed a caught and bowled chance at 12, the bowlers maintained control. With the score on 35 without loss, and with the innings 40 minutes old, heavy rain interrupted play for over an hour. Any chance of a Kent win now appeared remote. Seven wickets were still required with only an hour and a quarter left.

But this Kent team of 1913 was adept at skittling out the opposition in a very short space of time, especially on damp wickets, and, once again, they forced the win. And this despite Blythe bowling only a single over and Woolley, who was still hampered by his injury, taking no wickets in eight overs.

On the resumption, Fielder, from the Nackington Road end, removed Wilson's off stump with his second ball. Fairservice then had Albert Relf dropped by Huish but immediately bowled him with a ball that kept very low. The remainder of the afternoon belonged to Carr, who took 5-28 in only ten overs from the Pavilion End, including dismissing both Fender and Chaplin with his googly. Vine's resistance was ended by a fine leg-side catch by Woolley. Second time round, there were to be no heroics from the tail as the last seven wickets fell for just 29. Kent's handsome, if improbable, victory was sealed just 20 minutes before the scheduled close.

When they went to press, after the first day of the Nottinghamshire fixture, the *Kentish Gazette & Canterbury Press* adjudged the week thus far a "*distinct success*", contrasting Canterbury Week with both the "*disastrous festival*" of 1912 and the

Fred Huish and Bill Fairservice, two of Kent's generally unsung heroes who shared a bright partnership in the second innings

Joe Vine and Vallance Jupp

washout at Tunbridge Wells earlier in the season *"Practically three days' cricket was seen in the Sussex match, and the dramatic finish in Kent's favour gave a fillip of excitement which caused the interest in the game to be maintained up to almost the last moment. The prospective Champions scarcely 'found their legs' until the third day – but then they fully compensated for their moderate showing previously."*[1]

Sources

1   *Kentish Gazette & Canterbury Press* 9th August 1913

Nottinghamshire 1st Innings

G Gunn	c Dillon b Fielder	0
GM Lee	b Blythe	63
Mr AW Carr	c Seymour b Carr	58
JR Gunn	c Hubble b Blythe	55
WRD Payton	c Blythe b Carr	65
J Iremonger	c Woolley b Carr	21
WW Whysall	lbw b Carr	0
Mr GO Gauld *	c Carr b Blythe	15
TW Oates +	st Huish b Carr	22
TL Richmond	b Fielder	2
TG Wass	not out	2
Extras	(2 lb, 3 nb)	5
Total	(all out, 101.2 overs)	**308**

FOW 1st Innings 1-0, 2-99, 3-150, 4-211, 5-253, 6-253, 7-280, 8-293, 9-306, 10-308

Nottinghamshire 2nd Innings

	c Blythe b Woolley	4
	c Dillon b Blythe	1
	b Blythe	13
	c Humphreys b Blythe	2
	not out	3
	c Dillon b Blythe	4
	not out	0
	did not bat	
	did not bat	
	did not bat	
	did not bat	
	(1 b)	1
	(5 wickets, 12 overs)	28

FOW 2nd Innings 1-5, 2-5, 3-16, 4-22, 5-28

Kent bowling	O	M	R	W
Fielder	22	6	69	2
Fairservice	12	5	33	0
Carr	32.2	4	116	5
Blythe	28	5	66	3
Humphreys	1	1	0	0
Woolley	6	2	19	0

Kent bowling	O	M	R	W
Blythe	6	1	14	4
Woolley	6	2	13	1

Kent 1st Innings

E Humphreys	b Wass	9
HTW Hardinge	c JR Gunn b Wass	79
J Seymour	c and b Iremonger	67
FE Woolley	st Oates b Iremonger	50
JC Hubble	c Oates b Wass	11
Mr EW Dillon *	c G Gunn b Wass	13
FH Huish +	lbw b Wass	4
WJ Fairservice	c Carr b Wass	16
Mr DW Carr	c Gauld b Iremonger	16
C Blythe	c Whysall b Wass	8
A Fielder	not out	15
Extras	(2 b, 4 lb)	6
Total	(all out, 113.5 overs)	**294**

FOW 1st Innings 1-27, 2-154, 3-158, 4-189, 5-211, 6-221, 7-245, 8-260, 9-271, 10-294

Nottinghamshire bowling	O	M	R	W
Wass	45	12	113	7
Iremonger	40.5	9	108	3
JR Gunn	16	5	24	0
Richmond	10	1	34	0
Carr	2	0	9	0

Kent vs Nottinghamshire

St Lawrence Ground, Canterbury
Thursday 7th, Friday 8th & Saturday 9th August
Toss: Nottinghamshire
Match Drawn
Points: Kent 1 Nottinghamshire 3

AFTER A DISAPPOINTINGLY low attendance had witnessed the previous day's spectacular victory over Sussex, a record Ladies' Day crowd of 13,030 for a county match flocked to the St Lawrence Ground for the opening day of the second Championship game of Canterbury Week against Nottinghamshire. The 8,354 paying spectators were half as many again as in 1912, when Blythe and Woolley had combined to take 20 wickets in an innings victory over the same opponents. In addition to 760 motor cars, there were 39 "other vehicles" on the outfield. Aided by fine weather, the festival atmosphere was in full swing with Kent edging ever closer to that fourth title in eight years.

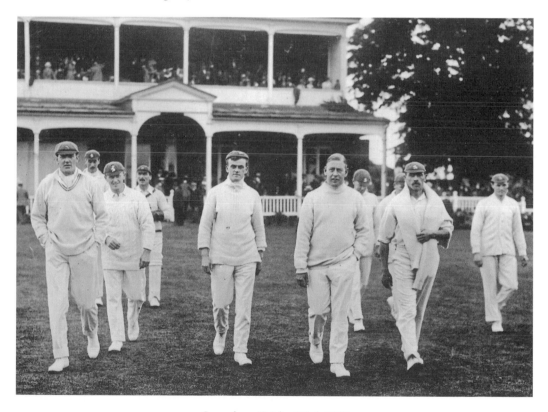

Canterbury Cricket Week 1913
Mr EW Dillon, Woolley, Hardinge, Huish, Blythe, Mr DW Carr, Fairservice, Humphreys, Fielder, Seymour
Photograph courtesy Mr & Mrs Richard Seymour

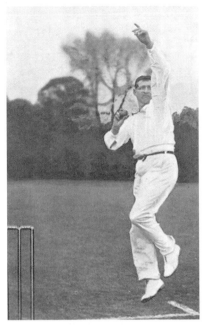

Tom Wass, 7-113 for Notts, and Douglas Carr, 5-116 for Kent

After winning the toss, Nottinghamshire batted but lost their first wicket without a run on the board when George Gunn, fresh from a century the previous day against Surrey, played a poor stroke to Fielder and was caught at slip. After such an inauspicious start, they would have been delighted when they had moved on to 211-3 later in the afternoon. Arthur Carr and Garnet Lee, the latter more expansive, settled the innings down with a second-wicket partnership of 99. But the Kent fieldsmen had colluded in their recovery. Fielder, who was extracting considerable bounce, induced Carr to play false strokes to successive balls, only to have the batsman's namesake at mid off, and Dillon at slip, drop the catches.

Lee's chanceless 63, which contained a six and nine fours, was ended when Blythe bowled him with the visitors one short of their hundred. The ultra-cautious Carr and John Gunn took the score to 131 at lunch. Carr had made 49 in two hours and a quarter by showing *"good judgement and considerable skill"*[1] in the eyes of the *Kentish Observer & Canterbury Chronicle* correspondent, but, two balls after reaching his half century, he was caught smartly by Seymour at slip off Carr.

Gunn and Wilfred Payton took the attack to Kent after Carr's dismissal, adding 61 in 55 minutes before Gunn, who had played several fine off drives, fell to a brilliant, leaping one-handed catch by Hubble at second slip off Blythe. By tea, Nottinghamshire had reached 243-4, and looked well placed for a formidable total. Fortunately for Kent, it didn't happen, as after James Iremonger had helped Payton to add 42 for the fourth wicket, the innings subsided and Nottinghamshire lost their last six men for just 55 runs, Carr and Blythe being the main wicket takers.

The leg spinner also held a skier to dismiss the visitors' captain, George Gauld. Payton, who played the innings of the day, was eighth out at 293 when Blythe repaid the compliment to his spin partner by holding a steepling catch. With the Nottinghamshire innings coming to a close after six o'clock, stumps were drawn.

On the following day the weather was less kind as there had been heavy rain overnight. This not only dampened the enthusiasm of those due to attend but brought about a significant change to the wicket. The crowd was significantly down on that of the previous day at "only" 5,191.

Play was delayed by three quarters of an hour and, after Kent had scored 11 in four overs, the rain came back to drive the players from the field. *The Sportsman* captured the frustration of the crowd admirably in referring to the *"company of three or four thousand chafing under a wait which seemed to them unduly drawn out."*[2] In fact, the adjournment lasted an hour, by which time the sun had appeared and the players took the field again. There was some anxiety amongst the Kent faithful as to how they would fare on a wet wicket against a Nottinghamshire attack that included the 1908 *Wisden* Cricketer of the Year, Thomas Wass, Iremonger and John Gunn. They need not have worried, however, as the sun was too weak to cause the batsmen any real discomfort and, in the end, the wicket dried naturally. It wasn't until the Nottinghamshire second innings that it began to offer any real assistance to the bowlers.

After losing Humphreys early, comprehensively bowled by the 40-year-old Wass, Hardinge and Seymour compiled a masterly partnership of 127 in 115 minutes for the second wicket, all the more impressive given that it was *"very hard to get the ball away."* The *Kentish Observer & Canterbury Chronicle* adjudged that Hardinge *"has seldom given a finer display than on this occasion. He was always master*

The St Lawrence Ground, Canterbury

CANTERBURY CRICKET GROUND.   *Photo by A.B. Collis, Canterbury*

St Lawrence Cricket Ground 1895
Photograph courtesy of Howard Milton

of the situation, his timing being perfect."[1] The stand was broken only when Seymour, who had "*played his usual vigorous and attractive game*" and hit six fours, gave a tame return catch to Iremonger. Hardinge followed almost immediately when he presented a catch to cover point from the first ball he received after tea. Was this the curse of the long partnership or the curse of taking a break? His "*flawless*" 79 in 160 minutes surpassed the 71 he made in the first game of the week against Sussex. It was clear that he was running into a rich vein of form and that a century – or five – was just around the corner.

Woolley dominated the remainder of the day with "*a display entirely worthy of his reputation*". As the wicket became trickier, his judgement on which ball to defend and which to hit was impeccable. Kent had reached 258-7 at stumps, exactly 50 behind their opponents. Despite interference from the weather, another intriguing final day was in prospect.

Saturday dawned bright and fair, with the prospect of an exciting finish and the chance for Kent to avenge their defeat against Nottinghamshire at Trent Bridge earlier in the season. Kent's hopes of a first innings lead were dashed almost immediately as, with the addition of only two runs, Woolley was smartly stumped off Iremonger. Fairservice, Fielder and Carr "batted pluckily" and added useful runs, but they eventually fell short of their opponents' total by 14 runs.

When Nottinghamshire batted again, they were quickly in trouble against Blythe and Woolley. The wicket by now was giving considerable help to spin and there were no two better bowlers in England to take advantage of these conditions. Both George Gunn and Lee were dismissed with the score at five. Lee fell to a wonderful catch by Dillon at silly point, who caught a full-blown drive which was otherwise destined for the boundary. Blythe in particular was proving "*virtually unplayable*", and with the fielders crouching close to the bat, the visitors were reduced to 28-5. It could have been worse for the visiting side as Seymour, rather uncharacteristically, missed Payton and Carr from successive balls at long off, and Blythe and Woolley also dropped chances off each other's bowling.

At one o'clock, however, play was halted when a storm broke over St Lawrence which brought an end to any further play in the match. The rain itself lasted until half past two, but the wicket had received a thorough soaking and couldn't be made fit for play again. Kent had been tantalisingly close to emulating their Maidstone Week double success. which would have given them an even firmer grip on the Championship.

The proceeds of this match went to "Punter" Humphreys in his benefit year, and a collection during the afternoon realised the handsome amount of £92, bringing the grand total for the season to £879 with one more to come at Dover.

On the final day of the game "Wanderer" in *The Sportsman* warned *"those who regard the championship race as all over bar shouting – Kent, it is true, can retain their leadership, defeat or two, and are the best side of the season, yet their recent form has been none too convincing, and neither at Leyton nor on the opening day at Canterbury did they do themselves justice. I think they admit this themselves. There was a lack of confidence, an element of luck in much of their batting, their catching was not safe, the ground-work at times slack. They have still one or two stiff fences to negotiate, notably Surrey at the Oval on Monday and Middlesex at Lord's later in the month."*[2]

Mr AW Carr and JR Gunn: two of Nottinghamshire's run makers in their first innings

St Lawrence circa 1902

He may not have been responding to *The Sportsman* directly, but a more optimistic Kent supporter took to verse in the *Kentish Gazette & Canterbury Press* to express his confidence:

> Prophet of ill not far we seek
> To prove thy foolish forecast wrong,
> For still our Canterbury Week
> Finds Kent victorious – and strong!
> Nor has she, spite of luck and weather,
> Lost from her plume a single feather.
>
> Hail, heroes of the bat and ball
> No grudging tribute may we yield,
> Whatever fortune may befall
> To you, who, on each tented field
> Still for your motto proudly claim
> "Fight to the last" and "play the game"[3]

Sources

1   *The Kentish Observer & Canterbury Chronicle* 9th August 1913
2   *The Sportsman* 9th August 1913
3   *The Kentish Gazette & Canterbury Press* 9th August 1913

8th August 1913	P	W	L	DWF	DLF	NC	Max	Pts	PtsPC
Kent	22	16	2	2	1	1	105	87	82.86%
Northamptonshire	19	12	2	1	4	0	95	67	70.53%
Middlesex	14	7	1	4	2	0	70	49	70.00%
Yorkshire	23	13	4	4	2	0	115	79	68.70%
Surrey	19	10	3	2	4	0	95	60	63.16%
Nottinghamshire	17	7	4	2	4	0	85	45	52.94%
Lancashire	22	6	9	7	0	0	110	51	46.36%
Warwickshire	20	7	9	2	2	0	100	43	43.00%
Sussex	23	6	10	4	3	0	115	45	39.13%
Hampshire	19	4	9	2	4	0	95	30	31.58%
Worcestershire	14	3	7	1	2	1	65	20	30.77%
Gloucestershire	17	4	10	1	2	0	85	25	29.41%
Derbyshire	17	3	10	2	2	0	85	23	27.06%
Somerset	12	2	8	2	0	0	60	16	26.67%
Essex	16	2	8	2	4	0	80	20	25.00%
Leicestershire	17	3	10	1	3	0	85	21	24.71%

A collage of illustrations of Canterbury Cricket Week drawn by Frank Gillett from *The Graphic* circa 1905

The Social Scene

A photograph of St Lawrence in 1908: Kent vs Sussex

KENT, PERHAPS ABOVE all other counties, has long been celebrated for the number and variety of its cricket weeks or festivals, combining attractive cricket in beautiful settings with a vibrant social scene. Not content with boasting the oldest and grandest of them all, at Canterbury, those at Tunbridge Wells and Maidstone have been praised by players and writers alike. While matches at Dover, Gravesend, Gillingham and Folkestone may not have had the same glamour, they were always major events in the town calendar, and are fondly remembered by the county's cricket followers. Sadly, only Canterbury and Tunbridge Wells remain though, at the time of writing, there are hopes that county cricket may, in a more modest form, return to Maidstone and Folkestone in the near future.

It is generally acknowledged that the cricket festival, and its accompanying social spectacle, was never more popular than during the period between Victoria's last years and the First World War, the era recognised as the "Golden Age of Cricket".

In 1913, there were five cricket weeks in Kent – at the Angel Ground in Tonbridge, the Nevill Ground in Tunbridge Wells, the Mote in Maidstone, the St Lawrence Ground in Canterbury and the Crabble Athletic Ground in Dover. While Canterbury had the prestige and glitz, drawing huge crowds, particularly on Ladies' Day, the others each had their own individual personality.

Hosting the county cricket team was an opportunity for the local burghers and townspeople to showcase their town, displaying bunting and illuminations from every available building. It was also the artistic high point of the year where local businesses put on shows and concerts for the entertainment of all the classes. And finally, it was an opportunity for local journalists to sharpen their pens and drag out their most purple prose in praise of their town. The main focus of this chapter is, inevitably, Canterbury, although it will also look in some detail at the "show" put on by the county town as well as recognising the splendid efforts being made at Dover – the youngest "festival" of them all. In 1913, unlike Tunbridge Wells, which was ravaged by rain, Maidstone, Canterbury and Dover were generally blessed with good weather, and the county team were also extremely successful on the pitch, winning four matches and drawing the other two.

CANTERBURY

Canterbury Week was the doyen of cricket festivals. It was one of the most important dates in both the cricket and social calendars, on a par with the Gentlemen vs Players, Varsity and Eton vs Harrow matches at Lord's. In 1913, it was still one of *the* events of the social season, and thousands of people would travel from London to attend. The London, Chatham & Dover Railway and South Eastern Railway would run special trains to the East, West and South stations. The gentry would stay at various country houses within carriage-driving distance of St Lawrence. During the day, they would parade in their finery and observe who else was in attendance. Just occasionally, some even paid attention to what was happening on the field. In the evening, they would attend Society Balls or performances given by The Old Stagers at the Orange Street Theatre. In his excellent book, *The Golden Age of Cricket*, George Plumptre likens this *"more relaxed but equally elegant occasion"* to *"the late summer race-meeting at Goodwood"*.[1]

At the Ground

While its still young pavilion (built in 1900) and even newer Annexe (1909) were fine sights, viewed from anywhere on the ground, it was the sweep of marquees occupying the curve of the Old Dover Road and Nackington Road that excited the most interest, and where alternative entertainment competed with the action out in the middle.

Tent holders included Lord Harris, the Mayor of Canterbury, Band of Brothers, I Zingari, the Old Stagers, the Buffs, the East Kent Club, the Canterbury Club, the Conservative Club and the Earl of Guilford and Viscount Chilston.

The most prestigious invitations of the Week were to dine at the marquees hosted by these prominent clubs and individuals. The 96th Archbishop of Canterbury, Randall Davidson, made a special trip from Lambeth to attend, and the local press delighted in listing the great and good who were present.

While most marquee pitches were granted almost by divine right, six were allocated by other methods, and for 1913 the lucky recipients were Viscount Chilston, Mr Frank Penn and Mr and Mrs Hatfeild, Mr Elmer Speed, Mr Deedes and Mr Samuelson. Those defeated in the ballot included Sir Arthur Markham, 1st Baron Markham of Arusha, East Africa and a Mrs Barnes.

When the occupants of the marquees had finished dining, and perhaps taken in a little cricket, they could saunter around the new rose garden recently planted by the County Club. But it was Ladies' Day on Thursday that provided the most glamorous spectacle of the Week, when, during the intervals in play, the ladies displayed themselves for the benefit of the crowd. While this tradition waned over the intervening decades as society became more democratic, the modern Club has attempted in recent seasons to resurrect it, on a less ostentatious scale, with a "Fashion on the Outfield" competition and "Ladies' Arcade".

Equally grand were the forms of transport in which the more prosperous visitors travelled to the Week and from which, when they weren't feasting themselves in the tents, they sometimes watched the cricket. Car ownership may have been increasing rapidly, but those that could afford it still preferred to arrive in style in their carriages, for which there was an elaborate framework of prices, dependent upon the size, capacity and length of stay on the ground.

For example, carriages *"sent on the ground to remain for a week"* were charged a fee of ten shillings, a healthy discount on the 2s. 6d. daily fee. A "subscriber", roughly equivalent to the member, friend and car category of modern times, who had paid the annual dues of a guinea (21 shillings), was only permitted to bring one carriage onto the ground. However, he was also allocated a *"servant's pass"* to enable a *"luncheon cart with not more than two servants"* to accompany him. While two servants per carriage were admitted free of charge, the people arriving by public transport, who occupied the benches at the upper end of the ground, were required to pay a shilling for a day's play, double the cost of attending any of the other Kent grounds.

But despite this inequity, it wasn't just the leading county families who enjoyed the special atmosphere of the Week as the *Kentish Observer & Canterbury Chronicle* claimed that *"all classes have derived a large mood of pleasure from the event"*.[2] And that may well have been the case – this was one of the rare opportunities for the lower classes to rub shoulders with society folk.

One is reminded of Dr John Spedding who, at Covent Garden in Vita Sackville-West's book, *The Edwardians*, was *"enjoying the sensation that around him were hundreds of spoilt, leisured people, soon to be on show like regal animals or plumaged birds, well-accustomed and seemingly indifferent to excited gaze"*.[3]

But while such deference still persisted and indeed still does today, England in 1913 was an increasingly volatile nation. The County Club was anxious that the suffragette movement, whose reliance upon violence reached its zenith in this year, and which we have already encountered at Tunbridge Wells, might use this event for a protest – or worse. It must have been a factor, along with large crowds and additional cars, in the decision by the Managing Committee to approve an increase in the level of security – *"engage more policeman, including an Inspector in place of a Sergeant"*.[4]

Band of Brothers

Formed in 1858, BB is the third oldest of the wandering cricket clubs after I Zingari (1845) and Free Foresters (1856). Differing from these two clubs, BB requires a territorial allegiance to Kent and will also admit *"Men of Kent and Kentish Men of distinction, good will and good sportsmanship"* in addition to those who play the game. The original bretheren were Sir Courtenay Honywood, Edward Pemberton, Henry Denne, Loftus Pemberton, Wykham Pemberton, Wyndham Knight and

Henry Pemberton. All but one were officers of the Royal East Kent Mounted Rifles. The name they chose was the title of a popular song of the day by the Christy Minstrels called 'The Band of Brothers'. BB took the colours of black and Kentish grey and played its first match on 12th August 1858 at Evington on Sir Courtenay Honywood's ground against a side from Torry Hill, "*and, quite properly, won it by 159 runs against 63.*"[5]

Lord Harris wrote: "*The original brethren were rather a boisterous crew, out to enjoy themselves when they did assemble but, as the founders got old and dispersed, the Club was nearing collapse. The only symptom of vitality displayed by the B.B. Club was the pitching of their tent on the St. Lawrence Ground and the display of their colours by the fair sisters in the ballrooms.*"[6]

The original Rules of BB are quite brief:

E. A. C. Druce.   R. H. Fox.   A. F. Leach Lewis.   J. R. Mason.   L. Weigall.   E. Dillon.   H. Z. Baker.
Hon. J. S. R. Tufton.   L. G. A. Collins.   S. Christopherson.   F. Marchant.   G. Marsham.   A. O. Snowden.   E. C. Stevens.
G. J. V. Weigall.   W. H. Patterson.   L. Wilson.   General Wykeham Leigh Pemberton, C.B.   Lord Harris.   K. McAlpine.   Rev. W. W. Rashleigh.
Major D'Aeth.   R. W. Mitchell.   Rev. F. A. G. Leveson-Gower.

A BB match: East Kent vs West Kent 1908
The photograph contains no fewer than 14 men who played first-class cricket,
five Kent captains, and three who played Test cricket[7]

1   That the annual subscription be £0.0.0. payable in advance.
2   That the entrance money be £0.0.0 payable within one month of election.
3   That wives and daughters of Brothers be themselves Brothers.
4   That the sisters of Brothers be admissible as Brothers upon undertaking to marry any Brother on demand.
5   That loss of temper be punished by immediate expulsion.
6   That three original Brothers form a quorum for the purpose of electing new Brothers but that the objection of any original Brother to the proposal of any party shall prove fatal.

There is, however, no known instance of Rule 4 being invoked and enforced.

It was Lord Harris who began the revival in 1879 and 1880 when the fixture list was restored to include regular games against The Royal Engineers, The Royal Artillery, The Mote, Bickley Park, West Kent, Shorncliffe Camp, Blackheath and The Weald of Kent. By 1913, BB was playing 20 matches a season, most of which were two-day games. The List of Matches, which now included fixtures against Eton Ramblers, Harlequins and the Royal Navy, entreated members *"to ask for places in matches and not to play against B.B. without first obtaining the permission of the Match Manager."*[5] The matter of obtaining "permission" to represent another club against BB was honoured rather more in the breach than the observance, but there are known instances where Lord Harris was the Match Manager when a BB member, who had failed to obtain the necessary permission, found himself batting at number 12 for BB against the side he had expected to represent – who played with ten men.

In the period following the turn of the century, BB was extremely strong, and although it never played first-class fixtures, as was the case with the so-called "senior" clubs of I Zingari and Free Foresters, it was able to call upon the services of any number of players who had played first-class, and, in some instances, Test match cricket. These included Cuthbert Pinky Burnup, Nigel Haig, Sammy Day, Kenneth Hutchings, Frank Marchant, Cloudesley Marsham, Jack Mason, Dickie Blaker, Lionel Troughton, William Sarel and Chris Hurst. Those who appeared for Kent in the 1913 Championship side were Edward Dillon, Douglas Carr, Eric Hatfeild, Arthur Day, Jack Mason and William Powell.

By this stage, Lord Harris had retired from first-class cricket but still turned out on a regular basis for BB. It was his involvement with both BB and the Kent club that led to the close connections that exist to this day. The outward manifestation of that connection today is the BB Tent which is pitched at both the Canterbury and Tunbridge Wells festivals.

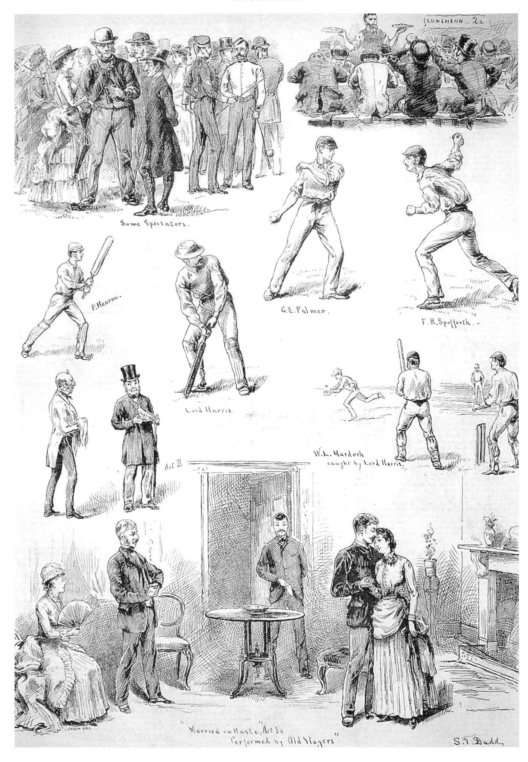

Some Spectators.

LUNCHEON. 2s.

F. Hearne.

G. E. Palmer.

F. R. Spofforth.

Lord Harris.

Act II.

W. L. Murdoch
caught by Lord Harris.

"Married in Haste," Act I.
Performed by "Old Stagers"

S. T. Dadd.

The Founders of I Zingari painted in 1897
Sir Spencer Ponsonby-Fane, John Lorraine Baldwin and Earl Bessborough

I Zingari

I Zingari – in Italian "the Gypsies" – were founded on 4th July 1845 by three Harrovians, John Lorraine Baldwin, Frederick Ponsonby (later 6th Earl Bessborough) and Spencer Posnsonby (later Sir Spencer Ponsonby-Fane), who were dining at the Blenheim Hotel and decided to form a club to foster the spirit of amateur cricket. IZ played some first-class matches against various opponents between 1849 and 1904, including matches against the Australians in 1882 and 1884. The colours symbolise the IZ motto of "out of darkness, through fire and into light".

The Old Stagers

The oldest amateur dramatic society in the world, the Old Stagers had first performed on 1st August 1842 during the inaugural Week when Kent played the Gentlemen of Kent at the Beverley Ground. They continue to provide evening entertainment to

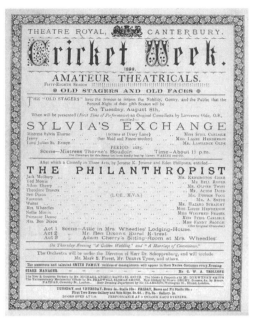

A playbill from the Theatre Royal Canterbury for 1899

this day. It was originally the idea of John Baker, then Secretary of the Kent Club and an ancestor of one of the current KCCC Committee, Mark Baker-White, Frederick Ponsonby (subsequently one of the founders of IZ) and Charles Taylor, a friend of Ponsonby's. Formed to provide evening entertainment during the Canterbury Festival, it originally involved several of the cricketing community with thespian inclinations, including Alfred Mynn. They share their colours with IZ because of the Ponsonby connection.

The Buffs

The other familiar tent on the outfield was home for the 1913 Week to The Buffs (The East Kent Regiment). In 1935 its name was graced with the "Royal" prefix and, following amalgmation with The Queen's Own Royal West Kent Regiment in 1992, it became the Princess of Wales' Royal Regiment. It retains "The Buffs" title, however, and proudly displays the colours at the tent it hosts still to this day.

Music

Another feature of the occasion was the playing of military music. During the 1913 week, The Royal East Kent Yeomanry *"discoursed pleasing music"* during the Monday afternoon's play. The tradition remains to this day, although it is now confined to the tea interval on Ladies' Day, the 1st Cinque Ports Rifle Volunteers performing in the 2012 Week. It would be invidious to suggest that the cacophonous, five-second bursts of "sound" heard at modern day T20 matches are part of this lineage.

In the City
The Outward Display

The air of celebration extended to the city centre where the *"main thoroughfare from St George's Gate to the West Gate"* presented *"a gay and festive appearance by day and a brilliant spectacle by night."* Mercery Lane, which leads directly from St Peter's Street to the Cathedral Gate, was also *"prettily decorated with baskets of flowers and illuminated with Chinese lanterns."*[2]

It was in 1913 that the Corporation decided to extend the scale of decorations and illuminations, notably along the avenue of the Dane John Gardens, which were lit for the first time for many years *"by tiny vari-coloured electric bulbs, the effect produced being enchanting"*.[2] The Band of the Royal Marines entertained on Monday, followed by the Royal East Kent Mounted Rifles on Tuesday and the Band of the 6th Dragoon Guards on the remaining three evenings. Around 6,000 seats were purchased in the course of the week.

Cricket Week Illuminations St Dunstans Canterbury Aug. 1906

Lodgings

"Wanderer" in *The Sportsman* lamented that the *"more general use of the motor vehicle has caused many of those who at one time had to make their residence there to return to their homes for dinner and to convey their house parties back to their country residences after theatre or ball."*[8] While this might well have been true, many still followed tradition and took residence in Canterbury for the duration of the Week. Such was the prestige that it ordained upon the city's hotels that they permitted their guest lists to be published in the local press. We learn, therefore, that the County Hotel entertained the gentlemen of the Sussex team and other notable personages, including Miss Roberta Dillon from Nashville, Tennessee and Mr and Mrs Percival Tattersfield of Philadelphia. It was a decade since Kent had toured Philadelphia and cricket was still a popular sport in the eastern United States.

The Rose, Fleur de Lis and Fleece hotels, along with Folkestone House, Longport House and 21 St George's Place, all provided accommodation for noted dignitaries, but it was the Royal Fountain Hotel, the headquarters of the Old Stagers, that housed the most prestigious names, including Lord and Lady Harris, along with assorted colonels, majors, lords, ladies, councillors, vicars, bishops, and possibly actresses.

The Theatre

Having already hosted their guests in their tent on the cricket ground, the Old Stagers turned their attention to providing the evening entertainment in the city.

Canterbury Cricket Week 1882

They opened their 72nd season on Monday 4th August 1913 with a production of *The Cap and Bells*, a comedy in three acts by Robert Vansittart, and *The Conspiracy*, a drama in one scene, by Robert Barr and Sidney Lewis-Ransom. A record audience, including Lord Harris and his party, the Earl and Countess of Guilford, together with other leading county families, crowded into the Theatre Royal. *The Cap and Bells* was repeated on Thursday, and on Tuesday and Friday evening, the company put on *Public Opinion*, a comedy in three acts by RC Carton, which had the packed house *"rocking with laughter"*. *The Kentish Gazette & Canterbury Press* delivered a somewhat backhanded compliment in arguing that the company *"exhibited no signs of decrepitude, and delighted large audiences with their admirable acting."*[9]

On the final evening, the main production was followed by the traditional Canterbury Week epilogue by Harold Whitaker and Paul Rubens, entitled *Enquire Without_____*, *" an extremely amusing farce, based upon the recent Marconi Enquiry ... unusually well flavoured with topical allusions"*. Set at a *"bored meeting of the Permanent Enquiry into Current Gossip Commission"*, it also made reference to the notorious Derby race of this year, the polo team in the United States and, closer to home, the *"question of dances for the ballroom."*[2]

The exploits of the cricket team were not forgotten either as *"Humphreys had a flattering reception, and the Kent amateurs, Lord Harris and others, were favourably greeted from the wings".*[2]

Film Screenings

Film historians may argue as much as their cricket counterparts over the origins of their subject, but the art of moving pictures was still in its infancy in 1913. The programme of films put on by the Electric Theatre in St Peter's Street would, therefore, have been extremely popular. One film with the unfortunate title of *Nigger Jim* was screened, equally unfortunately described in the *Kentish Express & Canterbury Gazette* as "*an exceptionally fine coloured film*", an assessment unlikely to appear in print today. The pun would also appear to have been lost on the newspaper's editor.

Other films shown included *The Convent of Subiaco* not, as might be presumed, a forerunner of Ken Russell's *The Devils* nearly sixty years later, but a series of "*beautiful coloured illustrations of ancient Italian architecture*", hardly likely to prevent any film censor from sleeping at night. And *The Stolen Purse* was "*quite one of the best comedy pictures seen at this Theatre*".[9]

In a "no expenses spared" strategy the management also provided "the phenomenal attractions of Will Evans in his famous sketch, "Harnessing a Horse", and George Gray as "The Fighting Parson", both popular London productions.[9] It should, of course, be remembered that these were thrilling and novel experiences for the pre-1914 audience.

County Balls

And then there were, perhaps, the highlights of the Week, at least for the well to do – the two County Balls held on Wednesday and Friday night at the Skating Rink, at which the colours of the Old Stagers, Band of Brothers and I Zingari intermingled brilliantly. The Band of the Royal East Kent Mounted Rifles supplied the music under Bandmaster Blake, and the list of participants included the usual cast of the Lords Harris, Guilford, Chilston, Camden, Sondes and Darnley as well as the un-ennobled families of Marsham and captain Dillon. The *Kentish Observer & Canterbury Chronicle* reported that it was a "*very successful affair, the fashionable element being well represented*".[2]

If there was any doubt that the balls had been a resounding success, evidence was provided at the County Club's General Committee meeting on 15th September when the Canterbury Committee reported the attendance figures and profits for the past 13 years. Although the attendance had risen from 521 in 1911 to 565 in the following year, increasing profits from £24 to £35, there had been an astronomical rise in 1913 when 684 people generated a threefold increase in profits to £106.[4] Whether the better weather, or the feeling of wellbeing engendered by the team's improved fortunes, or a little of both, was the main reason, it is difficult to say.

MAIDSTONE

Although the county town could not compete with Canterbury in terms of either history or prestige, it, nonetheless, portrayed in microcosm all the features of its older and bigger rival. The date of Maidstone Week might not have been so eagerly anticipated in the country houses as Canterbury, but the municipal authorities took great pride in putting on a show for the visitor. As the *Kent Messenger* reported: *"All the week-end the streets had been gay with streamers in lines which stretched along and across the streets, fluttering in the breeze, gleaming in the sun, or drenched in the untimely downpours which have marked our July"*.[10] And the town was even more welcoming in the evening when *"the effect was heightened by the brilliant illuminations, especially in the High Street where about 2,000 electric lamps – red, white and green predominantly – were used largely along the lines of the streamers, with special intersections at each end of the street. Along this scintillating thoroughfare thousands of people paraded in*

Arthur Fielder with the winner of the Decorated Cycles Competition in Maidstone 1913

the evenings, revelling in the glowing light and coyly throwing kisses and confetti and simulating the scene of a Continental town en fête."[10]

In 1913, the illuminations had been extended to cover Bank Street (with electrical stars) and also across Pudding Lane. The Town Hall comes in for specific praise. The weather vane on the cupola was red, the hemi-spherical part *"outlined in green"* and the pilasters white. Illuminated portraits of King George V and Queen Mary hung over the entrance with the *"letters 'GR' worked in green on either side and a crown in red over"*.[10] The Gas Office displayed an illuminated portrait of the year's beneficiary, Ted Humphreys at the wicket, and a large gas *"flare"* lit up the roof. The Star Hotel and the Conservative Club in Earl Street were also illuminated, *"while beautiful floral displays appear at the premises of the Kent Fire Office and at Messrs Blake and Sons."*[10] Many other establishments, including the Bull Hotel, Messrs Haynes Brothers, Drake and Fletcher and even the *Kent Messenger*, boasted their own decorations.

The Ground

The newspaper waxed equally, if not more, lyrically about The Mote itself: *"A broad sweep of velvet lawn, fringed in the far distance by glorious masses of foliage – a perfect symphony in green; in the near distance the terraces crowded with keen spectators, the array of motors, the stands wherein Dame Fashion shows herself in her latest and daintiest of confections, the pavilions packed with cricket's warmest supporters, the line of well-appointed tents, and, in juxtaposition, the benches whereupon the humbler follower of the game takes his case and criticises every move of the contest, all of which reminds one of the debt the public are under to Sir Marcus Samuel, and their expert groundsman, Mr Hickmott. Few grounds in England's garden are quite comparable with the Mote from*

The Mote during Maidstone Week

all the points of view that count in a cricket festival."[10] Sycophantic and over flowery though this may be, it was, after all, the style of the day.

As with St Lawrence, half of the perimeter of the ground was fringed with marquees, each booked and paid for by a prominent local individual or organisation. Private tents were taken in the names of the great and the good of Kentish society, including: The High Sheriff of Kent; The Band of Brothers; the MP for Mid Kent (Colonel Warde); The Royal West Kent Regiment; Mr J Campbell-Bannerman; Mr PF Warner; Baroness Orczy, novelist and playwright; Mrs Henry Lushington; Lady Dorothy D'Oyly-Carte and the Kent County Cricket Club Chairman (Mr FSW Cornwallis).

The *Kent Messenger* reported that *"many of the elite of the neighbourhood and others who were being entertained by various county families"* were seen in these *"exceptionally well furnished"* tents, many of which had been improved upon and extended since the last festival. Some had even been *"most artistically draped"*.[10]

For those to whom such things were important, an invitation to luncheon in one of the tents was something with which to regale one's acquaintances for the year to come. But only the most refined and wealthy received an invitation from Sir Marcus Samuel, 1st Viscount Bearsted, to accompany him in his pavilion. These included: Viscount and Viscountess Chilston; Lord and Lady Hothfield; Colonel and Lady Victoria Villiers; Lord and Lady Theobald Butler; Mrs H Deedes; Rev and Mrs Cloudesley Marsham; Mr and Mrs Campbell-Bannerman and Mr and Mrs Cornwallis.

An advertisement from the edition of the *Kent Messenger* that followed the cricket week. Probably a simple marketing ploy based on the normal selling price of 3/6, with a premium being added for having accommodated a better class of backside during the week.

The reader is then informed where, and with whom, many of the above eminent personages were staying for the duration of the Week. One of the hosts was Mr George Marsham, who although he had played only three games for the county nearly forty years before, was probably second only to Lord Harris in influence within Kent cricket. He served on the Committee for all but one year between 1879 and 1924, and was President in 1886. He accommodated, among others, Lord Harris, Sir Henry F Lennard and the amateurs of both the Kent and Lancashire elevens at his Hayle Cottage home. Mr J Campbell-Bannerman at Hunton Court, Mrs Tyrwhitt-Drake at Cobtree Manor, and the Rev TG Lushington at Park House also entertained esteemed guests too.

The middle, if not the lower classes need not have been completely excluded from enjoying this grandeur. There was an opportunity after the Week to purchase one or more of the *"comfortable"* and *"tasteful"* chairs for their own home or garden.

Theatricals

The *Kent Messenger* proclaimed that the *"finest treasures of the Festival were not, as to be expected, the duels between bat and ball on the resplendent Mote field, but the amateur theatrical performances given in the town after close of play. Indeed, it would be difficult... to imagine an adequate 'Week' without them"*.[10] Clearly, a journalist who had his mind on higher things than cricket.

Guests of Sir Marcus Samuel in The Tabernacle in 1911

On the evening of Thursday 24th June, following the extraordinary events at the Mote that afternoon, the Maidstone Palace Theatre produced *The Adventure of Lady Ursula*, a *"spectacular"* costume drama written by Anthony Hope and directed by Mr Alan Muckinnon of the Old Stagers.

We will spare the reader the gushing praise, and comprehensive plot description, provided by the same local newspaper. A brief extract will suffice: *"the work of a master craftsman… essentially romantic, but never cheaply sentimental; and the dialogue is sparkling and richly embellished with flashes of epigrammatic wit"*.[10] Those who were present that evening would probably have experienced some difficulty in identifying the play they watched from this description, but such was the duty of the provincial press journalist of the day that, if he wanted to keep his job, he was obliged to write such reviews.

Music

The Band of the 2nd Batallion Seaforth Highlanders (the Ross-shire Buffs – the Duke of Albany's Own) performed on several occasions in the Museum Gardens and Athletic Ground, culminating in a *"grand military concert"* at the Theatre on Saturday afternoon, the scheduled last day of the Week. The audience would have been swelled by those who would otherwise have been at the Mote. The newspaper does not record if they played at the ground itself during the cricket, and whether it was the sound of the pipes and drums of the band that caused Middlesex to collapse to 56 all out in their first innings, but it seems a possibility.

DOVER

Dover was the newest of the Kent cricket grounds, having been laid out, or perhaps it would be more correct to say carved out of a hillside, in River in 1897. County cricket was first played there in 1907 and the "week" was established the following year when two matches were allocated. By 1913, Dover was casting envious eyes northwards and westwards at Canterbury, Maidstone and Tunbridge Wells, and the Dover District Council, in conjunction with the Dover Club, had realised that here was an opportunity to create their own "festival" week and to promote both the venue and the town to a wider audience. One of the guests during 1913 was Francis

Francis Eden Lacey: MCC Secretary 1898 to 1926

Lacey, the longest serving of all the MCC Secretaries (1898–1926), who suggested to one journalist that a Test match might even be allocated to the ground in the near future. *"The MCC Secretary, Mr FC Lacey who was present during the first game of the week, expressed himself in highly appreciative terms at Dover's beautiful ground and it's accommodation. He also complimented Abbott, the groundsman, on the pitch and intimated to the local officials the probability that one of the next Test Matches might be allocated to Dover."*[11] Although the suggestion seems ridiculous today, a Test match had already been played at Bramall Lane, Sheffield, in 1902 which was not one of the, now, regular venues, so perhaps the idea wasn't so strange at the time. And one should always remember – people will always hear what they want to believe.

The Ground

This may only have been the sixth Cricket Week held at the Crabble Athletic Ground in Dover, but the town was not in awe of the grand dame to the north west. The holiday atmosphere was enhanced by the warm sunshine on the opening day of Thursday 21st August with Kent on the brink of their fourth Championship in eight years.

The amphitheatre setting of the Crabble gave the ring of tents an attractive look, especially when viewed from the highest point of the terraces. Apart from the usual patrons, the organisers had persuaded many local organisations to become part of the festival and these included the Dover Corporation, the Dover Club, the Royal Cinque Ports Yacht Club, the Royal Garrison Artillery, the Dover Carlton Club, the Dover Commercial Club and the Dover Institute.

An announcement of the Dover matches in the *Kentish Gazette & Canterbury Press* from July 1913

THE TOWN

The *Kentish Observer & Canterbury Chronicle* announced that *"the main streets of the town were brightly decorated, streamers of flags being extended from Venetian masts on either side of the road, and at night there were electrical illuminations along the route, similar to what was done in past years. A fair amount of private decoration had also been carried out by the trades-people and residents"*.[12]

The *Kentish Gazette & Canterbury Press* again – *"For the whole length of the thoroughfare from the Town Hall and right away down to the sea front, pretty streamers of bunting are suspended length wise along the pavements, the connections being provided by tastefully draped poles, surmounted with shields and small flags. Strings of electric lights have also been suspended above the streamers, and when these were lit last night's very pretty scheme of illumination was provided, which was pleasingly set off at the sea front and by the customary illuminations of the fountains"*.[13]

It was equally complimentary about the *"attractive and varied social programme"* organised by the Dover Cricket Week committee.[1]. On the first four evenings, the Dover Amateur Operatic and Dramatic Company presented a triple bill at the Town Hall of *"'The Dear Departed', a comedy in one act by Stanley Houghton; 'In Honour Bound', a play in one act by Sydney Grundy; 'Lights Out', a farce in one act by Max Pemberton."*[13]

On the following Monday, Tuesday and Wednesday Mr Gore Cusley laid on, at the King's Hall, *"the successful musical comedy in two acts – 'The Cingalee', by arrangement with the Cricket Week Committee (Book by Chas T Tanner, Author of 'Our Miss Gibbs' etc. Music by Lionel Monckton. Lyrics by Adrian Ross and Percy Greenbank. Additional Dialogues, Lyrics and Numbers by Paul A Rubens).*"[13] There were two performances at 6.30 and 8.45.

And on the final day of the Week, Wednesday 27th August, a "*grand carnival*" was held in aid of local charities. The decorations and illuminations were "*more lavish than usual*", with the Cricket Week Committee offering "*three prizes for the best decorated and illuminated business establishment and three prizes for the best decorated and illuminated private house*".[13]

Military band concerts were given in the Granville Gardens each evening, and during the afternoon the band of the 2nd Batallion Lancashire Fusiliers accompanied the cricket at the Crabble.

Not as grand or exclusive as Canterbury, Dover was already making a name for itself in social as well as cricketing circles. As the *Kentish Gazette & Canterbury Press* concluded: "*Dover, indeed, promises to establish on its own individual account an enviable reputation for the excellence of its festivities.*"[13]

Sources

1   George Plumptre, *The Golden Age of Cricket,* page 12
2   *Kentish Observer & Canterbury Chronicle*, 9th August 1913
3   Vita Sackville West, *The Edwardians*, page 143
4   Kent County Cricket Club Minutes Book 1913
5   Bryan Tassell, *Band of Brothers 1858–1958*, 1958
6   Lord Harris, *A Few Short Runs,* 1921
7   Fourteen with first-class experience AC Druce; JR Mason; EW Dillon; HZ Baker; JSR Tufton;
     S Christopherson; F Marchant; AO Snowden; GJV Weigall; WH Patterson; L Wilson;
     Lord Harris; K McAlpine; Rev W Rashleigh
     Five Kent captains; JR Mason; EW Dillon; F Marchant; WH Patterson; Lord Harris
     Three Test players; Lord Harris; JR Mason; S Christopherson
8   *The Sportsman* 9th August 1913
9   *Kentish Gazette & Canterbury Press* 9th August1913
10   *Kent Messenger* 26th July 2013
11   *Kent Messenger* 30th August 2013
12   *Kentish Observer & Canterbury Chronicle* 30th August 1913
13   *Kentish Gazette & Canterbury Press* 30th August 1913

Part of the pavilion and terraces at The Crabble during a meeting of the local cycling club

Kent 1st Innings

E Humphreys	c Strudwick b Hitch	4
HTW Hardinge	b Hitch	4
J Seymour	c Spring b Hitch	0
FE Woolley	b Hitch	0
JC Hubble	b Kirk	9
Mr EW Dillon *	b Hitch	33
Mr AP Day	c Strudwick b Hitch	35
FH Huish +	b Hitch	3
Mr DW Carr	b Kirk	4
C Blythe	b Hitch	0
A Fielder	not out	0
Extras	(1 b, 7 lb, 2 nb)	10
Total	(all out, 43.3 overs)	**102**

FOW 1st Innings 1-7, 2-9, 3-9, 4-10, 5-42, 6-66, 7-94, 8-98, 9-98, 10-102

Kent 2nd Innings

absent hurt		
C Hayes b Kirk		42
b Kirk		7
b Kirk		8
b Hitch		25
[1] b Kirk		135
b Hitch		63
c Spring b Hitch		27
c Spring b Hitch		0
not out		3
b Hitch		0
(14 b, 3 lb, 9 nb 2 w)		28
(all out, 125.5 overs)		**338**

FOW 2nd Innings 1-83, 2-96, 3-123, 4-212, 5-266, 6-327, 7-327, 8-338, 9-338

Surrey bowling	O	M	R	W
Hitch	19	6	48	8
Kirk	21.3	8	32	2
Spring	3	0	12	0

Surrey bowling	O	M	R	W
Hitch	39.5	9	115	5
Kirk	47	13	107	4
Spring	24	6	52	0
Bird	7	1	18	0
Hayes	7	1	14	0
Goatly	1	0	4	0

Surrey 1st Innings

TW Hayward	b Carr	17
JB Hobbs	c Huish b Blythe	115
EG Hayes	run out	27
HS Harrison	b Day	54
Mr DJ Knight	c Huish b Fielder	0
EG Goatly	b Woolley	76
Mr MC Bird *	c sub b Dillon	55
WA Spring	b Day	32
H Strudwick +	b Woolley	46
Mr EC Kirk	not out	29
JW Hitch	st Huish b Woolley	4
Extras	(15 b, 9 lb, 1 w)	25
Total	(all out, 131 overs)	**480**

FOW 1st Innings 1-40, 2-84, 3-196, 4-199, 5-242, 6-361, 7-368, 8-426, 9-464, 10-480

Kent bowling	O	M	R	W
Fielder	24	4	70	1
Day	31	5	103	2
Carr	8	0	47	1
Blythe	30	13	51	1
Woolley	30	3	128	3
Dillon	8	0	56	1

Surrey vs Kent

The Oval, Kennington
Monday 11th, Tuesday 12th & Wednesday 13th August
Toss: Kent
Surrey won by an innings and 40 runs
Points: Surrey 5 Kent 0

IF KENT HAD made the most of home advantage against Surrey in recent years, the record at The Oval was much more even. In the preceding ten years, each side had won four times with one tie and a draw. In 1913 it was Surrey's turn and they avenged themselves for their defeat at Blackheath five weeks earlier by winning in some style by an innings and 40 runs. Kent were, to some extent, unlucky in this match in that they effectively lost the use of two bowlers because of injury. Carr was only able to bowl eight overs in the Surrey innings and Humphreys not at all due to a badly damaged hand (he appears to have been injured while batting in the Kent first innings), which not only prevented him from taking any further part in the match but also kept him out of the side in the following match against Somerset. It would, however, be unfair to make too much of this as Surrey thoroughly deserved their win and outplayed Kent completely on the first two days.

Kent won the toss and elected to bat on a wicket which was generally described as good. Some light rain had fallen on the previous evening and in the early morning and *The Times* thought that *"Possibly the showers in the night and morning made the wicket 'pop' just a little at the start but it was not too difficult."*[1] Whatever the reason, some fine fast bowling by Bill Hitch from the Vauxhall End (in those days it was known as the Gasworks End) made short work of the top order and Kent found themselves reeling at ten for four after 45 minutes with Seymour and Woolley out for ducks. *"Hitch bowled very fast … the Kent batsmen are not noted for playing fast bowling well"*[1] just about said it all that day, and it was only when Hubble and Dillon came together that the visiting side made any progress at all. Their partnership was

The Pavilion at The Oval built in 1898

Bill Hitch

worth 32 runs before the fifth wicket fell at 42. "*Mr Day came next and after one bad stroke, he played well and confidently… Mr Day seemed to be seeing the ball very well and made several beautiful strokes.*"[1] Things began to look a little better for Kent while Hitch was rested, but when he was brought back for a quick burst before lunch, he quickly removed Dillon for 33. "*Mr Dillon is a determined batsman at a crisis and he played really well… he, at least, was not afraid to play right forward and surely, even in these days, it must be right to put the left leg forward to fast bowling on fast wickets.*"[1]

After lunch Huish stayed with Day, who continued to bat well, playing several fine shots until he got an edge to Hitch and was caught behind by Strudwick for 35. The rest of the wickets went down quickly with Hitch still bowling at high pace and Eric Kirk with great accuracy. "*Kent never recovered from their wretched start and they were all out in two hours and thirty five minutes for a paltry 102.*"[2]

This had been a fine performance by the Surrey attack, one of the few counties to have an array of decent fast bowlers. Hitch was having the best season of his career, and he was well supported that day by the amateur Kirk, who had played only three times previously in the 1913 season. He had bowled unchanged throughout the innings. Hitch's usual partner was Tom Rushby who, although not having the extreme pace of Hitch, was a fine bowler for Surrey and took 954 wickets in his career at 20 runs apiece. Rushby made way for Kirk in this match. Hitch had taken 8-48 in the Kent innings which, although not his best return of the season (he took 8-44 against Leicestershire), was his best against quality batsmen. "*He* (Hitch) *kept, for this pace, a consistent length and made the ball get up to the awkward body height, a thing which no one else could do that day. Moreover, he bowled many balls that rose straight over the stumps so that the batsman had to play them.*"[1] *Wisden* suggested that it was Hitch's bowling on the first day that effectively decided the match.[3]

By the time Surrey started their innings, the wicket had recovered from any effects of the previous night's rain and was at its best for batting. "*Surrey never looked at all likely to get into difficulties.*" Hobbs and Hayward made a good start against Fielder and Day, neither of whom were able to get the ball to rise as Hitch had done – "*the ball seldom rose more than stump high.*"[1] Dillon made a quick change, introducing Carr in place of Fielder. Hayward was immediately discomfited by his spin, and when Carr gave one some air, he was deceived in the flight and bowled for 17. Hobbs and Hayes played comfortably in a partnership of 84 before a smart piece of fielding run out Hayes for a tidy 27. There appears to be a little confusion as to the identity of the fielder, as in its report of the first day's play, *The Times* credits Humphreys with the run out, but on the following day, it is stated that he had not been able to take the field owing to a damaged hand. So it remains a mystery.

After Carr had bowled only eight overs, during which he was treated disdainfully by Hobbs, he too managed to damage his hand – "*to add to Kent's discomfiture, Mr Carr hurt his hand a little and was not able to do any more.*"[1]

In the meantime, Hobbs had been accumulating steadily and Blythe had been bowling over the wicket with most of his fielders on the leg side in an attempt to restrict the scoring. Despite his slow start, Hobbs was beginning to bat at his majestic best and once he reached his 50, he "*punished some of the bowling severely, especially that of Woolley and his batting at the end was glorious fun… there was only one ball that beat him; he was always the master of the bowling and the way the stroke is played at the very last moment is wonderful … when he was 92, he made a hook for 4 off a ball well outside his off stump which looked to be somewhere near a length and he reached his hundred from the next ball which he hit half-volley off the wicket to square leg. At this time, he gave the impression, just as does Mr Trumper, that it did not matter what the bowlers sent down, for he had three or four different scoring shots, which he could use at will for a ball of any length.*"[1] At close of play Hobbs was not out 107 and the score 183-2. The crowd of 14,000 had enjoyed a wonderful day's cricket and might have been reminded of the first few lines of Albert Craig's[4] tribute to Jack Hobbs which was written in 1906.

Joy reigns supreme amongst the Surrey throng,
Patrons break out in one triumphant song,
Young Hobbs we loved as hero of today
Gaily steers along his conquering way

John Berry Hobbs

Next morning, however, *The Times* declared rather sniffily that "*the cricket at the Oval yesterday was in a sense too one-sided to be interesting*".[5]

Kent struck back first thing on Tuesday morning with Blythe having Hobbs caught behind by Huish for 115 and then, three runs later, Fielder found the edge of Knight's bat to leave Surrey 199-4. At this point there was reason to hope that Kent might not start their second innings more than 200 runs behind, but although Day bowled Henry Harrison at 242, it was now the turn of the lower middle order to enjoy a perfect Oval wicket.

"*Goatly and Mr Bird made another long stand which put on 129. Towards the end of this partnership and afterwards, Mr Dillon very wisely did not give his most valuable bowlers too much work. It was a tremendous lead anyhow; the wicket was perfect and 50 runs more or less did not greatly matter.*" Nearly all the batsmen made runs "*and there was some amazing hitting especially when Spring was dealing with the bowling of Mr Dillon.*"[5] By half past three, when Bill Hitch was stumped off Woolley's bowling, Surrey had reached 480, leaving Kent the small matter of 378 runs to make the hosts bat again.

The bowling analysis makes interesting reading. Despite the carnage wrought elsewhere, Blythe had bowled 30 overs for 51 runs with 13 maidens, a "*testimony to wonderful control of length and skill in placing the field to keep runs down.*"[5] While his team mates conceded runs at 4.25 per over, Blythe yielded a miserly 1.66. Although

Herbert Strudwick and Ernest Hayes

not specifically mentioned, it seems probable that for a good period of his spell, Blythe was bowling his "leg theory".

With Humphreys unable to bat, Dillon promoted himself to open with Hardinge. The wicket was now good for batting and Hitch did not present the same sort of problem as on the previous morning. At least, not to Dillon, who took the responsibility of facing the quicker stuff while allowing Hardinge to become acclimatised by facing the lesser pace of Kirk. Hardinge was a fine batsman for Kent for upwards of 30 years but *it was said at the time and since, that Hardinge had no relish for fast bowling. The evidence is at best inconclusive.*[5] If this was the case, he was not alone in his dislike of the really fast stuff – few batsmen have a real liking for it – but it is often given as the reason why he did not play more than his one Test match. Dillon knew this well and on that day, he was happy to shield his partner from a bowler with his tail up. *"Hitch did not seem to have any real terrors for Mr Dillon, who played him really well with his bat close to his leg and took no risks with the off-ball. The scoring was naturally very slow. Hardinge was quite comfortable at Mr Kirk's end and he soon became happier against Hitch."*[5]

Having weathered the opening onslaught from Hitch, Bird began a rotation of his bowlers and, as often happens when a batsman relaxes against the change bowlers, Dillon gave two chances that were both dropped. *"It was curious that Mr Dillon, who had played the opening bowlers so well, made two bad strokes against the others."*[5] Kent were beginning to look as if they might make it through to the close without loss when Hardinge edged to slip where Hayes took the catch off Kirk, who had just been brought back from the Gasworks End. This brought Seymour to the wicket, and immediately Bird brought Hitch back on from the Pavilion End.

The light, by this time, was obviously indifferent as an appeal was made to the umpires but was rejected. As if to prove the point, Seymour then missed a straight ball from Kirk and was bowled with the score on 96. Woolley then joined his captain and another appeal against the light was made but, to the delight of the large crowd, it too was refused. Kent got through to the close without further loss at 115-2 with Dillon on 47 and Woolley on seven. Strangely enough, *The Times* says "*stumps were pulled up about ten minutes past six.*", which was 20 minutes before the scheduled finishing time, so either there was a further, successful but unrecorded, appeal or the umpires themselves decided not to continue.

The matter of appealing against the light was a sensitive subject at this time. Only the week before, Lord Harris had written to *The Times* suggesting that too many sides appealed against the light in circumstances where it could not really be justified, and called upon batsmen to remain at the wicket longer. The letter is reproduced opposite.

Yet, here was the Kent captain involved in two, perhaps three, such appeals that would have put him into direct conflict with his club Chairman.[6] It is most unlikely that either Seymour or the young Woolley would have made an appeal

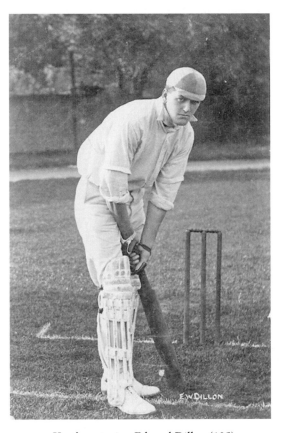

Kent's centurion Edward Dillon (135)

independently of Dillon, and it would be interesting to learn of the exchange between the captain and his Lordship at the next Committee Meeting. One thing is for certain: words would have been exchanged!

On the third day, play commenced at 11 o'clock, half an hour earlier than usual so that, with a half past five finish, Kent would have time to catch their train to Taunton to play against Somerset on the following day. With only two wickets down, they had reason to be optimistic that they might escape with a draw. The weather was unsettled and, indeed, there were interruptions on a number of occasions. There was, however, the little matter of the damage to Humphreys' hand which had prevented him fielding in the first innings and which, in the event, would keep him from batting in this innings and playing in the next match. At the same time, Carr had sustained an injury to a finger which, although it would not prevent his batting, may well have restricted his ability to bat properly. The odds were certainly long to say the least, but, as the day eventually played out, Kent weren't too far from saving the match.

Any hopes of forcing a draw were diminished after only eight runs had been added on the third morning when Woolley aimed to play the left-armer, Kirk, on the leg side and had his off stump removed. Hubble then joined Dillon, showing

BAD LIGHT AND INTERRUPTED MATCHES.

LORD HARRIS'S APPEAL TO CAPTAINS.
TO THE EDITOR OF THE TIMES.

Sir, - Some short time back, at the annual meeting of the Cricketer's Fund Friendly Society, I deprecated the modern practice of drawing for light, and stated that I could not remember any case of such a thing in the 30 years, 1870-1900, when I was actively engaged in first-class cricket.

A correspondent of the *Sporting Life*, signing himself "Long Leg" challenges the accuracy of my statement in a recent issue. I have therefore referred to Dr W. G. Grace, Mr A. N. Hornby, and Mr. A. P. Lucas, who all confirm the absolute accuracy of my statement. Dr Grace adds:--

"We never dreamt of appealing for bad light. I have played at the Oval when the gas lamps have been lighted."

I know well that it is very little use appealing to the umpires to display more independence; but surely the captains need not to be so timorous. I quoted at the above meeting two recent cases – Eton v. Winchester and Kent v. Surrey. In the former by staying at the wickets in a really abominable light, the Eton batsmen made their position practically safe; in the latter the Surrey batsmen, when well in, appealed for light when it was nothing like so bad as that at Eton and perhaps lost the match in consequence.

Faithfully yours
Belmont, Faversham, Aug 3. HARRIS

P.S.– By the way, at the same meeting I told a most charming story of my dear friend and old time comrade, Alfred Lyttelton which the reporters, for reasons best known to themselves, chose to omit all reference to.

In a Middlesex v. Lancashire match at Lord's Lyttelton was magnificently stumped by Pilling off Crossland's fastest ball breaking back between bat and leg. When the innings was over Lyttelton unostentatiously met Pilling at the players' entrance and slipped a sovereign into his hand as a token of a brother wicket-keeper's appreciation of a splendid piece of work

Lord Harris's letter to *The Times* dated 3rd August 1913
which was published on 7th August

"*admirable defence, and gave priceless support to Mr Dillon.*"[7] For the first time in the match, Hitch bowled poorly and was severely punished when he dropped short. He conceded 18 runs from his first two overs. Nevertheless, the Surrey bowlers managed to create chances which went begging. Hubble was dropped on seven and Dillon was missed by Bird in the slips on 70, and again shortly after from the bowling of Kirk. With his two best bowlers unable to force a further breakthrough, Bird tried Bill Spring, Hayes and himself to no effect. "*There was great enthusiasm when Mr Dillon, after having been batting for nearly four hours, completed his hundred with the score at 192. All this time, both batsmen played with patience and sound judgement, rarely attempting to hit unless they could do so with perfect safety.*"[7]

Having failed with the supporting acts, Bird reintroduced Hitch and Kirk and shortly after, Hitch bowled Hubble with the score at 212. His partnership with Dillon had added 89 runs in an hour and three quarters. "*At this point, Mr Day came in and began his great innings. From the first, he was full of confidence, nearly always hitting the ball in the middle of his bat.*"[7] By lunch, the score had reached 251-4 and, as the players left the pitch, rain had begun to fall. Unfortunately for Kent, the shower proved to be short and not particularly sharp so that after lunch play began on time but, only ten minutes later, a further shower delayed the action for half an hour. As matters turned out, although the rain had taken a little time out of the

Lord Harris

The Oval circa 1905

game, which in theory should have made Kent's attempt at survival easier, the effect of the rain on the wicket seems to have just freshened the surface sufficiently to assist the bowlers. "*Before Mr Dillon could settle down, again he was bowled by Kirk at 266. As has already been said, he played well ... but not so well as the day before; indeed he has seldom, if ever batted quite so finely as on Tuesday evening. Huish, who came next, received a very nasty blow on the thigh and another from Hitch's bowling but he went on batting most pluckily.*"[7]

Day and Huish stayed together until more rain interrupted play at around four o'clock with the score at 312-4. The players were off for 20 minutes which, because of the early finishing time, left Surrey only an hour and ten minutes to take the remaining six wickets – or was it only five as it wasn't entirely certain whether Humphreys would bat? Providing the wicket hadn't suffered, the balance had now swung back in Kent's favour but, for about the only time this season, they contrived to snatch defeat from, well, if not exactly the jaws of defeat, certainly the arms of safety. The end, when it came, came swiftly. Huish, who had batted for 70 minutes for his 27, was caught low down at slip by Spring off Hitch. The partnership with Day had been worth 61. A few balls later, Carr played at a long-hop from Hitch, got an edge and Spring took the catch. In Hitch's next over "*Mr Day was bowled in attempting to hit a ball from Hitch... Fielder was the next man. The first ball he received hit him on the thigh, the next one bowled him. As Humphreys was unable to bat, the game was over.*"[7]

Kent had been bowled out for 338, losing by an innings and 40 runs. Day's innings was particularly praised – "*The finest batting, however, was certainly that of Mr Day and, indeed, it would be impossible to overpraise his innings of 63. The way he stood up and played the bowling of Hitch was an object lesson in dealing with a very fast bowler.*"[8]

Hitch had taken the last four wickets in 17 balls for six runs. His match figures were 13-163. Kirk had bowled 47 overs in the Kent second innings, taking four for 107. Although his was, on the face of it, merely a supporting role, *The Times* says that Bird had given his two strike bowlers *"far too much work to do"* and *"Mr Kirk's record... does not suggest anything very remarkable but the figures are utterly misleading. He bowled magnificently... keeping up his pace in an astonishing way and never losing his length; moreover, he bowled without any luck to encourage him. The chief honours in this game are due to Hitch and Hobbs, but Mr Kirk had far more to do with winning the game than the score sheet reveals."*[7]

After a poor start to the match, and with bad luck having deprived them of one all-rounder in Humphreys and one bowler who could bat a bit for the best part of the match (Carr), Kent had made Surrey work hard to avenge their Blackheath defeat.

As the side made the short journey across London to the GWR London Terminus at Paddington to catch the train to Taunton, they had time to reflect on their biggest defeat of the season and the fact that in their past two outings, they had only secured one point from the ten available. The loss at The Oval had narrowed the gap between first and second place as a result of Yorkshire's victory over Middlesex to 9.09%. Kent had five matches remaining and the Championship was still theirs to lose.

Mr Arthur Percival Day

The Oval circa 1909

Sources

1   *The Times* 12th August 1913
2   *The Dundee Courier* 12th August 1913
3   *Wisden* 1914
4   Albert Craig (1849–1909), generally known as The Surrey Poet, was a Yorkshireman by birth. He was a regular at The Oval and also at Kent grounds.
5   *The Times* 13th August 1913
6   Lord Harris was Chairman of the Kent Committee from 1906 until his death in 1932
7   *The Times* 14th August 1913
8   *Manchester Courier* 14th August 1913

14th August 1913	P	W	L	DWF	DLF	NC	Max	Pts	PtsPC
Kent	23	16	3	2	1	1	110	87	79.09%
Northamptonshire	19	12	2	1	4	0	95	67	70.53%
Yorkshire	24	14	4	4	2	0	120	84	70.00%
Middlesex	15	7	2	4	2	0	75	49	65.33%
Surrey	20	11	3	2	4	0	100	65	65.00%
Nottinghamshire	18	8	4	2	4	0	90	50	55.56%
Lancashire	22	6	9	7	0	0	110	51	46.36%
Warwickshire	20	7	9	2	2	0	100	43	43.00%
Sussex	24	7	10	4	3	0	120	50	41.67%
Gloucestershire	18	5	10	1	2	0	90	30	33.33%
Worcestershire	14	3	7	1	2	1	65	20	30.77%
Hampshire	20	4	10	2	4	0	100	30	30.00%
Derbyshire	17	3	10	2	2	0	85	23	27.06%
Essex	16	2	8	2	4	0	80	20	25.00%
Somerset	13	2	9	2	0	0	65	16	24.62%
Leicestershire	18	3	11	1	3	0	90	21	23.33%

Kent 1st Innings

Mr EW Dillon *	c Braund b Bridges	0
HTW Hardinge	c Newton b Bridges	19
J Seymour	b Bridges	0
FE Woolley	c Newton b Bridges	28
JC Hubble	c Newton b Bridges	40
DW Jennings	c Newton b Robson	33
GC Collins	c Newton b Bridges	13
FH Huish +	c Braund b White	17
WJ Fairservice	c White b Robson	17
C Blythe	b Robson	28
A Fielder	not out	8
Extras	(10 b, 4 lb, 4 nb)	18
Total	(all out, 62 overs)	**221**

FOW 1st Innings 1-2, 2-2, 3-39, 4-52, 5-114, 6-137, 7-166, 8-168, 9-198, 10-221

Kent 2nd Innings

	c White b Bridges	0
	lbw b White	75
	c Hylton-Stewart b White	82
	not out	101
	b White	47
	c White b Bowring	1
	c Hyman b White	2
	c Braund b White	7
	c Johnson b Bowring	7
	c Hyman b Bowring	5
	did not bat	
	(1 b, 3 lb, 2 nb, 2 w)	8
	(9 wickets declared, 77.1 overs)	**335**

FOW 2nd Innings 1-2, 2-152, 3-183, 4-284, 5-287, 6-292, 7-307, 8-324, 9-335

Somerset bowling	O	M	R	W
White	22	5	87	1
Bridges	21	8	44	6
Robson	14	1	45	3
Hylton-Stewart	5	0	27	0

Somerset bowling	O	M	R	W
White	27	3	120	5
Bridges	21	2	63	1
Robson	11	1	53	0
Hylton-Stewart	5	0	27	0
Garrett	8	1	40	0
Bowring	5.1	0	24	3

Somerset 1st Innings

Mr PR Johnson *	b Fielder	1
W Hyman	c Huish b Fielder	1
LC Braund	c Huish b Fielder	7
Mr RE Hancock	c Woolley b Fielder	8
CJ Bowring	b Fairservice	5
Mr BD Hylton-Stewart	c Hubble b Fielder	3
E Robson	c Dillon b Fairservice	22
Mr HF Garrett	c Dillon b Fielder	8
Mr JC White	b Blythe	1
Mr AE Newton +	c Seymour b Fielder	7
JJ Bridges	not out	11
Extras	(6 b, 2 lb, 4 nb)	12
Total	(all out, 42.2 overs)	**86**

FOW 1st Innings 1-1, 2-3, 3-14, 4-19, 5-22, 6-48, 7-57, 8-58, 9-70, 10-86

Somerset 2nd Innings

	not out	55
	c Hubble b Seymour	35
	did not bat	
	did not bat	
	did not bat	
	did not bat	
	did not bat	
	did not bat	
	did not bat	
	did not bat	
	did not bat	
		0
	(1 wicket, 45.5 overs)	**90**

FOW 2nd Innings 1-90

Kent bowling	O	M	R	W
Fielder	21.2	5	50	7
Fairservice	13	7	16	2
Blythe	8	3	8	1

Kent bowling	O	M	R	W
Fielder	7	2	22	0
Fairservice	13	7	29	0
Blythe	9	5	12	0
Woolley	8	4	6	0
Collins	1	1	0	0
Dillon	6	1	19	0
Jennings	1	0	2	0
Seymour	0.5	0	0	1

Somerset vs Kent

The County Ground, Taunton
Thursday 14th, Friday 15th & Saturday 16th August
Toss: Kent
Match Drawn
Points: Somerset 1 Kent 3

KENT WERE OBLIGED to make changes for the match at Taunton because of injuries sustained at The Oval. Humphreys and Carr had damaged a hand and fingers respectively, and Day was not available for the jaunt to the West Country. Fairservice, Jennings and George Collins came into the side in their place. This was to be George Collins' only match of the season and, at the end of it, like Henry Preston, his services were dispensed with despite featuring respectably in the second XI.[1] He was re-engaged by Kent after the war and played until 1928.

The showers that affected the final afternoon at The Oval had been more severe in the West Country, so that the wicket favoured the bowlers from the start. Kent, nevertheless, decided to bat on winning the toss. Because of Humphreys' absence, Dillon took the advice of *The Times* correspondent at the Oval match and opened the batting with Hardinge, but was back in the pavilion almost immediately without scoring. Seymour was then also dismissed for a duck. The wicket was proving very interesting for the batsmen *"for the ball broke a good deal and got up awkwardly but even allowing for this, the bating was a great deal worse than it need have been. There was a general tendency to go for the off ball."*[2]

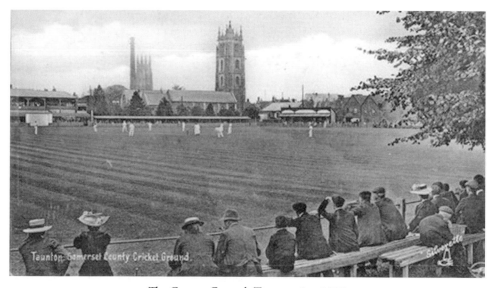

The County Ground, Taunton circa 1919

Ernie Robson: top scorer in the Somerset first innings with 22, and "AE" Newton: the Somerset wicketkeeper who played for the county from 1880 to 1914, a total of 35 seasons

Woolley made a few good strokes in his 28 but was caught behind just when he looked set. Then Hubble and Jennings put on 62 for the fifth wicket, the best partnership of the innings. Apart from this, most of the Kent batsmen struggled. Fairservice and Blythe added a valuable 30 for the ninth wicket with some fierce and lucky blows being struck by the left-arm spinner, of whom it is sometimes said that he could bat much better than his average would indicate. Kent were all out for 221. Jimmy Bridges was the main wicket taker for Somerset with 6-44 and the veteran Somerset keeper, the Etonian Arthur Newton, *"did brilliantly and brought off five catches in the Kent innings."*[2]

If Kent's start had been bad, then Somerset's can only be described as dire. Fielder, relishing the life in the pitch, snapped up the first four wickets to leave Somerset reeling at 19-4. This soon became 22-5 when Fairservice bowled Charles Bowring for five. The only batsman who reached double figures was Ernie Robson. He was out for 22 from the final ball of the day *"splendidly caught by Mr Dillon close to the boundary on the leg side,"*[2] with Somerset 70-9 at the close and still needing one run to avoid the follow-on.

Kent had dropped several catches. Seymour dropped Robson twice in one over and he was also missed at third man by Collins. But for this generosity, Kent would have finished off Somerset much sooner and had them batting again on that first evening. In the event, it could be argued that these missed catches cost Kent maximum points.

The last Somerset wicket added 16 runs in 30 minutes on the next morning before Fielder wrapped up the innings to finish with 7-50. Kent led by 135 on the first innings.

Kent's centurion and leading wicket taker: Woolley (101 not out) and Fielder (7-50)

Despite the improvement in the wicket, which had dried out overnight, Kent lost Dillon, with the score at two for a pair in the match – definitely a case of "after the Lord Mayor's Show" following his innings at The Oval. Thereafter, the Kent batsmen put on a fantastic display of stroke making, scoring at nearly four and a half runs per over. *"Hardinge and Seymour put on 150 runs together in an hour and 40 minutes for the second wicket, but although they actually scored so fast, they never seemed to be making runs at any great pace."*[3] Seymour's 82 included 11 fours and Hardinge, whose innings lasted for two hours and ten minutes, hit nine fours in his 75.

Woolley and Hubble then plundered the bowling for 101 in less than an hour, but when Hubble was out to Jack White, wickets fell quickly as the later batsmen tried to maintain the breakneck scoring rate. *"Woolley carried out his bat for 101, made in an hour and thirty five minutes including thirteen fours."*[4] The Kent innings was declared on 335-9 shortly before half past five, which set Somerset a most unlikely target of 471 with a day plus an hour to bat. Jack White was the best bowler for Somerset with 5-120 from 27 overs with Bowring taking 3-24. By the close of play, the home side had reached 53 without loss.

Next morning, Somerset set about their target of 418, and by half past twelve had scored another 37 runs when the rain arrived. Peter Johnson had reached 55 and Bill Hyman had just been dismissed by Seymour, who was having

Kent's other Taunton run makers – Wally Hardinge and Jim Seymour

one of his rare spells as a bowler that day. His one wicket was, technically, sufficient to take him to the top of the Kent bowling averages that year with 2.5 overs, one wicket for three runs.

The rain persisted throughout the afternoon, and shortly before tea, it became apparent that, even if the rain stopped immediately, the pitch would not be fit for play before stumps. The match was abandoned as a draw. Kent had, at least, secured three points, two more than they had taken from their last two fixtures combined.

Kent's immediate lead in the Championship table suffered slightly as a result of Yorkshire taking five points from their victory over Surrey. Kent could still be overtaken, but it required them to lose two of their last four matches while Yorkshire needed to win all three of their remaining fixtures. The two points dropped at Taunton were, however, the last points Kent would drop during the 1913 season as they won every one of their remaining matches.

Sources
1   KCCC Blue Book 1914 p 276
2   *The Times* 15th August 1913
3   *The Times* 16th August 1913
4   *Manchester Courier* 16th August 1913

Mr PR Johnson – top scorer for Somerset at Taunton

16th August 1913	P	W	L	DWF	DLF	NC	Max	Pts	PtsPC
Kent	24	16	3	3	1	1	115	90	78.26%
Northamptonshire	20	13	2	1	4	0	100	72	72.00%
Yorkshire	25	15	4	4	2	0	125	89	71.20%
Surrey	21	11	4	2	4	0	105	65	61.90%
Middlesex	16	7	3	4	2	0	80	49	61.25%
Nottinghamshire	18	8	4	2	4	0	90	50	55.56%
Lancashire	23	7	9	7	0	0	115	56	48.70%
Warwickshire	21	7	10	2	2	0	105	43	40.95%
Sussex	25	7	11	4	3	0	125	50	40.00%
Gloucestershire	19	6	10	1	2	0	95	35	36.84%
Hampshire	21	5	10	2	4	0	105	35	33.33%
Leicestershire	18	4	10	1	3	0	90	26	28.89%
Worcestershire	15	3	8	1	2	1	70	20	28.57%
Derbyshire	18	3	11	2	2	0	90	23	25.56%
Essex	16	2	8	2	4	0	80	20	25.00%
Somerset	14	2	9	2	1	0	70	17	24.29%

Kent 1st Innings

E Humphreys	c Shields b Skelding	22
HTW Hardinge	b Skelding	6
J Seymour	c Sharp b Coe	61
FE Woolley	c and b Geary	47
JC Hubble	c Shields b Coe	21
Mr EW Dillon *	b Geary	0
DW Jennings	st Shields b Geary	1
FH Huish +	c Sharp b Geary	31
WJ Fairservice	b Coe	1
C Blythe	c Coe b Geary	1
A Fielder	not out	0
Extras	(1 b, 8 lb, 1 w)	10
Total	(all out, 55 overs)	**201**

FOW 1st Innings 1-12, 2-65, 3-140, 4-144, 5-144, 6-146, 7-190, 8-194, 9-195, 10-201

Kent 2nd Innings

	b Geary	31
	not out	154
	c and b Shipman	39
	c Skelding b Geary	24
	b Geary	5
	b Riley	32
	c and b Riley	1
	retired hurt	23
	b Skelding	19
	st Shields b Coe	0
	not out	1
	(9 b, 8 lb, 2 nb, 1 w)	20
	(8 wickets declared, 98 overs)	**349**

FOW 2nd Innings 1-67, 2-123, 3-165, 4-171, 5-250, 6-256, 7-345, 8-348

Leicestershire bowling	O	M	R	W
Shipman	12	1	51	0
Skelding	21	3	72	2
Geary	16	2	61	5
Coe	6	3	7	3

Leicestershire bowling	O	M	R	W
Shipman	13	2	52	1
Skelding	25	3	88	1
Geary	30	4	88	3
Coe	24	4	72	1
Wood	3	0	17	0
Riley	3	0	12	2

Leicestershire 1st Innings

Mr CJB Wood	c Huish b Fairservice	2
Mr J Burgess	c Hardinge b Blythe	23
JH King	b Blythe	16
Mr CE de Trafford	b Woolley	15
S Coe	b Fielder	12
Mr AT Sharp	lbw b Blythe	17
Mr WN Riley	c Woolley b Blythe	21
W Shipman	c Seymour b Blythe	38
Mr J Shields *+	c Dillon b Blythe	4
G Geary	c Jennings b Blythe	21
A Skelding	not out	14
Extras	(3 b, 6 lb)	9
Total	(all out, 59.3 overs)	**192**

FOW 1st Innings 1-3, 2-44, 3-45, 4-67, 5-86, 6-98, 7-137, 8-146, 9-157, 10-192

Leicestershire 2nd Innings

	c Woolley b Blythe	34
	b Blythe	25
	c Woolley b Fairservice	25
	b Fairservice	4
	c Seymour b Fairservice	0
	c Dillon b Woolley	0
	c Woolley b Blythe	0
	c sub b Blythe	2
	not out	1
	b Blythe	3
	lbw b Blythe	0
		0
	(all out, 35 overs)	**94**

FOW 2nd Innings 1-33, 2-68, 3-81, 4-81, 5-81, 6-82, 7-88, 8-92, 9-94, 10-94

Kent bowling	O	M	R	W
Fielder	18	1	63	1
Fairservice	5	0	21	1
Blythe	24.3	6	54	7
Woolley	12	2	45	1

Kent bowling	O	M	R	W
Fairservice	10	3	16	3
Blythe	18	4	40	6
Woolley	7	1	38	1

Kent vs Leicestershire

St Lawrence Ground, Canterbury
Monday 18th, Tuesday 19th & Wednesday 20th August
Toss: Kent
Kent won by 264 runs
Points: Kent 5 Leicestershire 0

WITH THEIR TITLE campaign having suffered something of a setback, following an innings defeat at The Oval and a frustrating draw at Taunton, Kent hosted Leicestershire, who were fresh from a magnificent victory over Worcestershire. Humphreys returned in place of Collins, but otherwise the team was unchanged from the one that had outplayed, but been unable to finish off, Somerset because of the weather.

Winning the toss, Dillon chose to bat in cold and dark conditions in front of a crowd estimated to be between 800 and 1,000 hardy souls. It was hard to imagine that, just 11 days previously, more than 13,000 people had enjoyed Ladies' Day at the same venue.

Given the amount of rain that had fallen overnight, it was a tribute to the groundsman that the game was able to start on time.

Kent posted a moderate total of 201, despite being 140-2 with Seymour and Woolley apparently well set. Indeed, the *Kentish Gazette & Canterbury Press* concluded that Kent's batting had, with the exception of the aforementioned batsmen and the brief partnership of Hubble and Huish, been *"not only colourless but in instances quite feeble"*.[1]

The first wicket went at 12 when Hardinge was done for pace by Alec Skelding, described by the same correspondent as *"that most promising young trundler."* Humphreys and Seymour played some finely judged strokes to take the score to 65-1 at exactly a run a minute, at which point Humphreys was unluckily out, brilliantly caught wide down the leg side by the Leicestershire captain and wicketkeeper, John Shields.

With Woolley in especially sparkling form, the third-wicket pair took Kent to lunch at 86-2, and in one 15-minute spell before and after the interval, they thrashed 50 runs through a combination of the left-hander's powerful driving and Seymour's cutting and leg-side placement. They were separated, however, at 140 when Seymour edged a turning ball to slip. His 61, in an hour and 40 minutes, had included an all-run five and six boundaries.

Three further wickets went down with the addition of only six runs, starting with Woolley who, after scoring 47 in 45 minutes with six fours, gave George Geary a simple return catch. Dillon's run of ducks extended to three following his wonderful century at The Oval, a striking example of the fickleness of form, and two runs later

Jennings was stranded out of his crease as the ball rebounded off the wicketkeeper's pads onto his stumps.

Hubble and Huish batted brightly, primarily at Skelding's expense, adding 44 in 20 minutes. But the return to the attack of the 40-year-old slow left-armer, Sam Coe, immediately brought about the downfall of Hubble. The second, more excusable, collapse of the innings began when *"Geary was brought on to bowl for the second time, took five of the last eight wickets to fall at a cost of 38 runs."*[2]

Leicestershire started badly. John Burgess (playing in place of Harry Whitehead who was indisposed) *"ought to have been caught and bowled before a run had been scored"*[2] but Fairservice missed the chance. *"Mr Wood was out in the same over"* caught behind by Huish. Burgess and John King *"then hit out finely and put on 41 runs for the second wicket"*. The introduction of Blythe saw Burgess's sprightly knock ended when, from the second ball of his spell, he was caught by Hardinge in the long field. Three balls later, Blythe bowled King to leave the visitors on 45-3. By this time, the light was becoming a problem but, before it caused a stoppage, Woolley finally bowled Charles de Trafford, who had already given a couple of chances off his bowling, to leave Leicestershire on 67-4. The poor light caused play to be interrupted at half past five, but after a brief resumption, *"stumps were pulled up"*[2] at 79-4, still behind Kent's first innings total by a daunting 122 runs.

There were a few light showers first thing on Tuesday morning which did not affect the wicket unduly, but the still damp outfield proved a handicap for the bowlers. Fielder made the first breakthrough of the day when, after seven runs were added, he uprooted Coe's off stump. Then Blythe *"came to the rescue of his side, and, varying his pace and flight of the ball with all his old skill, captured the last five wickets. Fielder bowled uncommonly well too, but had wretched luck."*[3]

George Geary circa 1914: Mr Cecil Wood and John King: the mainstays of the Leicestershire 2nd innings

William Riley and Bill Shipman steadied matters with a stand of 39 at a run a minute before they presented mid off and silly point with simple catches. At 157-9, it looked as if Kent would secure a decent first innings advantage, but Geary and Skelding contributed 35 for the final wicket in a valiant attempt to secure the first innings lead. *"Geary showed fine defence and courage was ably backed up by Skelding… by very determined cricket"*,[3] before the former, trying to hit Blythe out of the ground, was caught at long off by Jennings. Blythe finished with seven for 54. With the weather looking unsettled, the nine-run lead had at least secured three points in the Kentish cause.

The Kent openers negotiated a testing quarter of an hour before lunch, which was taken with the score at 11. After the interval Kent took full advantage of a wicket playing faster than at any other time in the match. Hardinge, who had threatened a big score in recent weeks, played a *"wonderfully fine knock"*, reaching an unbeaten 114 by the close, his first century at the St Lawrence Ground. Among *"many magnificent strokes, one, veritably dazzling cut past point off Skelding was the best"*.[3]

His opening partner, Humphreys, was unfortunate in playing on when appearing well set, after the pair had put on 67. Seymour once more played attractively until, like Woolley in the first innings, he gave Shipman his first wicket of the game by lobbing the ball back into his grateful hands. The bowler, who was struggling with a side strain, must have been doubting the wisdom of taking the catch shortly afterwards, when Woolley took 16 off an over. It was only a stunning catch by Skelding at deep mid on from a *"terrific smack"* that cut short the master's onslaught. Geary was equally fortunate when Hubble chopped a wide ball onto his stumps.

This brought in the Kent captain, who was without a run to his name from his previous three outings. The affection in which he was held was evident in the *"sympathetic cheer"* he received on emerging from the pavilion, and the *"volume of cheering"* that greeted his boundary to long leg off Geary. This gave Dillon the confidence to play several more forcing leg-side strokes in a bright innings of 32. Meanwhile, Hardinge moved to that elusive hundred with an all-run five. He had batted for three hours and 20 minutes. Huish stayed with him in poor light to help Kent finish the day at 272-6, a healthy lead of 281.

The final morning of the match saw Kent in search of quick runs and a declaration. Helped by two dropped catches by the 49-year-old de Trafford in the slips, Kent added 77 in an hour. Before the declaration came, however, Huish was obliged to leave the field to receive treatment to a cut which he sustained when he edged a rising ball from Geary into his chin. He received several stitches and was unable to play any further part in the game. Hubble, who was to become the first-choice wicketkeeper after the war, took his place behind the stumps. Hardinge's unbeaten 154 lasted four and a half hours and included a five and 16 fours.

Left to score 359 in four and three quarter hours to win, Leicestershire had about an hour's batting before lunch was taken. With the sun beginning to break through, it would not be long before the wicket became truly difficult, and the two amateurs at the top of the order decided to attack the Kent bowling. They were at first successful, largely due to some uncharacteristically poor bowling from Woolley. Three weeks earlier, against Essex at Leyton, Woolley had damaged the spinning finger on his left hand and was, evidently, still troubled by it as he conceded 32 runs in just four overs. Burgess was the first to leave, bowled by Blythe for an aggressive 25 but Cecil Wood and King took the score to 67 when Fairservice had King caught at slip and then, a few runs later, bowled the former captain, de Trafford for just four. Lunch arrived with Leicestershire on 81-4 with Blythe finding the edge of Wood's bat to give Woolley another slip catch.

During lunch, the sun *"became very powerful"*[4] and by the time play resumed, the wicket had been transformed into a true "sticky dog". Blythe took four wickets for five runs as Leicestershire lost their remaining wickets for only 13 runs. *"The luck was certainly with Kent, but they took full advantage of it."*[4] Blythe's 7-54 gave him match figures of 13-94.

One interesting snippet gleaned from the *Kent Messenger* report of the final day was that as a result of the injury to Huish, Kent fielded a certain AP Freeman as 12th man. "Tich" Freeman[5] would make his first-class debut during the following season but on that final afternoon at St Lawrence had to be content with the anonymity of "sub" when he caught Shipman at mid off from Blythe's bowling.

Despite the win, not all Kent followers were entirely happy with events. A reader calling himself "An old subscriber and cricketer" wrote to the editor of the *Kentish Gazette & Canterbury Press* a few days after the game finished. The letter is shown below.

One hundred years later, at a time when the county's home fixtures are played principally at a redeveloped St Lawrence Ground, one is more likely to hear the residents of West Kent putting forward the counter argument.

Dear Sir,

I think every cricket supporter in East Kent regretted that such wretched weather conditions prevailed in the course of the Kent v. Leicestershire match at our ancient cricket ground this week. To my great astonishment, I learn, from a side wind, that through this weather and the consequent small attendance, the usual third cricket match is in danger of being lost to Canterbury next year. Where is Kent's Managing Committee's and officials' gratitude to Canterbury for past support! East Kent subscribers could tell how unsuitable was the date for the Committee to expect a good gate this year. How many old subscribers were chagrined (as I was) to hear "the powers that be" declaiming against the Canterburians and district attendance compared with – well, say, other places in Kent. Now, Sir, I claim that Canterbury and East Kent subscribers are entitled to a third match – apart from the poor Leicestershire attendances – and the West Kent subscribers are already well catered for without scratching our extra match. Give Canterbury the last Kent match on the last three days of the week, and you will see where Kent's supporters are. Further, I hope the Championship may hang on the result.

Yours etc
Name and address supplied

Blythe: 13 for 94 at St Lawrence

Wally Hardinge circa 1922

As it happened, the rumour turned out to be true and, when the 1914 fixtures was published, Canterbury had only two matches. However, by the time Canterbury Week arrived, war had been declared (28th July 1914), and a general mobilisation was already afoot. The Crabble Athletic Ground had been requisitioned by the military and the matches scheduled for the Dover Week were transferred to Canterbury. So, at least in 1914 our disappointed "Canterburian" got his wish, although perhaps not quite for the reason he might have argued for in the first place.

Sources
1   *The Kentish Gazette & Canterbury Press* 23rd August 1913
2   *The Times* 19th August 1913
3   *The Times* 20th August 1913
4   *The Times* 21st August 1913
5   Tich Freeman had arrived at Kent via a few games for Essex Club and Ground. He was taken on to the Tonbridge Nursery Staff and in 1913 played all his cricket for the 2nd XI. This match at Canterbury was the first reference to his participation at senior level, although he did not make his first-class debut until 1914. See also the notes under Worcestershire vs Kent at Amblecote (pp 60) and Essex v Kent (pp 164) earlier in the season.

Kent 1st Innings

E Humphreys	c Stone b Newman	106
HTW Hardinge	c Mead b Kennedy	117
J Seymour	c Bowell b Newman	85
FE Woolley	c Kennedy b Newman	27
JC Hubble	b Newman	12
Mr EW Dillon *	not out	29
FH Huish +	st Stone b McDonell	23
WJ Fairservice	st Stone b McDonell	3
Mr DW Carr	b Brown	0
C Blythe	b Brown	4
A Fielder	c Tennyson b Kennedy	1
Extras	(6 b, 9 lb, 2 w)	17
Total	(all out, 112 overs)	**424**

FOW 1st Innings 1-192, 2-298, 3-340, 4-354, 5-359, 6-402, 7-406, 8-419, 9-423, 10-424

Kent 2nd Innings

c Stone b Brown	3
not out	105
c Bowell b Kennedy	77
c Brown b Kennedy	10
c and b McDonell	4
not out	24
did not bat	
did not bat	
did not bat	
did not bat	
did not bat	
(5 b, 5 lb, 1 w)	11
(4 wickets declared, 60 overs)	**234**

FOW 2nd Innings 1-4, 2-159, 3-190, 4-197

Hampshire bowling	O	M	R	W
Brown	18	4	66	2
Kennedy	34	7	112	2
McDonell	16	1	77	2
Mead	15	0	69	0
Newman	29	6	83	4

Hampshire bowling	O	M	R	W
Brown	9	0	44	1
Kennedy	28	7	88	2
McDonell	13	0	58	1
Newman	10	1	33	0

Hampshire 1st Innings

Mr AC Johnston	c Huish b Fairservice	27
HAW Bowell	c Huish b Blythe	79
Hon LH Tennyson	c Huish b Blythe	38
CP Mead	c Fielder b Blythe	33
Mr EM Sprot *	c Hubble b Fielder	26
Lt CH Abercrombie	c Seymour b Carr	44
G Brown	b Fielder	4
J Stone +	run out	4
Mr HC McDonell	lbw b Carr	17
JA Newman	lbw b Blythe	16
AS Kennedy	not out	2
Extras	(4 b, 6 lb)	10
Total	(all out, 92 overs)	**300**

FOW 1st Innings 1-55, 2-115, 3-174, 4-210, 5-210, 6-222, 7-228, 8-267, 9-294, 10-300

Hampshire 2nd Innings

st Huish b Carr	7
c Huish b Carr	70
c Woolley b Carr	8
b Blythe	30
c Dillon b Fairservice	58
c Hardinge b Woolley	4
b Woolley	2
b Woolley	9
st Huish b Carr	0
not out	1
c Seymour b Woolley	0
(7 b, 4 lb)	11
(all out, 53.4 overs)	**200**

FOW 2nd Innings 1-30, 2-42, 3-78, 4-181, 5-185, 6-190, 7-190, 8-198, 9-200, 10-200

Kent bowling	O	M	R	W
Fielder	13	1	49	2
Fairservice	18	5	61	1
Carr	26	4	80	2
Blythe	28	6	74	4
Woolley	7	1	26	0

Kent bowling	O	M	R	W
Fielder	8	2	35	0
Fairservice	14	4	41	1
Blythe	11	0	50	1
Carr	14	3	43	4
Woolley	6.4	0	20	4

Kent vs Hampshire

Crabble Athletic Ground, Dover
Thursday 21st, Friday 22nd & Saturday 23rd August
Toss: Hampshire
Kent won by 158 runs
Points: Kent 5 Hampshire 0

THE CRABBLE ATHLETIC GROUND in Dover was constructed in 1897 by a consortium of local businessmen. The ground, which was carved out of a hillside through a process of cut and fill, created a natural amphitheatre which provided excellent viewing for the public. It had been purchased in 1902 by Dover District Council for £5,000 (less than half the original cost of construction) when the original owners got into financial difficulty.[1]

The Crabble became a venue for first-class cricket when, in 1907, Kent played a single Championship match against Gloucestershire. Although they suffered a 96-run defeat, the experiment was deemed a success, and two matches were allocated to the ground the following year. The Dover Cricket Week or Festival was now effectively established – the *"youngest but not the least important of the Kent festivals."*[2]

Kent made the 14-mile trip down the Dover Road knowing that six days' solid work would see them confirmed as County Champions for 1913, well before they arrived at Lord's for their final match against Middlesex. They actually required a

The Crabbe Athletic Ground, Dover

229

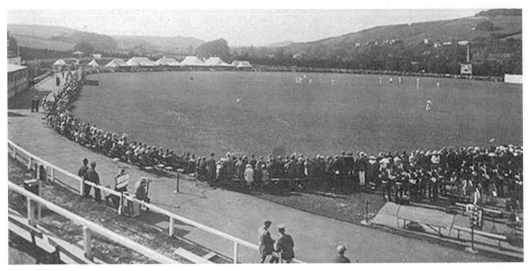

The Crabble Ground circa 1913

total of six points from their last three matches to ensure they could not be overtaken by Yorkshire.

In contrast to the first few years of the Dover Week, warm sunshine graced proceedings throughout the three days of this match. The *Kentish Gazette & Canterbury Press* believed that "*In a summer remarkable for gloom rather than rain, it really does seem as if the captious clerk of the weather, conscious of past delinquencies, is at this late period of the season bent on rehabilitating himself in the good graces of cricket habitués in this particular neighbourhood,*"[2] a statement which would have guaranteed inclusion in Pseuds Corner – had *Private Eye* existed in those days – and, although it wasn't untypical of the prose at the time, it certainly rankles today.

Kent made one change, bringing in Carr for Jennings. Carr had sustained a finger injury at the Oval, but was fit again and probably relishing the prospect of the Dover wicket that was already established as a happy hunting ground for spinners. Hampshire fielded their strongest side with all three of their talented amateur batsmen on show – The Hon Lionel Tennyson[3], Alexander Johnston and the Scottish rugby international, Lt Cecil Abercrombie.

The first day crowd of 5,228 was treated to one of Kent's best batting displays of the season as they posted 419-8 in a little over five hours. Hardinge's second successive century, which he completed before lunch, was the highlight of the innings. The openers were completely dominant during the morning session, and the score stood at 188 by lunch. *The Star* correspondent gushed that "*boundary followed boundary with riotous speed.*"[4] On the resumption, however, Hardinge's "*sparkling*" knock, which contained 19 fours, ended when Mead caught him at slip off the bowling of Alec Kennedy. Seymour and Humphreys maintained the momentum with another century stand and Humphreys' three-hour hundred included some beautiful strokes, but did includes three "lives". He hit only five boundaries, his relatively circumspect approach contrasting sharply with Hardinge's more adventurous innings.

With Kent just short of 300 and only two wickets down, this seemed the ideal platform for Woolley as he strode out to bat. But, not for the first time of late, he played a handful of glorious strokes and then got out. The *Kentish Gazette & Canterbury Press* reporter speculated, not unreasonably, that he seemed to be "*suffering from an attack of hit-it-itis*" as he followed up hitting Mead out of the ground by nicking one to slip.

Seymour's fine innings ended contentiously as the batsman stood his ground, unconvinced that Horace Bowell had taken a fair catch at cover. Indeed, *The Kentish Gazette* claimed there was "*grave doubt*" as to whether he had gathered the ball cleanly before it touched the ground, adding that "*many people in a good position to judge were of the opinion that a flagrant mistake had been made.*"[2] From 340-2, Kent had slipped to 359-5, but still, an imposing score late on the first day.

Dillon and Huish, always fine men for such a crisis, restored Kent's fortunes with a stand of 43 for the sixth wicket, before the veteran wicketkeeper was smartly stumped by Jimmy Stone off the bowling of McDonell. Although Fairservice and Carr gave their captain no support, Kent ended an excellent day at 419-8.

The Hampshire bowlers stuck to their task well in the face of this onslaught "*and the fielding was always excellent. Stone, especially, distinguished himself behind the*

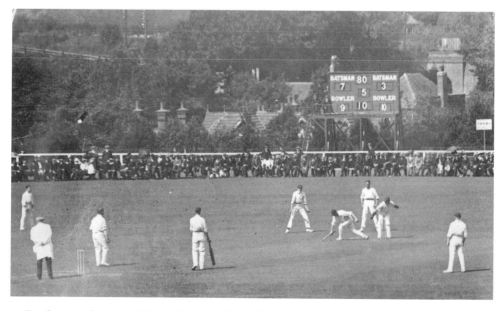

Jim Seymour batting at Dover. The date of this photograph is unknown but it cannot be before 1914 as the large scoreboard dates from that year.
(Photograph courtesy of Richard and Helen Seymour)

August 23, 1913.　　CRICKET: A WEEKLY RECORD OF THE GAME.　　555

HAS THE KENTISH 'PLANE TOO LONG A LEAD?

stumps."[2] According to the *Kentish Gazette & Canterbury Press*, the exception was George Brown, whose "*mission it seemed was to make the ball fly past the batsman's head.*"[2] Clearly, his mood had not improved significantly since the match at Portsmouth.

The following morning was dull and cloudy and there was a strong wind blowing down the ground. Kent lost their last two wickets for just five runs. Jack Newman was the pick of the Hampshire bowlers with 4-83 from 29 overs. "*The pitch was just as good as on Thursday and the outfield was, if anything, rather faster, so that it seemed more than likely that Hampshire's formidable batting side would make a very large score.*"[5] But matters didn't turn out quite as predicted. Their reply, although initially solid, fell away from an impressive 130-2 at lunch and 230-3 at tea to a disappointing 300 all out.

Johnston, though not at his best, put on 55 for the first wicket with Bowell. When he was out, Tennyson carried on the good work, hitting four fours and a six in a bright 38. Bowell, who survived a simple stumping chance at 56, was the third man out when he was caught by Huish. His 79, which combined "*clean hitting with good sense*", included ten boundaries. Mead was less fluent than usual and fell to a fine catch at deep point by Fielder.

Tennyson, however, "*began to score freely at once; for so forcing a batsman his back play is very severe, and he watches the ball very closely on to his bat. His methods are certainly attractive; he seldom plays forward, relying on hard forcing drives and very hard back play. By delightful cricket, he scored three quarters of the runs made while he was in and had bad luck in being caught off a good length ball from Blythe, which 'popped' and just touched the handle of his bat.*"[5]

Wally Hardinge – two hundreds at Dover making four in a row for the Kent opener
(Photograph courtesy of Richard and Helen Seymour)

Lionel Tennyson was one of the great eccentrics of the game. It was said he once attempted to amuse his fellow fielders during a dull passage in a Gentlemen vs Players match at Lords by laying odds of 10-1 that his grandfather had written *Hiawatha* and, "*as Hampshire captain, was never clear in his mind if he had hired his valet as wicket keeper or his wicket keeper as his valet.*"[6]

Blythe bowled his leg theory to Mead (as he often did to left-handers), with as many as seven fielders on the leg side, which restricted the scoring during the afternoon session. Late order stands between Abercrombie and Harold McDonell and then, when Carr trapped him lbw, Abercrombie and Jack Newman, added a further 30 before the innings was brought to a close at 300 at around a quarter past five. Blythe was the most successful bowler with 4-74 from 28 overs, reflecting the tight control he had maintained over the batsmen during the afternoon session.

"*The splendid Kent attack was skilfully handled by Mr Dillon. Hardinge's outfielding and return of the ball to the wicket was quite the feature of the day's play and Mr Dillon's return from the outfield to run Stone out was also a fine piece of work.*"[5]

Jim Seymour: 77 & 85   Douglas Carr: 6-143   Colin Blythe: 5-124

Kent had about an hour to bat before the close, and were tested by some very fast and aggressive bowling from Brown from the pavilion end. His effort was rewarded when Humphreys got an edge and was caught behind with the score on four, but Hardinge and Seymour stood firm for the rest of the session and ended the day on 69-1.

Kent began the final day with their lead at 193 and a declaration around lunchtime in their sights. Hardinge and Seymour batted to plan in scoring 90 in the first hour, and were only separated when the partnership had reached 155 in an hour and three quarters. Bowell took a fine catch falling forward to account for Seymour, whose 77 had contained ten boundaries – "*his play this year has improved in a marked degree.*"[7] Any hopes that the crowd may have had of a cameo innings from Woolley were again quickly dashed, and Hubble followed shortly afterwards. The *Evening News* reporter remarked that it was "*strange to see such a fine hitter scraping about for runs whilst his partner (Seymour) was scoring with ease.*"[7] Meanwhile, Hardinge proceeded serenely to his second century in the match, and his third in successive innings. "*Twice before in his career he has played two separate innings of a hundred in a first-class match – in 1911 against Hampshire also and in 1908, against Essex. He seems to have very much the same temperament as the late Arthur Shrewsbury and he and Seymour may on their form this season and particularly in this match, be compared as first and first wicket batsmen to Shrewsbury and William Gunn.*"[7]

At a quarter past one, play was interrupted by a sharp shower. On the resumption, and beneath clearing skies, the pair added a further 19 before Dillon declared, setting Hampshire 359 to win in three and a half hours – "*practically an impossible task against such a fine bowling side as Kent.*"[8]

EDWARD HUMPHREYS.

Edward Humphreys: Kent's other centurion at Dover

If Hampshire had any thoughts of chasing down the target, they were quickly dispelled when Johnston and Tennyson both fell to Carr in the space of 12 runs. Johnston was lured from his crease and stumped, and Tennyson edged one to slip where Woolley took the catch. Mead joined Bowell with the score at 42-2 and struck 30 out of 36 in just 20 minutes before being bowled by Blythe, who turned one through the gate. It was to be his only wicket of the innings.

The partnership between Bowell and the Hampshire captain, Edward Sprot, saw the best batting of the innings, as they took the score from 78 to 181 for the fourth wicket, and seemingly as near safety as made no odds. Kent had bowled well during the afternoon but the fielding was extremely lax. "*Three or four catches – not easy ones – were dropped, Mr Carr being the main sufferer, and the ground fielding was none too good; in fact several runs were given away by bad misfielding on the offside.*"[8] It was Fairservice who made the breakthrough by dismissing Sprot. He was caught by Dillon at deep long on from a soaring drive which not even the strong wind blowing down the ground could carry over the boundary. It was this dismissal that was the turning point of the match as "*one or two of the Hampshire batsmen appeared to lose their heads against Mr Carr, who was spinning the ball, especially from leg, far more quickly than he did before the interval.*"[8]

Dillon, who always seemed to have the happy knack of knowing which bowler was best suited to the moment, then removed Fairservice and brought

The Hon Lionel Hallam Tennyson

Woolley on from the River End. "*In a very few overs, the game was over amidst scenes of tremendous enthusiasm. The Kent bowling was very good indeed. Fairservice bowled well against the wind without any luck, and Woolley, who in conjunction with Mr Carr, did the mischief in the last half hour of the game, kept a wonderful length and was not apparently troubled by his injured finger. But it is to Mr Carr that the greatest credit is due; bowling from the pavilion end, he so unsettled the batsmen opposed to him.*"[8]

Woolley, described by the *Kentish Gazette & Canterbury Press* as Blythe's "*faithful understudy*", had experienced a relatively lean period with the ball since Maidstone, due largely to the finger injury he had been carrying. His four-wicket haul was a timely and welcome return to form.

The local press was understandably ecstatic over the result. The *Kent Messenger* described the collapse as "*sensational*" and complemented Kent for fielding "*like champions*" – Seymour's catch to finish off the innings was exceptional.[8] And the *Kentish Gazette & Canterbury Press* hailed a "*splendid snatched victory against one of the most powerful batting sides of the country.*"[9] The win "*delighted the crowd immensely*".[9] This is a very good example of the slightly one-eyed view taken by the county's press which we often encountered in the research for this book. The dropped catches and poor ground fielding referred to in the earlier quotation by *The Times* had been completely overlooked in the euphoria surrounding the moment of victory.

The game had been a huge commercial success too, as it was seen by more than 12,000 people who contributed to gate receipts of £266 18s 11d.

Sources

1   *Cricket Grounds of Kent* – Howard Milton: ACS 1992

2   *Kentish Gazette & Canterbury Press* 23rd August 1913

3   The Hon Lionel Hallam Tennyson was the grandson of the poet Alfred, Lord Tennyson and became the 3rd Baron on the death of his father in 1928. He played nine Test matches for England between 1913/14 (in South Africa under Johnny Douglas) and 1921 – when he was captain for three of the matches against Australia. As a result of his 1913 season he was one of *Wisden*'s Cricketers of The Year in 1914.

4   *The Star* 22nd August 1913

5   *The Times* 23rd August 1913

6   Benny Green *Some Cricket Eccentrics* Barclays World of Cricket 1980

7   *The Evening News* 23rd August 1913

8   *Kent Messenger* 30th August 1913

9   *Kentish Gazette & Canterbury Press* 30th August 1913

23rd August 1913	P	W	L	DWF	DLF	NC	Max	Pts	PtsPC
Kent	26	18	3	3	1	1	125	100	80.00%
Yorkshire	26	16	4	4	2	0	130	94	72.31%
Northamptonshire	20	13	2	1	4	0	100	72	72.00%
Surrey	24	11	4	5	4	0	120	74	61.67%
Middlesex	18	8	3	4	3	0	90	55	61.11%
Nottinghamshire	20	8	5	3	4	0	100	53	53.00%
Lancashire	25	7	10	7	0	1	120	56	46.67%
Sussex	26	8	11	4	3	0	130	55	42.31%
Warwickshire	23	7	11	2	3	0	115	44	38.26%
Gloucestershire	20	6	11	1	2	0	100	35	35.00%
Hampshire	23	6	11	2	4	0	115	40	34.78%
Worcestershire	18	4	8	1	4	1	85	27	31.76%
Derbyshire	19	4	11	2	2	0	95	28	29.47%
Leicestershire	20	4	12	1	3	0	100	26	26.00%
Essex	18	2	9	2	4	1	85	20	23.53%
Somerset	15	2	10	2	1	0	75	17	22.67%

Northamptonshire 1st Innings

Mr WH Denton	b Blythe	22
Mr JS Denton	lbw b Carr	41
RA Haywood	c Day b Carr	12
Mr SG Smith *	lbw b Carr	51
GJ Thompson	c Huish b Carr	7
CN Woolley	lbw b Carr	20
J Seymour	b Blythe	7
FI Walden	c Dillon b Carr	7
W Wells	c Woolley b Blythe	23
WA Buswell +	b Blythe	10
JV Murdin	not out	2
Extras	(5 lb)	5
Total	(all out, 65.2 overs)	**207**

FOW 1st Innings 1-54, 2-70, 3-87, 4-98, 5-156, 6-157, 7-167, 8-181, 9-205, 10-207

Northamptonshire 2nd Innings

	b Fielder	0
	c Huish b Fielder	35
	c Blythe b Carr	14
	b Day	108
	c Carr b Fielder	67
	c Blythe b Fielder	5
	lbw b Day	8
	lbw b Blythe	9
	c sub b Carr	17
	c Dillon b Blythe	8
	not out	4
	(10 b, 7 lb, 2 nb)	19
	(all out, 77.1 overs)	**294**

FOW 2nd Innings 1-3, 2-21, 3-119, 4-235, 5-243, 6-252, 7-256, 8-279, 9-289, 10-294

Kent bowling	O	M	R	W
Fielder	7	1	19	0
Day	5	0	23	0
Blythe	27.2	4	72	4
Carr	26	2	88	6

Kent bowling	O	M	R	W
Fielder	16	3	58	4
Day	17	0	56	2
Blythe	26.1	3	87	2
Carr	14	1	64	2
Humphreys	4	1	10	0

Kent 1st Innings

HTW Hardinge	c Seymour b Thompson	107
E Humphreys	c JS Denton b Murdin	58
J Seymour	b Wells	5
A Fielder	c JS Denton b Smith	8
JC Hubble	b Thompson	23
Mr EW Dillon *	c Buswell b Thompson	0
Mr AP Day	c Buswell b Thompson	23
FE Woolley	c Haywood b Wells	6
FH Huish +	not out	6
C Blythe	b Thompson	0
Mr DW Carr	run out	0
Extras	(1 b, 1 lb, 2 nb)	4
Total	(all out, 79 overs)	**240**

FOW 1st Innings 1-126, 2-151, 3-171, 4-204, 5-204, 6-217, 7-230, 8-234, 9-234, 10-240

Kent 2nd Innings

	b Wells	3
	c Buswell b Smith	54
	not out	114
	did not bat	
	lbw b Murdin	13
	lbw b Smith	0
	4b Murdin	54
	did not bat	
	[7] not out	1
	did not bat	
	did not bat	
	(17 b, 4 lb, 2 nb)	23
	(5 wickets, 76.3 overs)	**262**

FOW 2nd Innings 1-20, 2-125, 3-229, 4-255, 5-256

Northants bowling	O	M	R	W
Wells	17	1	44	2
Thompson	24	4	72	5
Smith	20	5	45	1
Woolley	6	1	16	0
JS Denton	7	0	43	0
Murdin	5	2	16	1

Northants bowling	O	M	R	W
Wells	23	7	75	1
Thompson	23	4	92	0
Smith	20	5	46	2
Murdin	10.3	3	26	2

Kent vs Northamptonshire

Crabble Athletic Ground, Dover
Monday 25th, Tuesday 26th & Wednesday 27th August
Toss: Northamptonshire[2]
Kent won by 5 wickets
Points: Kent 5 Northamptonshire 0

KENT MADE ONE change to the side that had beaten Hampshire the previous week, bringing in Day for Fairservice as they began their quest for the single point that would secure the 1913 Championship title.

There seems to be some question as to who won the toss in this match. *Cricket Archive* says it was Kent, who then elected to field, whereas *The Times* of 26th August 1913, says, "*Northamptonshire won the toss on what appeared to be a beautiful run getting wicket.*"[1] The *Kent Messenger* also says the toss was won by Northamptonshire. Given the reluctance of most captains during that era to insert the opposition, even on really wet wickets, it is perhaps asking a lot to believe that Dillon would have inserted the opposition in the circumstances that existed on that late summer day in Dover.[2]

The bowling was opened by Fielder and Day against the Denton brothers, Jack and Billy, (who, with the Seymours and Woolleys, made up the third set of

Sidney Smith – 51 & 108 to add to his 133 & 21 against Kent at Northampton

Douglas Carr: 6-88 & 2-64

brothers engaged in this match). After only half an hour, Dillon turned to his spinners for the rest of the innings (pun intended). The Dentons compiled 54 at over a run a minute for the first wicket, though Jack Denton was missed by Day in the slips in Fielder's opening over. During the course of their partnership, Frank Woolley sustained a thumb injury in attempting to take a catch, and although he returned to the action later in the innings and took another catch, he was unable to field on the second day when Northamptonshire batted for a second time. This injury also kept him out of Kent's final match at Lord's.

The introduction of Carr and Blythe, 16 runs later, changed matters immediately. Jack Denton, who had been particularly strong on the leg side, was the first to go, leg before to a full-length ball from Carr. His brother, who reached his 1,000 runs for the season for the first time during his innings, played on to Blythe. With Robert Haywood pouched by Day and Thompson superbly caught wide down the leg side by Huish, the visitors had been reduced to 98-4, with Carr taking three of the wickets. The Trinidad left-hander, Sidney Smith, and Frank Woolley's brother, Claude, steered the side to 136 by lunch for no further loss.

Smith, unquestionably the most successful batsman against Kent this season, having already made 133 and 21 in the fixture at Northampton, drove magnificently in his innings of 51 which contained eight fours. The partnership with Woolley stretched to 58 in three quarters of an hour before both were out in a single over from Carr. Then 156-5 became 207 all out as Blythe joined the party in taking three of the last five wickets to fall. Bowling an excellent length, he probably deserved better figures.

The Four Hundreds Club Members as at 1913
Tom Hayward, Wally Hardinge and Charles Fry

Despite good bowling and enthusiastic fielding from the visitors, Humphreys and Hardinge posted a century partnership in an hour and 20 minutes in the Kent reply. The former, who had hit five fours, was caught in the slips off the fourth change bowler, John Murdin. When Seymour played on at 151 shortly before the close, Dillon, already without the services of Woolley, chose to deploy a night-watchman, in this case Fielder rather than Blythe, who was the usual first choice in this role. The fast bowler did his job and Kent finished a thoroughly satisfactory first day at 158-2.

Starting the second morning on 90, Hardinge gave two chances, an easy catch to the first ball of the day and a stumping, before he completed his fourth successive century, which included 14 fours and took him 160 minutes. The *Evening News* reported that he received a "*remarkable ovation*". With his outstanding feat, attained in a week, he joined CB Fry in 1901 and Tom Hayward in 1906, although Charles Fry went on to make six centuries in a row. When Hardinge was fourth out at 204, Kent were in a formidable position, only four runs short of a first innings lead. But, notwithstanding some fine off-side strokes from Hubble and Day, the last six wickets made just 36, mainly because of an outstanding performance from the former England bowler George Thompson, who took 5-72. Woolley, who batted at number eight, was clearly incapacitated by his thumb injury and made only six, a victim of the other opening bowler, William Wells, who also had creditable figures of 2-44 from 17 overs. The pitch was becoming increasingly dry but this cannot be held up as an adequate excuse for the prospective Champions' collapse.

Northamptonshire would have been delighted to start their second innings with a deficit of just 33. Despite losing Billy Denton, who had his leg bail removed by Fielder with the score at three, and Robert Haywood on the stroke of lunch to a smart catch by Blythe off Carr 18 runs later, they spent the remainder of the second day constructing a challenging target for the home side to chase in the fourth innings. This was largely due to Sydney Smith, who topped his first innings half century by scoring a century.

Jack Denton, adopting the anchor role, helped the man who was proving to be the scourge of Kent bowlers this season, to add 98 for the third wicket before Fielder had him caught behind. This brought in Thompson who followed up his fine bowling with a brilliant 67. Made in and an hour and a half, *The Sportsman* reported it as " *full of lusty driving*",[3] as he assisted his captain, Smith, in a stand of 116. At the fall of his wicket, Northamptonshire were 235-4, with a lead of 202, and undoubtedly in the driving seat.

But without Woolley, the Kent attack stuck to its task. Day made the breakthrough, removing Smith's middle stump and following it up by trapping John Seymour leg before. Smith's superb 108 was made in two and a half hours and contained one six (off Blythe) and 13 fours. The spinners then finished off the innings, completing a creditable comeback by the home county. Four bowlers had shared the ten wickets, the last six of which had fallen for 59 runs. Although the innings had rather fallen away, 294 was a formidable total. Indeed, the *Kent Messenger* asserted that they had "*pulled the game round in remarkable fashion*".[4] With the final Northamptonshire wicket falling a few minutes before the scheduled close, stumps were drawn.

Kent had a complete day in which to score the 262 required to secure the Championship title. The *Kentish Gazette* expressed the general feeling amongst the Kent faithful, which numbered 6,983, at the end of the second day, that it was still a daunting task "*on a pitch upon which over 700 runs had been scored and which in the course of the two previous days' play had shown more than a suspicion of crumbling*".[5] Moreover, although

George Tompson: 5-72, and Arthur Fielder: 4-58

James Seymour – Kent's match winner against Northants at Dover
Seen here with his wife at St Lawrence, Canterbury later in his career
Courtesy of Mr & Mrs Richard Seymour

he had batted, at number eight in the first innings, Woolley's thumb injury was likely to prevent him making a significant contribution to the run chase.

The Times suggested that at the start of the final day "*Very few capable judges had any but the faintest hopes (or apprehensions as the case might be) that Kent would obtain 262 runs on a wicket that was showing distinct signs of wear; without any rain to bind it there was, indeed, good reason to suppose it would become worse.*"[6] Such misgivings about Kent's capacity to reach their target seemed to be justified when Hardinge was bowled by Wells after batting for 25 minutes for just three runs. Shrugging off this setback, Humphreys and Seymour played brightly, hitting 105 in 75 minutes. The driving of Humphreys, who made 20 in two overs off Thompson, was particularly impressive, but he fell to a "*lofty catch at the wicket*" off Smith. Day joined Seymour and the pair put on 104 in 70 minutes with brilliant stroke-play. "*Humphreys, Seymour and Mr A P Day all played like heroes and it was the magnificent batting of Seymour and Mr Day after the luncheon interval which practically gave Kent their victory.*"[5]

At 229, just 33 short of their target, Day, who had hit seven fours, became a victim of the worn wicket, when he played on to a ball that kept very low. Hubble, with 13, then helped Seymour to take Kent to within seven runs of the win before he was trapped leg before by John Murdin. Smith then dismissed Dillon in the same manner for his second "pair" in less than a fortnight, but these two wickets falling for the addition of only a single run was very much a case of too little, too late for Northamptonshire. Huish and Seymour collected the remaining six runs needed to complete their victory and as they made their way back to the pavilion 3,000 people "*cheered them to the echo*".

Of Seymour, who had batted for three hours and hit 12 boundaries, the *Kent Messenger* wrote that "*considering the conditions under which he played, a greater innings has seldom been seen. He batted for close upon three hours, and timed the ball so perfectly that he only made two false strokes, both of which were almost chances in the slips*".[4]

The Times was just as effusive, if perhaps a little more technical, about Seymour's innings: "*Seymour's play this year, and especially this month, has shown a wonderful improvement for a player of some 13 or 14 seasons. He gets over the rising ball with the greatest precision and has quite given up the plan of hanging his bat out on the offside at the beginning of an innings which so often used to lead to his downfall. He is far more upright in his position at the wicket and rivals Hobbs in the extraordinary number of strokes he has at his command. There were periods when he was none too comfortable especially when he attempted to force Mr Smith's spinning deliveries on the off side and he gave a chance, a difficult one, at slip to which Thompson did not move quickly enough but his was a great performance and he kept his hand splendidly.*"[6]

The scene in front of the pavilion was "*peculiarly soul-stirring and nerve thrilling*".[4] Each Kent player was loudly called for "*and as these smilingly appeared in turn deafening cheers were raised*". The crowd, magnanimous in victory, also called for the "*eminently sporting Northants side*" who were "*none the less heartily received*".[4]

The Times said, "*Mr Dillon and the Kent eleven are to be heartily congratulated on their victory, which in the circumstances was perhaps their best performance of the year, although their batting at Canterbury in the second match against Nottinghamshire runs it very close.*"[6]

Kent's two supporting batting acts: Arthur Day and Ted Humphreys – 54 each

The Denton twins: WH & JS

Sources

1   *The Times* 26th August 1913
2   Following discussions with *Cricket Archive* on the apparent discrepancy over the toss, they agreed to amend their records in the face of the evidence of the newspaper reports in *The Times* and the *Kent Messenger*.
3   *The Sportsman* 27th August 1913
4   *The Kent Messenger* 30th August 1913
5   *The Kentish Gazette & Canterbury Press* 28th August 1913
6   *The Times* 28th August 1913

28th August 1913	P	W	L	DWF	DLF	NC	Max	Pts	PtsPC
Kent	27	19	3	3	1	1	130	105	80.77%
Yorkshire	28	16	4	4	3	1	135	95	70.37%
Surrey	26	13	5	4	4	0	130	81	62.31%
Northamptonshire	22	12	4	1	5	0	110	68	61.82%
Nottinghamshire	20	8	5	3	4	0	100	53	53.00%
Middlesex	19	7	5	4	3	0	95	50	52.63%
Sussex	28	10	10	4	3	1	135	65	48.15%
Lancashire	26	7	11	7	0	1	125	56	44.80%
Gloucestershire	21	8	10	1	2	0	105	45	42.86%
Warwickshire	24	7	11	3	3	0	120	47	39.17%
Worcestershire	20	6	9	1	3	1	95	36	37.89%
Hampshire	25	6	11	4	4	0	125	46	36.80%
Derbyshire	18	4	10	2	2	0	90	28	31.11%
Leicestershire	21	4	13	1	3	0	105	26	24.76%
Essex	18	2	9	2	4	1	85	20	23.53%
Somerset	16	2	11	2	1	0	80	17	21.25%

Kent 1st Innings

E Humphreys	c Murrell b Weston	26
HTW Hardinge	lbw b JT Hearne	110
J Seymour	b Weston	3
Mr AP Day	b Weston	9
Mr JR Mason	b JW Hearne	11
Mr EW Dillon *	c Saville b JT Hearne	12
DW Jennings	lbw b JT Hearne	0
FH Huish +	lbw b Tarrant	20
Mr DW Carr	not out	25
C Blythe	b Tarrant	10
A Fielder	c Weston b JT Hearne	5
Extras	(4 b, 1 lb)	5
Total	(all out, 118.3 overs)	

FOW 1st Innings 1-50, 2-58, 3-70, 4-93, 5-135, 6-135, 7-182, 8-210, 9-225, 10-236

Kent 2nd Innings

	lbw b Tarrant	49
	c Murrell b Weston	1
	c JW Hearne b Weston	4
	c Tarrant b Weston	33
	b JW Hearne	4
	b Tarrant	2
	b JW Hearne	2
	b JW Hearne	8
	c Hendren b JW Hearne	0
	b Tarrant	1
	not out	3
	(12 b, 5 lb)	17
	(all out, 49.5 overs)	

FOW 2nd Innings 1-7, 2-29, 3-81, 4-94, 5-99, 6-102, 7-112, 8-113, 9-114, 10-124

Middlesex bowling	O	M	R	W
JT Hearne	26.3	11	50	4
Weston	34	7	81	3
JW Hearne	32	7	70	1
Tarrant	26	15	30	2

Middlesex bowling	O	M	R	W
JT Hearne	14	4	27	0
Weston	15	3	27	3
JW Hearne	7.5	0	34	4
Tarrant	12	4	18	3
Haig	1	0	1	0

Middlesex 1st Innings

Mr WP Robertson	b Fielder	15
FA Tarrant	c and b Day	6
JW Hearne	c Carr b Blythe	22
Mr PF Warner *	c Mason b Day	15
EH Hendren	c Huish b Blythe	2
Mr FT Mann	c Huish b Blythe	15
Mr SH Saville	c Huish b Day	10
Mr NE Haig	c Day b Blythe	8
Mr H Weston	not out	22
HR Murrell +	c Mason b Day	8
JT Hearne	b Fielder	2
Extras	(4 b, 2 lb)	6
Total	(all out, 44.4 overs)	**131**

FOW 1st Innings 1-21, 2-29, 3-57, 4-64, 5-75, 6-80, 7-94, 8-106, 9-116, 10-131

Middlesex 2nd Innings

	st Huish b Carr	47
	c Huish b Carr	15
	c Huish b Fielder	96
	st Huish b Carr	4
	c Huish b Humphreys	13
	c Day b Humphreys	0
	c Jennings b Humphreys	7
	[9] b Fielder	8
	[8] c Mason b Day	16
	b Day	9
	not out	1
	(5 b, 1 lb, 2 nb)	8
	(all out, 73.1 overs)	**224**

FOW 1st Innings 1-37, 2-99, 3-103, 4-129, 5-129, 6-151, 7-192, 8-207, 9-221, 10-224

Kent bowling	O	M	R	W
Fielder	7.4	1	30	2
Day	22	3	58	4
Blythe	15	1	37	4

Kent bowling	O	M	R	W
Fielder	10	4	21	2
Day	10.1	1	24	2
Blythe	24	6	59	0
Carr	20	2	84	3
Humphreys	9	2	28	3

Middlesex vs Kent

Lord's Cricket Ground,
St John's Wood
Thursday 28th, Friday 29th & Saturday 30th August
Toss: Kent
Kent won by five runs
Points: Middlesex 0 Kent 5

KENT TRAVELLED STRAIGHT to Lord's from Dover. Their previous visit to St John's Wood at the start of the season had been a less than happy occasion when they were beaten by MCC by an innings inside two days. This time, they arrived as Champions to play out what was the closest and probably the most exciting match of the season.

Kent made two changes to the side that played at the Crabble. Hubble and Woolley (who had sustained an injury to a thumb) were replaced by Mason and Jennings. This was Jack Mason's penultimate Championship match (he played one more against Gloucestershire the following year at the Mote), and his last match at Lord's. He played in two more games during the 1913 season for the Gentlemen vs Players and for Kent against Lord Londesborough's XI at Scarborough.

Dillon won the toss and had no hesitation in batting on a hard, fast wicket, in front of a paying crowd of 6,000. The batsmen, however, seemed in no hurry to put up the sort of score the occasion and circumstances called for. Humphreys and Hardinge had to bat well in the face of good bowling from "Old Jack" Hearne and Henry Weston, who bowled left arm at a slow-medium pace. The opening partnership was worth exactly 50 when Humphreys was caught behind by Joe Murrell for 26. Weston then bowled Seymour and Day in quick succession; *"the ball that bowled Seymour was a fine one that came up the hill some inches"*[1] to leave Kent 70-3. Mason followed shortly after, bowled by "Young" Jack Hearne.

Lunch was taken at 93-4 and *The Times* suggests *"it was the correct and sound batting of Hardinge that very likely prevented a collapse. After the luncheon interval*

The grandstand at Lord's 1898

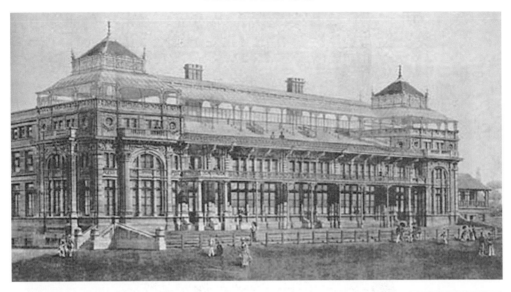

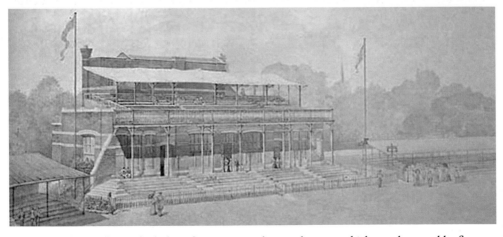

The Lord's Pavilion, which dates from 1890, and its predecessor, which was destroyed by fire

Wally Hardinge: fifth century in six innings

Mr Dillon was badly missed in the slips before he had scored and it was fortunate for Middlesex that they had not to pay a heavy penalty; but Mr Dillon never seemed to time the ball properly"[1] and after making 11, he was caught by Saville off the bowling of "Old Jack" Hearne.

Jennings went lbw to the same bowler for a duck and it fell to Huish and Carr to provide Hardinge with some much-needed support, so that he was able to complete his century before falling lbw to "Old Jack" Hearne. His 110, rather unusually, took four and a half hours and contained only eight fours. *The Times* describes his innings as *"a sound defensive innings and rather dull to watch... He crouches at the wicket but watches the ball all the way; his back play was exceedingly good but he is one of those batsmen who never really let themselves go for the ball."*[1] Not, perhaps, the kindest of remarks to make of a batsman who had just completed five hundreds in the course of his last six innings, and who had earlier been praised for preventing a batting collapse. *The Times* correspondent then goes on to say it was a relief to see the remaining batsmen (Carr and Blythe) *"hit the ball to the boundary"*.[1]

Kent were all out for 236 shortly after half past five and Middlesex survived around 12 minutes batting without loss, but not without some discomfort to the openers, William Robertson and Frank Tarrant, as Fielder, in particular, made them hop around. It was suggested that the ability of Fielder to get such lift out of the pitch must have made the Middlesex side wish they had a bowler of his pace. Middlesex did, however, have "Old Jack" Hearne who, in the course of the Kent innings, took the 3,000th wicket of his career. *"JT Hearne has probably bowled more balls in first-class cricket than any other bowler that has ever lived. He has never bowled a bad over..."*[1] At the time of this match, he was in his 47th year and did not retire from first-class cricket for another ten years – although he hardly bowled at all after 1914. In the course of his 35-year career, he took 3,061 first-class wickets at 17.65 each. He played for England ten times, taking 49 wickets at 22.08 each. His record would eventually be eclipsed by Charlie Parker (3,278), Tich Freeman (3,776) and Wilfred Rhodes with 4,204 wickets.[7]

The following morning, there was a heavy shower at around ten o'clock which, because the wicket was so dry, only delayed matters by 30 minutes, and play got underway shortly after noon. *The Times* says, *"Tarrant and Robertson went on with their innings but, as may be judged from the score, there is little to say about the Middlesex batting."*[2] The bowling, however, was testing. Day took a smart caught and bowled to remove Tarrant who had *"started to hit before he was set"*[2] and then Fielder bowled Robertson for 15. After this, Blythe and Day bowled accurately, and waited for the batsmen to make mistakes, which they did at frequent intervals.

By lunch, Middlesex were 94-6 and *"it must be said, the batting was indifferent. It was not a fast wicket but the batsmen shaped badly at the fast bowling of Mr Day. JW Hearne had batted well and then got under one from Blythe and was caught by Carr at mid-off."*[2]

While lunch was being taken, the rain returned again and play could not restart until a quarter to three when, after Blythe had removed Nigel Haig (the

The Middlesex veteran JT "Old Jack" Hearne, who took his 3,000th first-class wicket in the Kent first innings

nephew of Lord Harris), "*Mr Saville and Mr Weston played with confidence but then Mr Saville fell into the same trap as many of his colleagues and was caught at the wicket off a ball that got up a little.*" Weston continued to play well, hitting cleanly in playing "*the best of the side*"[2] but ran out of partners when Day had Murrill caught at slip by Mason and Fielder returned to clean bowl "Old Jack" Hearne. "*The bowling of Kent was, however, very good, and Huish's wicket-keeping was really fine*".[2] Day had taken 4-58 from 22 overs and Blythe 4-36 from 15. Fielder's workload had been light with 7.4 overs which yielded 2-30. *Wisden* comments that "*with the light defective and the ball rising awkwardly, Middlesex had little chance of getting on terms.*"[3]

By the time Kent batted for a second time, the weather had deteriorated to the extent that the light was "*very bad*" and rain showers interrupted play on several occasions. *The Times* says that the light was never good during the whole afternoon. The question of bad light prompted reference to a small controversy that had arisen a few weeks previously. On 7th August 1913 (during Canterbury Cricket Week), *The Times* had published a letter from Lord Harris regarding the matter of bad light [4]

The Times says: "*this letter has had its effect, for there was no appeal and, so far as could be seen, not once did the batsmen seem to experience any difficulty arising from the poorness of the light. This goes to show that the modern habit of stopping a game for bad light is, in nearly every case, unnecessary and uncalled for, and umpires are absurdly weak in allowing so many interruptions.*"[2] It is of course, possible that Lord Harris was at Lord's for the Kent match, and was watching from his traditional place in the

Two Middlesex "stars": Mr "Plum" Warner and Francis Tarrant

Arthur Day, in the nets at Lord's, and Ted Humphreys

Committee Room but, in any event, the matter would have been discussed with Ted Dillon following the appeals made against bad light during the final afternoon of the Surrey match at The Oval, only a few days after his Chairman's letter. No doubt the message would have been to the effect that Kent needed to set some kind of example.

Hardinge's purple patch came to an end when he was caught behind off Weston for a single, followed soon after by Seymour, who "*hit under a short ball from Mr Weston which was going up the hill with the bowler's arm and was caught at long-leg*" by "Young Jack" Hearne. This brought Day in to bat with Humphreys, and they put on 52 together. "*Mr Day is a most attractive batsman to watch. He comes down on the ball, making the most of his height and he could generally score off a short ball and his style resembles that of Mr C T Studd in the '80's.*"[2] High praise indeed. Day was out to what was the last ball of the day, edging Weston to Tarrant at slip to leave Kent on 81-3 with Humphreys not out 31. The Kent lead was 186 and *The Times* correspondent suggested, "*If no more rain falls, Kent's lead may prove not too large but the match is undoubtedly in their favour so far.*"[2]

The final day of the Championship season had the best weather of the match, but Middlesex made the most of the early morning dew which had freshened the wicket. This little bit of "juice" helped them sufficiently to take the remaining three wickets in about an hour for the addition of only 43 runs. "*Tarrant and J W Hearne carried all before them.*"[5]

Humphreys had batted stoically for his 49 but, apart from his partnership with Day, the innings was very disappointing. Kent's total of 124 all out set Middlesex 230 to win in a little under five hours. The wicket had offered the bowlers some assistance in the morning, although not as much as on the previous day, but, by the time the dew had evaporated, it was playing well again.

Kent opened the bowling with Fielder and Day, but Robertson and Tarrant scored freely, and after half an hour, the score stood at 37. Fielder was removed from the attack and Blythe came on to bowl economically. Carr was introduced at the other end and was immediately successful, persuading Tarrant to cut at a ball turning away from the off stump which he edged to Huish. Robertson and "Young" Jack Hearne then batted soundly to take the score to 77-1 at lunch.

After the interval, the batsmen played with more freedom as the wicket dried out further and batting became even easier, but on 99, Robertson was out "*to a smart piece of stumping*" by Huish off the bowling of Carr. "*Mr Robertson had played splendid cricket for 85 minutes and his driving and cutting had been especially good.*"[5] Four runs later, "Plum" Warner was also stumped by Huish to leave the home side

Two of the Kent wicket takers in the final match against Middlesex at Lord's, 1913:
"Punter" Humphreys and "Daddy" Carr

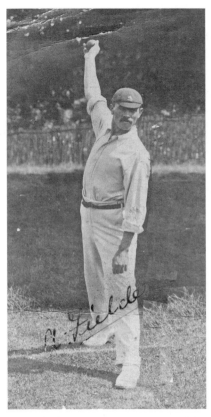 

The other two Kent wicket takers in the final match against Middlesex at Lord's, 1913:
"Pip" Fielder and "Happy" Day

on 104 for three and needing a further 126 to win. The dismissal brought Patsy Hendren to the wicket, who together with Hearne scored freely enough to persuade Dillon to remove Carr from the attack.

With the score at 120-3, the introduction of Humphreys meant left-arm orthodox spin from both ends as Blythe was still wheeling away and conceding very few runs at the other end. The move proved immediately successful as Humphreys dismissed Hendren, caught behind for 13 and, with his next ball, had Frank Mann *"brilliantly caught high up with his left hand by Mr Day, who ran from cover point to behind point"*[5] to reduce Middlesex to 129 for five and leave the match evenly poised. Middlesex needed 101 runs with half their wickets remaining, but with "Young Jack" Hearne batting well. Stanley Saville helped him add 22 runs before being caught by Jennings off Humphreys. Weston, who had batted so well in the first innings, was promoted and again proved a thorn in Kent's side. He and Hearne added 41 for the seventh wicket.

It was around this time that the Kent captain had to leave the field through an injury to his right hand. Mason took over the captaincy and brought Fielder back into the attack (he had been indisposed for much of the day). Early in his spell, Hearne, who looked as if he was going to win the match for the home side, got a thin edge and was caught by Huish four short of a well-deserved hundred. One hundred and ninety-two for seven. Thirty-three to win – with three wickets to fall.

"*Mr Mason… kept Fielder on at one end and changed Mr Day and Mr Carr very skilfully at the other*"[5] but gradually, despite the wiles of the veteran skipper, Weston and Haig edged the score upwards to 206-7 at tea. At that stage, Middlesex looked to be firm favourites but, immediately afterwards, the balance swung decisively in Kent's favour. *The Times* said, "*as so often happens, this* (the interval) *proved disastrous for the batting side. Only one more run, a leg-bye, was scored when Fielder bowled Mr Haig with a beautiful ball.*"[5] It was now 207-8. Twenty-three to win – two wickets to fall!

Fourteen more runs had been added when Fielder produced a ball which moved late to find the edge of Weston's bat and the ever reliable Mason took the catch at slip. 221-9. Nine to win – one wicket to fall !

Two overs later, with four more runs added and Middlesex needing only six to win, Day deceived wicketkeeper Murrill, who mistimed his shot and was bowled off the first ball of the over to give Kent their 20th and final victory of the Championship season. Carr with 3-84 and Humphreys with 3-28 had been the main wicket takers with two each for Fielder and Day. Strangely, Blythe went wicketless in the second innings but his steadiness in the late morning and afternoon had allowed Dillon and Mason to attack with the other bowlers. Despite failing to take a wicket in his 24 overs, Blythe too had played his part in this fine team performance.

The display of Fred Huish behind the stumps had been outstanding, securing him eight victims in the match for the second time in the Championship this season (the other being Leicestershire at Leicester). In the final match of the season against

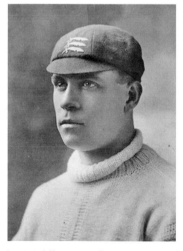

Another Middlesex worthy: Patsy Hendren

Lord Londesborough's XI at Scarborough, he would repeat the feat. On three other occasions, his victims numbered six and *"his share in gaining the Championship was an important one."*[5]

This had been, with the possible exception of the Warwickshire match at Tonbridge, the most exciting game of the season and in a way it was a shame this match couldn't have determined the outcome of the Championship. *Cricket Magazine* put it thus:

"Kent very nearly came a cropper in their last game of the season. It would have been distinctly a pity if they had done so, for they have most worthily earned the honours of the season. Day in and day out, plumb pitch or wet wicket, they have proved themselves the side of the year. Gloucestershire and Nottinghamshire beat them inside ten days; but these happenings left us wondering – they were not at all according to the book of form. And Surrey beat them in an innings at The Oval, a result less surprising. But when one remembers that match somehow the splendid efforts of Dillon and Day to save the game bulks larger in the memory than anything else – which may be unfair to Surrey, but is a sign of the glamour which Kent exercises even upon the mind of one whose dearest cricket interests are elsewhere than in the Garden of England." [6]

As *Cricket* says, Kent had been too consistent throughout the season and despite their reverses, they were never really under any significant threat of being overtaken. Although they languished in second place for about 14 days in June after "dropping" two points against Yorkshire at Bradford, it was a virtual "pillar to post" victory. Something *Cricket Magazine* summed up quite well in saying: *"Kent very nearly came a cropper in their last game of the season. It would have been distinctly a pity if they had done so, for they have most worthily earned the honours of the season. Day in and day out, plumb pitch or wet wicket, they have proved themselves the side of the year. Gloucestershire and Nottinghamshire beat them inside ten days; but these happenings left us wondering – they were not at all according to the book of form. And Surrey beat them in an innings at The Oval, a result less surprising. But when one remembers that match somehow the splendid efforts of Dillon and Day to save the game bulks larger in the memory than anything else – which may be unfair to Surrey, but is a sign of the glamour which Kent exercises even up on the mind of one whose dearest cricket interests are elsewhere than in the Garden of England."*

Sources

1   *The Times* 29th August 1913
2   *The Times* 30th August 1913
3   *Wisden* 1914 Middlesex matches p114
4   See chapter on Surrey vs Kent at the Oval for the letter of Lord Harris dated 3rd August 1913
5   *The Times* 1st September 1913
6   *Cricket Magazine* 6th September 1913
7   See Authors' Notes regarding Wilfred Rhodes' total wickets

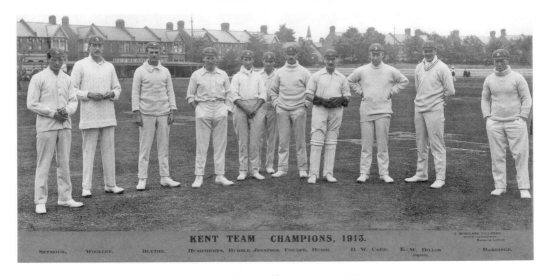

KENT TEAM — CHAMPIONS, 1913.

SEYMOUR, WOOLLEY, BLYTHE, HUMPHREYS, HUBBLE, JENNINGS, FIELDER, HUISH, D. W. CARR, E. W. DILLON, HARDINGE.

Kent as County Champions in 1913
J Seymour, FE Woolley, C Blythe, E Humphreys, JC Hubble, DW Jennings, A Fielder, FH Huish
Mr DW Carr, Mr EW Dillon, HTW Hardinge
The photograph is of the side that played against Essex at Leyton at the beginning of
August, long before the outcome of the Championship was properly determined.
Photograph courtesy of Mr and Mrs Richard Seymour

30th August 1913	P	W	L	DWF	DLF	NC	Max	Pts	PtsPC
Kent	28	20	3	3	1	1	135	110	81.48%
Yorkshire	28	16	4	4	3	1	135	95	70.37%
Surrey	26	13	5	4	4	0	130	81	62.31%
Northamptonshire	22	12	4	1	5	0	110	68	61.82%
Nottinghamshire	20	8	5	3	4	0	100	53	53.00%
Middlesex	20	7	6	4	3	0	100	50	50.00%
Sussex	28	10	10	4	3	1	135	65	48.15%
Lancashire	26	7	11	7	0	1	125	56	44.80%
Gloucestershire	22	8	11	1	2	0	110	45	40.91%
Hampshire	26	7	11	4	4	0	130	51	39.23%
Warwickshire	24	7	11	3	3	0	120	47	39.17%
Worcestershire	20	6	9	1	3	1	95	36	37.89%
Derbyshire	18	4	10	2	2	0	90	28	31.11%
Leicestershire	22	4	13	1	4	0	110	27	24.55%
Essex	18	2	9	2	4	1	85	20	23.53%
Somerset	16	2	11	2	1	0	80	17	21.25%

Three days after Kent's match with Middlesex was concluded, **on 3rd** September 1913, *Vanity Fair* published a caricature of the Kent Captain, **Edward** Wentworth Dillon under the title of "The Champion County". Dillon is drawn by Owl (whose identity has never been established), resting his weight on his bat dressed in cricket kit, wearing his Band of Brothers blazer and Kent cap. The text on the adjoining page read:

MR EDWARD WENTWORTH DILLON

Kent's yearly challenge for the County Championship dates from Mr Dillon's acceptance of the captaincy in 1909. In that year and in 1910, Kent were Champions. In 1911 they were second in the list and in 1912, third. This year they are Champions again.

Mr Dillon began playing cricket for Kent in 1900 when he was still at Rugby. He was in the Oxford XI's of 1901 and 1902. His university career, like that of many other great men, was abbreviated.

He has a way of making a pair of spectacles and has accomplished this feat twice this season. But he is still fonder of making a "duck" in the first innings and a century in the second. This is almost a hobby with him.

His bowling average is remarkable and, if he was not too good a sportsman to care about averages, the topic might become irksome. It will suffice to say that he does not head the list. Mr Dillon is captain of the most sporting county. I wish him luck

1913
Men of the Day No 2399

VANITY FAIR Supplement, No. 2339.

MEN OF THE DAY.

"The Champion County"

Lord Londesborough's XI 1st Innings

JB Hobbs (Surrey)	lbw b Fairservice	1
W Rhodes (Yorks)	c Mason b Carr	19
JW Hearne (Middx)	c Troughton b Blythe	102
AE Relf (Sussex)	lbw b Mason	32
Mr GA Faulkner (Transvaal)	c Huish b Fielder	17
Mr GL Jessop * (Glos)	c Huish b Fielder	116
JW Hitch (Surrey)	st Huish b Carr	12
MW Booth (Yorks)	c Huish b Carr	0
Mr HL Simms (Sussex)	c Jennings b Carr	0
SF Barnes (Staffs)	c Huish b Fielder	7
Mr WS Bird+ (Middx)	not out	0
Extras	(19 b, 2 nb, 1 w)	22
Total	(all out, 65.1 overs)	**328**

FOW 1st Innings 1-1, 2-52, 3-141, 4-185, 5-187, 6-220, 7-220, 8-248, 9-323, 10-328

Lord Londesborough's XI 2nd Innings

	c Huish b Humphreys	27
	c Mason b Fielder	6
	c Carr b Humphreys	45
	c Huish b Carr	4
	c Humphreys b Carr	24
	c Huish b Carr	8
	c Mason b Carr	5
	not out	26
	c Hubble b Fairservice	36
	c Fairservice b Mason	17
	c Fairservice b Mason	10
Extras	(1 b, 6 lb, 5 nb)	12
Total	(all out, 46.2 overs)	**220**

FOW 2nd Innings 1-14, 2-66, 3-85, 4-105, 5-116, 6-124, 7-128, 8-185, 9-204, 10-220

Kent bowling	O	M	R	W
Fielder	17.1	1	83	3
Fairservice	11	1	21	1
Carr	12	1	79	4
Blythe	16	1	72	1
Mason	8	1	40	1
Humphreys	1	0	11	0

Kent bowling	O	M	R	W
Fielder	11	1	36	1
Fairservice	11	1	50	1
Humphreys	12	0	64	2
Carr	9	2	41	4
Mason	3.2	0	17	2

Kent 1st Innings

Mr JR Mason*	b Booth	0
E Humphreys	c Faulkner b Barnes	8
J Seymour	b Barnes	2
JC Hubble	lbw b Rhodes	51
Mr LHW Troughton	c Relf b Booth	15
DW Jennings	b Booth	0
FH Huish +	c Hitch b Booth	5
WJ Fairservice	c Relf b Booth	1
Mr DW Carr	b Rhodes	2
C Blythe	run out	6
A Fielder	not out	0
Extras	(14 b, 4 lb, 1 nb)	19
Total	(all out, 39.2 overs)	**109**

FOW 1st Innings 1-0, 2-5, 3-18, 4-66, 5-66, 6-83, 7-85, 8-99, 9-105, 10-109

Kent 2nd Innings

	c Bird b Barnes	2
	c Relf b Booth	2
	c and b Barnes	12
	b Barnes	2
	c Barnes b Hitch	34
	c Rhodes b Barnes	16
	st Bird b Barnes	7
	b Hitch	14
	not out	6
	b Hitch	0
	b Barnes	1
	(6 b)	6
	(all out, 32.2 overs)	**102**

FOW 2nd Innings 1-4, 2-6, 3-13, 4-26, 5-42, 6-54, 7-80, 8-101, 9-101, 10-102

Lord Lond'gh bowling	O	M	R	W
Barnes	15	5	40	2
Booth	18	2	38	5
Relf	5	2	3	0
Rhodes	1.2	0	9	2

Lord Lond'gh bowling	O	M	R	W
Barnes	16.2	6	39	6
Booth	4	0	18	1
Relf	3	1	5	0
Hitch	9	0	34	3

Lord Londesborough's XI vs Kent

North Marine Road, Scarborough
on Tuesday 8th, Wednesday 9th & Thursday
10th September 1913
Toss: Lord Londesborough's XI
Lord Londesborough's XI won by 337 runs

WITH THEIR FOURTH Championship in eight years secured, Kent set about tidying up the season with a series of "festival matches" and dinners to celebrate their win.

Having finished at Lord's on 30th August, most of the side travelled to the market town of Attleborough in Norfolk to play for Mr JR Mason's XI at Buckenham Hall against Mr Lionel Robinson's XI in a match starting on 1st September. Lionel Robinson was an extremely wealthy Australian stockbroker who had purchased the estate with a view to creating the facilities to indulge his passion for sport which centred on cricket, shooting and racehorses. He engaged the former England captain Archie McLaren as his cricket manager and a mixture of first-class and other fixtures were played at Buckenham Hall between 1911 and 1921. The opponents included the South African touring XI in 1912 and the Australian touring side in 1921. The match against JR Mason's XI was played over three days and was deemed first class. No play was possible on the first day and the match was drawn. Jim Seymour scored 69 for the former Kent captains' XI which brought up his 2,000 first-class runs for the season.

A few days off was followed by a trip north to play Lord Londesborough's XI at the Scarborough Festival on 8th, 9th and 10th September.

William Francis Henry Denison, 2nd Earl Londesborough, was one of the largest landowners in Yorkshire and a major patron of cricket and other sports in the

Marine Parade, Scarborough in 1913

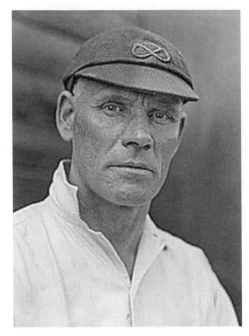

Captain of Lord Londesborough's XI, Mr Gilbert Jessop and Sydney Barnes, the main wicket taker with 8-79

county. He lived at Blankney Hall, which the first Earl (as Baron Londesborough) bought from Sir Henry Chaplin, "The Squire of Blankney", in 1882. His interest in cricket was fostered by his father, the first Earl, who arranged the first recorded Lord Londesborough's XI fixtures against Harrow Wanderers at Grimstone Park, Tadcaster and Scarborough Visitors XI at the Castle Hill Ground, Scarborough, both in 1871.

First-class matches were played against the Australians in 1886, 1888 and 1890. The 2nd Earl succeeded to the title in 1900 and the Londesborough patronage of the end of season festival resumed eight years later when his XI played MCC. Thereafter, Lord Londesborough's XI played the touring party or an MCC XI based on the side to tour, either South Africa or Australia, every year up to the war. The only exception to matches against the tourists was in 1913, when the opposition was Kent.

Troughton, Jennings and Fairservice replaced Hardinge, Day and Dillon from the side that played at Lord's. This was Lionel Troughton's second appearance in the Kent XI during the summer, his previous outing having been at The Parks against Oxford University. His season had been spent captaining the 2nd XI. By this stage of the season, it was already known that Ted Dillon was to retire as captain and that Troughton was to take his place in 1914. This was one of the few instances of an uncapped player being appointed to lead the county, although Kent later made similar appointments with John Evans in 1927 and David Clark in 1947.

Those ranged against them at Scarborough were as near an England side as made no difference: Jack Hobbs, Wilfred Rhodes, "Young" Jack Hearne, Albert Relf, Mr Aubrey Faulkner, Mr Gilbert Jessop (captain), Bill Hitch, William Booth, Mr Herbert Simms, Sydney Barnes and Mr Wilfred Bird.

Jessop won the toss and batted in delightful weather in front of a large festival crowd. Kent made early inroads into His Lordship's batting by dismissing Hobbs and Rhodes relatively cheaply for 52. Jack Hearne, however, gave "*a great batting display... he went for the off ball far oftener than he usually does and some of his off-drives off Fielder were so well timed that they were almost worthy of Tyldesley.*"[1] The real fireworks of the innings, unsurprisingly, came from Jessop, who arrived at the wicket with the score at 185-4. His hundred came up in only 55 minutes and the innings contained 19 fours and four sixes. "*Besides placing the ball out of harm's way so cleverly, Mr Jessop scored many 4's by hitting some well-pitched balls on the off side along the ground to deep square leg. He also made several slicing drives off Fielder which went off the face of the bat over the slips heads, an apparently dangerous stroke, which he executed with perfect safety.*"[1] He was dropped once when he had scored 53 from a mishit off Carr, but in his next over, he hit three sixes and two fours – two square cuts and three off drives out of the ground. This was to be Jessop's last first-class hundred – the 53rd of his career. The next year saw him play only nine matches for Gloucestershire plus the two Gentlemen vs Players matches and once for MCC. A fitting conclusion to a sparkling career.

Lionel Troughton

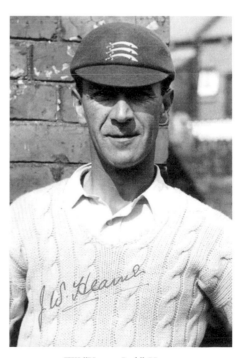

JW "Young Jack" Hearne

Marine Parade, Scarborough looking towards the pavilion

The innings closed at 328 with Carr taking 4-70, despite his mauling at the hands of Jessop. Kent made a pitiful start to their innings, losing Mason, Humphreys and Seymour for 18 runs before Hubble and Troughton stood firm until stumps were drawn at 37-3.

The next morning dawned much colder, with a strong east wind blowing across the ground. The sun still shone but the first signs of autumn were in the air. *"Except for a fine innings by Hubble, the last seven Kent wickets offered a poor resistance in their first innings. Mr Troughton shaped fairly well and hit a fine golfing straight drive for 6 off Booth."*[2] There had been some rain overnight and this was sufficient to assist Barnes and Booth – not that Barnes needed any help at any time in his career, and Booth was enjoying his best season in which he took 181 wickets, which earned him a place on the 1913/14 tour to South Africa, together with Frank Woolley.

"These two bowlers made the ball get up to a nasty height well above the stumps, so that they were very difficult indeed to play, and any attempt to force the ball away always involved considerable risk of a catch in the slips."[2] The innings closed for a miserable 109 before lunch. *"Hubble's innings was a fine display of well timed off side play. For so short a man Hubble uses his height wonderfully well in getting over the ball and timing it with ease and his style is certainly very attractive especially when playing fast medium or fast bowling."*[2] Booth returned the excellent figures of 5-38 from 18 overs.

Jessop decided not to enforce the follow-on despite Kent being 219 in arrears, and the batsmen pressed on with a view to a declaration after tea. Hearne, Simms and Booth were the main contributors to the second innings total of 220, scored at over 4.75 runs per over. Carr was again the best bowler with 4-41 from nine overs. Mason picked up the last two wickets for 17 and also made two splendid catches to dismiss Rhodes and Hitch.

Kent had 30 minutes' batting before the close, were reduced to 13-3, but improved to 32-4 by stumps, with Barnes collecting the wickets of Mason, Seymour and Hubble, while Booth had Humphreys caught at slip by Relf. "*Lord Londesborough's England XI were too good for the moderate Kent side and at the close of play they needed 408 runs to win with six wickets in hand – practically an impossible task against the splendid bowling of the England XI.*"[2]

There was little respite for Kent on the next morning as Barnes, with the support of Hitch, picked up the remaining six wickets with little trouble; "*and but for a very plucky and sound innings by Mr LHW Troughton, the batting was really bad.*" The margin of victory was a huge 337 runs. "*The form of the Kent eleven was certainly not worthy of a great side, nor even a good one. Kent lost a good deal by losing the toss it is true but with the exception of Hubble and Mr Troughton they all batted with an air of desperation which proclaimed them a beaten side early in the game.*"[3]

At the time, this was the highest "runs" defeat in the history of Kent but, unfortunately, it has since been relegated to the third highest.

Sources

1   *The Times* 9th September 1913
2   *The Times* 10th September 1913
3   *The Times* 11th September 1913

Aubrey Faulkner, the South African leg spinner

Kent & Yorkshire XI 1st Innings

E Humphreys (Kent)	c Jessop b Smith	16
W Rhodes (Yorks)	lbw b Barnes	17
J Seymour (Kent)	c Strudwick b Smith	4
A Drake (Yorks)	c Jessop b Barnes	23
GH Hirst (Yorks)	lbw b Barnes	0
JC Hubble	c Relf b Smith	4
MW Booth (Yorks)	not out	38
FH Huish + (Kent)	b Relf	16
Sir AW White * (Yorks)	b Hearne	14
C Blythe (Kent)	c and b Hearne	2
A Fielder (Kent)	c Hearne b Barnes	10
Extras	(4 b, 6 lb)	10
Total	(all out, 69 overs)	**154**

FOW 1st Innings 1-31, 2-37, 3-45, 4-45, 5-64, 6-68, 7-104, 8-128, 9-130, 10-154

Kent & Yorkshire XI 2nd Innings

	lbw b Barnes	7
	c Hitch b Barnes	9
	run out	0
	b Barnes	4
	c Hitch b Smith	9
	c Gunn b Barnes	2
	c Strudwick b Barnes	20
	not out	10
	c Hearne b Barnes	0
	run out	0
	st Strudwick b Barnes	5
	(1 lb)	1
	(all out, 32.2 overs)	**67**

FOW 2nd Innings 1-13, 2-13, 3-19, 4-28, 5-30, 6-31, 7-62, 8-62, 9-62, 10-67

The Rest bowling	O	M	R	W
Barnes	32	12	59	4
Smith	22	4	53	3
Relf	7	3	12	1
Hearne	6	1	17	2
Hitch	2	1	3	0

The Rest bowling	O	M	R	W
Barnes	16.2	10	20	7
Smith	13	5	32	1
Hearne	3	0	14	0

The Rest 1st Innings

JB Hobbs (Surrey)	c White b Booth	23
G Gunn (Notts)	b Booth	25
JW Hearne (Middx)	c White b Booth	14
Mr PF Warner (Middx) *	b Drake	28
CP Mead (Hants)	b Hirst	43
Mr GL Jessop (Gloucs)	c Booth b Fielder	9
Mr SG Smith (Northants)	c Booth b Humphreys	32
AE Relf (Sussex)	c Hubble b Humphreys	17
JW Hitch (Surrey)	c Booth b Blythe	18
SF Barnes (Staffs)	not out	17
+H Strudwick	c Blythe b Humphreys	18
Extras	(9 b, 10 lb, 3 nb)	22
Total	(all out, 83.4 overs)	**266**

FOW 1st Innings 1-53, 2-71, 3-84, 4-120, 5-133, 6-189, 7-197, 8-216, 9-235, 10-266

Kent & Yorks bowling	O	M	R	W
Blythe	20	6	65	1
Drake	14	2	33	1
Hirst	10	2	32	1
Booth	13	2	26	3
Fielder	9	2	21	1
Rhodes	7	0	26	0
Humphreys	10.4	1	41	3

The Rest vs Kent & Yorkshire

Kennington Oval
Tuesday 15th, Wednesday 16th, Thursday
17th September 1913
Toss: The Rest
The Rest won by an innings and 45 runs

WHILE THE GAME at Scarborough was in progress, it emerged that the match scheduled for the following week, in which Kent, as the Champion County, would play The Rest at The Oval, was in doubt because Kent would be unable to field a representative side due to injuries to, and unavailability of, key players. As a result of some last-minute negotiation between Kent, Surrey and Yorkshire, it was decided to field a combined Kent & Yorkshire XI. It was originally intended the side would be captained by Lionel Troughton, but eventually it was the Yorkshire skipper who would lead the team, which, with the exception of himself, was composed entirely of professionals: Mr Archie White (captain), Ted Humphreys, James Seymour, Colin Blythe, Arthur Fielder, Fred Huish, George Hirst, Wilfred Rhodes, David Denton, William Booth and Alonzo Drake.

The Rest were scarcely less formidable than the side Kent had faced at Scarborough: Jack Hobbs, George Gunn, "Young" Jack Hearne, Mr Pelham Warner (captain), Philip Mead, Mr Gilbert Jessop, Mr Sydney Smith, Albert Relf, Bill Hitch, Sydney Barnes and Herbert Strudwick.

The match started on Monday 15th September and was scheduled to last four days. There had been rain in London over the weekend and again on the morning of the match, so that play was delayed until midday. Further rain in the afternoon limited play to only two and a half hours. "Plum" Warner won the toss, and in a change from the normal convention at the time, invited Kent to make first use of a wet wicket. Humphreys and Rhodes made a fair start against Barnes and Smith, but with the score at 31, Smith *"lured Humphreys out to hit. He hit the ball hard and low to extra cover point, and Mr Jessop, who during part of the innings was one of the trio of great offside fieldsmen, Hobbs and Hitch being the others, made a good catch."*[1]

Seymour came in at three, and after hitting a four off Barnes, was caught at the wicket off Smith. None of the batsmen could make much of the bowling on the damp pitch, and wickets fell at regular intervals. At 68-6, Booth and Huish came together to make 36 for the seventh wicket, the highest partnership of the innings. Booth played well for his 27 not out at stumps, leaving just Fielder to bat in the morning with Kent & Yorkshire on 130-9.

The Times said Booth *"had played a valuable innings for his side. He is not an attractive bat to watch and he does not appear to play the stroke right although he watches the ball well, and he made some good drives and got Mr Smith's bowling away on the leg side cleverly. The Rest of England, who have a fine batting side, are in a good position, but there is no telling what the wicket may do ...if it is difficult, Blythe may be too good for the best of batsmen. Records and averages may easily be made too much of, but they do possess interest for a large section of the cricket public, and many of these at the Oval are keenly interested as to whether Mead or Hobbs will score the highest aggregate of runs for the year, who will head the batting averages, and other such questions, all of which this match will decide."*[1]

Booth and Fielder delayed the inevitable for a short while on the second morning, adding a valuable 24 for the last wicket. At 154, Barnes had Fielder caught by Hearne to secure his fourth wicket at a cost of 59 runs.

By the time The Rest began their innings, the wicket had dried and Hobbs and Gunn experienced little difficulty against Blythe and Drake. Drake gave way to Booth at the Pavilion End and had Hobbs caught for 23 at mid on, when he attempted to play to square leg and got a leading edge. Gunn was bowled round

The Rest of England vs Kent & Yorkshire at The Oval 1913
JB Hobbs, Mr PF Warner, G Gunn
JW Hearne, CP Mead, Mr GL Jessop, Mr SG Smith, AE Relf
JW Hitch, SF Barnes, H Strudwick

his legs by Booth – "*he is apt to step in front of his wicket in the modern style, and he paid the penalty.*" Lunch was taken at 84-2, and afterwards "*the play was not very enlivening… Sir A White took a fine catch at mid off over his head from a hard drive by Hearne… but two more wickets fell before the Counties score was passed, those of Mr Warner and Mr Jessop who, to the general disappointment, failed.*" Eventually, Hirst bowled Mead for 43 and, soon afterwards, Smith was caught at short leg off Humphreys. "*Mr Smith's defence is curious to watch. He hardly lifts the bat at all and seems to play the stroke with a flick at the last minute. But he has good wrists and he made some fine straight drives.*"[2]

Before the next batsman could arrive at the wicket, the players were driven off by rain, putting an end to play for the day with The Rest at 197-7 – a lead of just 43. The "*average watchers*" found something to interest them too. "*Hobbs, Mead and Gunn are all candidates for the highest batting average of the year. Hobbs and Gunn both brought theirs down, as also did Mead, but in a lesser degree. When Hobbs went in yesterday, he was two behind Mead in the aggregate of runs for the season; when he was out, he was 21 ahead, and then Mead, by scoring 43, put himself 22 in front again.*"[2]

There was heavy overnight rain in London, and play could not get underway at the Oval until two o'clock – and by five o'clock, the match was over. The Rest decided on quick runs, and added 69 in 45 minutes before being bowled out for 266. Relf, Hitch, Barnes and Strudwick all contributed with Hitch hitting Blythe for two huge sixes. Apparently, it was a case of "do unto others, before you are done unto."

When the combined counties batted again, the wicket had already become more difficult, and it was really a case of whether they could make The Rest bat for a second time. In the event, they never really looked like making a fight of it. Six wickets went down for 31 with Barnes exploiting the helpful surface. For the second time in the match, Booth and Huish provided some resistance, putting on 31 for the seventh wicket with some aggressive strokes; "*it was a wicket on which hitting paid.*" After Booth was well caught by Strudwick, the rest of the innings folded quickly for 67 in only 32.2 overs.

"*It was a pity the match came to an end so soon, but at the same time a great performance by the greatest bowler of the day was no bad finish to the first-class cricket season. Barnes had, of course, a wicket that suited him, an unpleasant wicket to bat on, no doubt, though perhaps not quite so difficult as to excuse a score of 67. Barnes bowled unchanged and took seven wickets in 16.2 overs for 20 runs. After he secured his first wicket, that of Rhodes, he took the other six in 12.2 overs for 10 runs and four of these 10 runs were hit by Fielder from the last but one ball of the game. In the match, Barnes took 11 wickets for 79 runs.*"[3] Over two weeks Sydney Barnes had played against Kent in three matches (including the match for Lionel Robinson's XI against JR Mason's XI), taking a total of 26 wickets at under ten each.

Sydney Barnes
"the greatest bowler of the day" – The Times

Even though Kent had finished the season with a sizeable defeat, it couldn't take away their Championship title, but it must have been a disappointing end to what had otherwise been a fine season. Kent's 1913 Championship title is sometimes regarded as the least of their four titles in this era. That does not entirely accord with our own impressions of the season for reasons that will become clear later. It is certainly true that the last two matches produced disappointing results, and this may have detracted from the overall impression of their achievements in the eyes of some commentators. In defence of Kent at Scarborough, and the combined side at The Oval, the sides they met in these two matches were virtually full England sides. It was not unusual for the Champion County to receive something of a drubbing in this, the final match of the season and, with the majority of the side being from Yorkshire, Kent's culpability in defeat could be seen as relatively minor!

Sources
1   *The Times* 16th September 1913
2   *The Times* 17th September 1913
3   *The Times* 18th September 1913

The Spoils of War

AT THE END of the season, the players were fêted and given the usual formal dinners at Canterbury and elsewhere. As in previous Championship years, they were also presented with a memento of the season by the County Club, a silver page turner by Henry Wigfall of Sheffield. Each of the gifts was personally engraved with the player's name. The picture shown below is of the page turner presented to Wally Hardinge which, having cost 40s (£2) in 1913, was sold at auction by Graham Budd Auctions in May 2007 for £800.

A total of 19 players, seven amateurs and 12 professionals, received this memento. In addition, a bonus of £10 each was awarded to the ten professionals who played frequently. Collins and Preston, who both appeared in only one match, did not qualify for the bonus.

In previous "Championship" years, the gifts had been: 1906, a silver cigarette case and gold cufflinks; 1909, a silver inkwell and, in the following year, a pair of silver candlesticks based on stumps, bat and ball.

In June 2010, a collection of some of these awards which had been presented to Bill Fairservice was entered for sale at Bonhams Chester. The cufflinks sold for £1,380 (apparently to a Kentish connection), the page turner for £660, the cigarette case for £660 and the inkwell for £780.

A pair of the 1910 silver candlesticks (above) came up for auction towards the end of 2012. They were the pair presented to David Jennings and were estimated at £1,500 to £1,800. They went unsold and were offered again on 22nd May 1913 – estimate £1,000 to £1,500. They fetched £1,845, including the buyer's premium.[3]

The Case for the Opposition

IN THE COURSE of our researches for this book, we uncovered a number of examples of inter-county rivalry which provided amusement. These were largely fomented by a provincial, and therefore partisan, press. A good example of this was the intrusion into private grief in the piece published in the *Hull Daily Mail* following Kent's first defeat of the season at Bristol – "*Kent has fallen from its proud estate ... Verily, Achilles has shown a tender heel.*"[1]

This traffic in barbed leg pulls wasn't entirely one way, and it cannot be claimed that Kentish newspapers always rose above temptation in such circumstances, as with the *Kent Messenger* when they published the Jack Stokes cartoon of the Kentish yokel guarding the Championship bone.

On a national level, but not really in the same spirit, was the graphic that appeared in *Cricket: A Weekly Record of The Game* on 23rd August showing two biplanes chasing each other – the one in the lead is marked Kent and the one following is Yorkshire. The caption poses the question: "*Has the Kentish Plane too long a lead?*" By and large though, this was harmless stuff in the best traditions of knockabout journalism and, after all, Yorkshire were always fair game.

On one occasion during 1913, however, the age-old local rivalry between Surrey and Kent surfaced at the end of a match: the scenes of unrest at Blackheath when the Surrey skipper, Morice Bird, was roundly booed following his retaliation when he was "jostled" as the players left the field. The incident was reported in the *Kent Messenger*, which referred to the Kent crowd as "*miscreants*", a rare example of the absence of home bias.

But it was when trawling the local press in the Maidstone Archive that we found the best example of a bad loser amongst the opposition. A Surrey supporter living in Kent, Mr Basil MacDonald Hastings, was so incensed by the attitude of the Kent supporters and Kentish press over their Championship victory, he was obliged to unscrew his fountain pen and give full vent to his feelings in a letter to a magazine called *Town Topics*. That letter was spotted by a journalist from the *Kent Messenger*, who took it upon himself to uphold the honour of the Kentish supporter and to have a little fun at the same time. The piece is reproduced overleaf.

CRICKET.

The "Sycophants" of Kent

———

AN "ORGY OF ADORATION"

———

A SURREYITE'S OUTBURST

———

Susceptible supporters of Kent cricket who have read the current issue of Town Topics have been somewhat infuriated by an article entitled "Plain Speaking about Kent Cricket", by Basil Macdonald Hastings, a Surreyite resident somewhere in the Weald of Kent. He, apparently, finding little to say against the Kent team itself, has fallen foul of its eulogists.

Here are a few examples of his tirade:

"While tendering my congratulations, may I offer a few words of advice not to the Kent team nor to the County Club, but to those verbal and vocal supporters who are never tired of sounding the team's praises in the Press, in the club and, let it be added, in the parsonage?

"When is all this fulsome, and to my mind, quite revolting flattery to cease? When is this orgy of adoration to find its close time? When is this saturnalia of toe-licking to reach exhaustion?

"Both verbally and vocally, year in year out, we are treated to the same old cry that Kent is the county of sportsmen, that Kent plays sporting cricket, that Kent plays for sport – and, by inference – that there is no sport elsewhere, that other county cricketers are not sportsmen and do not play sporting cricket.

"I happen to know how this nauseous and apparently immortal sycophancy disgusts the leading members of the Kent eleven. Kent play cricket in the only way cricket should be played – and so does every other county. Admitted that every county has its off-days when its play is listless and uninspired, but Kent just as many of these days as other counties. And Kent knows it. And Kent would be very much obliged to be saved from its blind friends.

"Give a certain type of journalist a band, a tent, and a sprinkling of girls with sunshades, and he exclaims, 'Ah, here is sporting cricket.' If he ever stopped to think – I mean that very kindly – he would realise he wasn't talking of cricket at all, but of the surroundings. Give him a return ticket to Canterbury, Maidstone, Dover, Tunbridge Wells or Tonbridge, let the weather be warm and the feminine abundant, he will watch his idols bat feebly and field sluggishly (what time the band plays Robert E Lee), and yet joyously write at the head of his copy 'This is Cricket with a capital C'"

We hope Mr Hastings feels better for having thus relieved his feelings, as he no doubt did when the champions were beaten by "my county" the other day at Kennington, while he should have felt better still on Wednesday evening on learning that Kent had fallen victims at Scarborough by 357 runs. We have no fault to find with the trend of his argument. An ever adulatory and sycophantic Press is to be despised, whether in cricket or politics, but what will puzzle the Kentish reader is where to go to find this immortal flattery with regard to the hop county.

Year after year it has been evident that many reports of Kent cricket have been written with a bias against the county, and whereas Surrey has been glorified, the doings of Kent have been deprecated as much as possible. A Cricket Week as known at Canterbury, Tonbridge and Dover is apparently a crime against the game, but we are not such Spartans and Puritans in Kent as to deny ourselves the sight of a sunshade on our cricket grounds. Really, there is very little in Mr Hastings' complaint. He is a self confessed-Surreyite strayed into the heart of Kent, where the praise of Kent must be as galling to his Surrey susceptibilities. Isn't his ostensible candour – to parody one of his own phrases – only a bit of bilious bigotry? He should get away to Yorkshire for a week or two, where he might find balm for his troubled spirit.

Although a valiant attempt at the defence of his own profession and his own county, it is not entirely convincing and, on balance, a points victory for the "Surreyite". It would not be long before Surrey was able to celebrate its seventh Championship, as in 1914, when cricket was abandoned following the declaration of war on Germany, the men in brown caps were awarded the title with two matches to go. Kent, under their new captain, Lionel Troughton, were never quite up with the pace during that season and finished third.

Sources
1   *Hull Daily Mail* 26th June 1913
2   *Kent Messenger* 1913
3   John Nicholson Auctioneers 22nd May 1913

The Season in Review

SO, HOW HIGHLY does the 1913 Championship victory rank among the four that Kent won in that golden decade before the Great War? Was it deserved? Who were the outstanding performers? And what part did luck play?

Wins in their first four Championship games put them firmly in the box seat, and despite briefly losing the lead to Middlesex in June, there was little likelihood that they would relinquish their grip. While, as the *Kent Messenger* confessed, *"there was just a possibility that the honour would slip through their fingers and fall to Yorkshire"* with around three weeks to go, victories in their last four matches obliterated any faint doubts surfacing after the setbacks in the second game of Canterbury Week, at the Oval and Taunton.[1]

There were some grumbles around the county circuit, and in the media, that Kent had received more than their share of good fortune during the season when the weather, and its effect on the pitch, played into the hands of the lethal partnership of Blythe and Woolley. Even the most "one-eyed" Kent supporter would concede that the elements played their part in the win against Worcestershire at Amblecote, when the hosts were bowled out for 43 on the second afternoon. Similarly, ten days later at Tonbridge, Warwickshire made just 16 in their second innings although, in this instance, there may have been an element of "pilot error" with Frank Foster selecting the heavy roller before they batted. On the other hand, Kent were denied almost certain victories against Nottinghamshire at Canterbury and Somerset at Taunton when rain caused the matches to be abandoned.

The most common of all sporting clichés – that luck evens itself out over a season and that sides make their own luck – were possibly never more relevant. The *Kentish Gazette & Canterbury Press*, however, would have none of it, exclaiming that a *"glance at the records reveals that the Hoppers have won their high honour by merit alone, fortune playing little or no part in their success"*.[2] Unsurprisingly, the loyal *Kent Messenger* felt *"that they deserve the position will scarcely be disputed by anyone"*.[1] If our researches in the course of writing this book have taught us anything, it is not to expect true objectivity from the local press when assessing their heroes' exploits.

Major Philip Trevor, a respected commentator on the game of the time, acknowledged in the *Daily Telegraph* that it *"is only fair to say that the Kent eleven have never promised to be lower than first on the list. From the beginning of May to the end of August they have played consistently well".* He went so far as to attribute much of the *"revival of public interest in county matches"* to Kent's desire to win every game. In a nod to Kent's second place in 1911, he goes on: *"Any points system which put Kent in any place but first in 1913 would be a seriously defective one."* Trevor attested to the high esteem in which the team was held by the cricketing public, not only *"in their own county"* but in being *"the most popular of visiting teams."*[3]

The *Kentish Gazette & Canterbury Press* argued that the doom merchants that had predicted the decline of the game at the start of the season could *"now look back and smile."* Cricketers had *"set out to score as brightly and quickly as circumstances would legitimately permit, and the result has been a thoroughly interesting, if not highly exciting, programme of games"*. A *"generally higher level of excellence"* had *"prevailed all round"* and the example of Kent had played no little part in that development.[2]

The strength of the Champions lay in the range of skills and strength of character possessed by both each individual and the team as a whole. This enabled them to adapt successfully to any conditions or game situation. Though Woolley's star continued in the ascendant, the team contained neither passengers nor prima donnas. They were *"essentially match-winners"*, imbued with a determination that complemented their ability.[2] With the understandable exceptions of the "festival" games at the end of the season at Scarborough and The Oval, they never knew when they were beaten, nor believed that victory was ever quite beyond them.

The consensus among cricket historians is that the 1906 side was the more flamboyant and exciting to watch, and that its extraordinary run of 11 straight victories in the latter half of the season will rarely be equalled. Moreover, its achievements were so memorable that it spawned a book of its own by Clive W Porter. But, without making invidious comparisons between the two teams, a look at some statistics from the 1913 Championship campaign reveals just how dominant the county was in Dillon's last year in charge. Aside from the nail-biting climax to the season at Lord's, where Middlesex were beaten by just five runs, most of Kent's 20 Championship victories were by substantial margins – three by an innings, ten by five or more wickets and five by 100 runs or more. That only leaves that thrilling game at Lord's and a 60-run success at Leyton, in itself hardly a close run thing!

Kent compiled over 300 runs on 13 occasions, while conceding that figure only twice. At the other end of the scale, they failed to reach 100 just once compared to six times by their opponents, and less than 200 eight times as against an astonishing 28 occasions. Against their 18 centuries, opponents notched just three, one by Hobbs and the other two by Sidney Smith of Northamptonshire. Not once were they on the receiving end of a declaration, while they closed their own innings on six occasions, nor were they ever obliged to follow on. They gained a first innings lead in 24 of the 27 matches where both knocks were completed, including doing so in two of the three games they lost!

Kent were bowled out twice in a match seven times while they inflicted it 21 times on their opponents. On nine occasions Kent's bowlers took ten wickets in a match while they were only on the wrong end of such a feat on one occasion – Bill Hitch's 13-163 in the innings defeat to Surrey. There are many other indicators that would substantiate Kent's dominance that year.

Dillon may not have been able to recapture his prolific form of 1905 and 1906 with the bat, though he tended to get runs when they were most needed, but he led his predominantly professional team with great aplomb. The *Kentish Gazette & Canterbury Press* attributed the "*happy family*" feeling in the Kent camp to the mutual respect that his captaincy engendered. It even went so far as to say that, had a "*well-understood technicality*" not disbarred them, the professionals under his command would have made worthy members of the Band of Brothers – praise indeed! Dillon's decision to retire at the end of the season to concentrate on his business commitments was a sad but understandable one.[2]

The top four in the order – Hardinge, Seymour, Humphreys and Woolley – were remarkably consistent, and when one or two of them did fail, others invariably delivered. Between them they amassed 6,814 Championship runs, with Hardinge and Seymour having their best seasons to date, and the last two, Humphreys and Woolley, only falling short by 62 and 18 runs respectively.

Woolley had an outstanding season with bat and ball, and only his injury at Dover prevented him from topping 2,000 runs for the season. Hardinge amassed the highest ever aggregate of runs in a season by any batsman for Kent to date. Only Woolley, Fagg, Ashdown and Hardinge himself have since surpassed his total of 2,018 runs in all matches. His four successive centuries in a little over a week in August earned him a permanent place in the game's record books.

After an indifferent 1912 (which admittedly was interrupted by awful weather), when he managed only half the number of runs he had in the previous year. Seymour scored 1,804 Championship runs at 42.95. On occasions, he even outshone Woolley with the brilliancy and range of his stroke play. Later that year he was informed by the Club's General Committee that, in response to his request for a benefit in 1914, he had been granted one in the year after that. Another five years would elapse before he was finally able to reap the rewards of his long, distinguished service, and only then after a famous court case that changed county cricket forever.[4]

Another consistent performer who, like Seymour, and Burnup before him, never wore an England cap, was Ted Humphreys, who was the season's Beneficiary[5] and also had an excellent year with 1,554 Championship runs at 36.13.

Hubble, usually batting at five, didn't need to perform too often. Nevertheless, despite making his highest number of runs in a season to date (818), he had another modest year. As the *Kent Messenger* reminds us, however, he often had to "*sacrifice his wicket after heavy scoring by his predecessors*"[1] His one and only thousand-run season was only 12 months away.

In his ten matches Arthur Day made only an occasional impact with a couple of half centuries and a handful of occasionally explosive spells of bowling. He did, however, succeed in maintaining his 100 per cent winning record when called upon to captain the side at Blackheath in the absence of Dillon. After not playing in 1912, the former captain, Mason, returned to play one especially fine innings in a losing cause at Trent Bridge. He made an important contribution at Lord's in the final match when Dillon was obliged to leave the field through injury. Mason took over the captaincy of the side at a critical moment on the final afternoon. His shrewd handling of the Kent attack possibly made the difference in securing a thrilling victory.

Jennings was given fewer opportunities than many, and the media particularly, would have liked, but his time would surely come, or so it was thought at the end of this and the following season. His death in 1918 is believed by some to be an even greater loss to Kent cricket than the lives of Blythe and Hutchings, and given that both players had probably played their last cricket for Kent, this may well be so. One who thought highly of him was the historian, RL Arrowsmith, who believed that "*In the 1920's he would have been invaluable. He was a compact, neat, aggressive batsman, somewhat in the style and build of Hendren and one of the great covers of his generation.*"[5] Although he played 11 matches, Hatfeild was unable to secure a regular place in the side, having found it difficult to make the transition from school to adult cricket. Arrowsmith says of him: "*As a small boy at Eton, he had been a phenomenal slow left-hander, but he never developed into a first-class bowler … he played mainly because he was thought a possible future captain.*"[5] Powell, too, showed glimpses of his talent with both bat and ball, but remained no more than what today we would call a squad player.

At the start of the season there was genuine anxiety among the Kent faithful that the attack would not be potent enough on all wickets to mount a successful title challenge. While the spin department, principally Blythe and Woolley, could be relied upon at least to contain on good wickets and wreak havoc on bad, the pace attack, and especially its spearhead, Fielder, did not instil the same confidence. The veteran quick bowler's form had declined sharply in 1912 when he took only 28 Championship wickets at 35.75 with a wicket every 12 overs, although given his tendency to overstep the crease, and the fact that, in those days, no balls were not debited to the bowler, it was probably nearer a wicket every 13 overs.

In the previous six seasons he had collected 639 victims with a wicket every six overs, and in three of those years topped 100, and in two, took 150 wickets. He would turn 36 in mid season, and most believed his best days were behind him. His emphatic return to form was, therefore, both welcome and crucial. He took 105

Championship wickets at 18.77, his best average since 1907, with a wicket every six overs. He took five wickets in an innings eight times and ten wickets in a match twice. The *Kent Messenger* attributed his success to his cutting his pace to concentrate on accuracy.[1] Remaining generally fit, he only missed six of the 28 Championship games and bowled nearly twice as many overs as in the previous year.

Blythe was as reliable and deadly as ever, taking 145 Championship wickets at 15.54, including ten wickets in a match three times and five wickets in an innings fourteen times. His "understudy", Woolley, took a further 83 at 17.61. They bowled unchanged throughout the innings on four occasions, demolishing the opponents' batting in helpful conditions. Only the injury to his thumb originally sustained at Maidstone prevented his achieving his third double in four years.

In having his best season since 1908, the redoubtable Fairservice provided solid support and Carr delivered his now obligatory 47 wickets in just eight matches, though his average was the highest since he had arrived "overnight" at the age of 37 four years earlier. The *Kent Messenger* actually speculated that he might have been "found out" at last, and was no longer the mystery bowler he had once been. The *Kentish Gazette & Canterbury Press* preferred to marvel at his consistency, hailing an achievement *"that must put him among the first flight of trundlers in the kingdom."*[2] But, after the game against Lord Londesborough's XI at Scarborough, where he had creditable match figures of 8-120, he was destined to play just one more game for the county in the following year when Hobbs and Hayward savaged him for 134 runs in 28 wicketless overs, whereupon he retired from first-class cricket.

Collins and Preston played just one game each and neither picked up a wicket in the short spells they bowled. Preston actually finished top of the Second XI bowling averages but was released at the end of the season, turning down the offer of a Lord's ground staff role to take up a post at Nelson in the Lancashire League. The 23-year-old Collins, who did not play at all in 1914, would become a stalwart of the post-war side for a decade.

As the match reports attest, the catching was not always up to the standard of recent years, though the ground fielding was generally good. Seymour at slip and Hardinge in the outfield were the outstanding performers. As remarkable as Fielder's renaissance had been, the performance of the ever-present Huish behind the stumps was equally astonishing. Still quick and alert, even at the age of 43 and in his 19the year in the side, he topped his 1911 record of 101 dismissals in a season – when he had been the first keeper to accomplish the feat – with 102 (32 stumped and 70 caught). Hubble would have to wait until after the war before he had the opportunity to assume the role of first choice wicketkeeper.

We return to that first question of where the 1913 team might rank among the four that won the title in this era. Cricket historians have tended to overlook their achievements in favour of the 1906 side, even though, in 1913, they won more games than any other in the county's history. After all, there was no Hutchings, no Blaker, no Marsham and no Sammy Day, and Mason only played in three competitive games. The amateur influence, at least on the pitch, of the late Victorian, and let it be remembered, unsuccessful, era, had faded into memory.

Still, of course, captained by an amateur, albeit an enlightened one, the side was now essentially professional, displaying above all the will to win, though still capable, especially when Woolley and Seymour were in full flow, of scoring runs at a furious pace. The only department in which it is generally acknowledged that it fell short of the 1906, 1909 and 1910 teams is in the fielding, and specifically catching. The margin of the title victory might have been still larger had the previous high standards, epitomised by Hutchings and Mason, been maintained.

Comparisons are difficult, particularly at such a distance. Even today, there is no agreement as to whether the 1970 Kent side was better than that of 1977 or 1978, and it is perhaps best to let such a debate lie. What is undeniable, however, is that Kent's 1913 Championship winning team was a happy, well-organised and, on occasions, quite brilliant unit that thoroughly deserved its triumph.

Sources

1   *Kent Messenger* 6th September 1913

2   *Kentish Gazette & Canterbury Press* 6th September 1913

3   *Daily Telegraph* 30th August 1913

4   Seymour's Benefit: This was a milestone legal case that is still thought to be binding today. The facts are broadly that James Seymour (whose benefit request for 1914 had been denied by KCCC and postponed until 1915) received a benefit in 1920. The Inland Revenue, in the form of a Mr Reed, challenged the right of the cricketer to receive the benefit sum without deduction of Income Tax. The case was initially heard in the High Court where the decision went in favour of Seymour. The Revenue appealed and the Court of Appeal reversed the High Court decision. That decision was then taken to the House of Lords, who restored the original ruling of the High Court. The action was funded partly by Lord Harris and partly by several other of the first-class counties as it is likely that the amount incurred on legal fees would have exceeded the sum raised by the Benefit itself.

5   From the Kent CCC Minutes Book – "The Managing Committee of the County Club agreed at its meeting on 10th March 1913 to award Ted Humphreys a benefit this season when *all the moneys received, whether in gate-money or donation, should be invested with the Trustees of the Club, during the pleasure of the Committee, and that the Club would guarantee him 4 per cent interest*". At the Managing Committee meeting on 24th November it was announced that the total amount received to date had been £1,316 11s.10d, and, as was customary at the time, it was in the gift of the County Club, rather than hand the money over to the player, to invest it on his behalf in stocks and shares. In Humphreys' case it was decided that the following monies should be invested:
£300 Canadian Pacific Railway 4% Perpetual Consolidated Debenture Stock;
£400 Canadian North Ontario Railway 3½% Dominion Guaranteed Debenture Stock 1961;
£400 South Eastern Railway 3% Perpetual Debenture Stock; and
£216.11s. 10d. New Zealand Government 4% Inscribed Stock 1943/63"
However, this was not entirely a done deal. *"Humphrey's approval to be first obtained"* – as if he really had a choice.

6   RL Arrowsmith – *A History of County Cricket: Kent* – Arthur Barker Ltd London 1971

Summary of Results

Date	Opposition	Venue	Match Scores	Individual Contributions	Result
12th, 3th & 14th May 1913	Sussex	The County Ground, Hove	Sussex 141 & 101 Kent 207 & 36-1	Mr HP Chaplin 40; AE Relf 29; Blythe 6-63 Mr HL Wilson 33; GR Cox 20; Fairservice 5-40 HTW Hardinge 43; J Seymour 68; Mr CE Hatfeild 29; RR Relf 5-30; Mr HL Simms 3-68	Kent won by 9 wickets Kent 5 Points Sussex 0 Points
15th, 16th May 1913	Marylebone Cricket Club	Lord's Cricket Ground, London	Kent 107 & 116 MCC 118 & 111-4	Mr CE Hatfeild 20; JW Hearne 3-8 HTW Hardinge 30, Mr EW Dillon 30, Mr WA Powell 25; Mr JWHT Douglas 3-19; Tarrent 3-30 Mr TAL Whittington 30; C Blythe 4-38 Mr NE Haig 39*; Mr TAL Whittington 31	MCC won by 6 wickets
19th, 20th & 21st May 1913	Oxford University Cricket Club	The Parks, Oxford	Kent 480 Oxford 225 & 154	FE Woolley 224*; J Seymour 96; Mr EW Dillon 39 Mr IPF Campbell 70; C Blythe 5-68 C Blythe 4-27; E Humphreys 3-36	Kent won by an innings & 101 runs
22nd & 23rd May 1913	Leicestershire	Aylestone Road Leicester	Kent 318 & 11-0 Leics 132 & 195	E Humphreys 77; HTW Hardinge 56; Mr EW Dillon 49 Skelding 3-67; Shipman 3-73 G Geary 42; A Fielder 7-50 H Whitehead 43; W Shipman 42; Mr J Shields 35; A Fielder 6-69	Kent won by 9 wickets Kent 5 Points Leics 0 Points

Summary of Results

Date	Opposition	Venue	Match Scores	Individual Contributions	Result
6th, 27th & 28th May 1913	Somerset	Private Banks Ground, Catford	Kent 233 & 389-5 dec; Somerset 146 & 122	HTW Hardinge 38; JC Hubble 36; Mr JC White 7-83; J Seymour 118; HTW Hardinge 105; E Humphreys 70; FE Woolley 60; FP Hardy 42; Mr JC Daniell 33; A Fielder 4-37; Mr JC Daniell 30; FE Woolley 5-21	Kent won by 354 runs; Kent 5 Points; Somerset 0 Points
29th, 30th & 31st May 1913	Northamptonshire	The County Ground, Northampton	Northants 298 & 141; Kent 40 & 39-0	Mr SG Smith 133; W East 43; JS Denton 39; Fl Walden 38; A Fielder 6-50; J Seymour 91; Mr EW Dillon 53; Mr WA Powell 48; JC Hubble 37; W Wells 4-110	Kent won by 10 wicket; Kent 5 Points; Northants 0 Points
2nd, 3rd & 4th June 1913	Yorkshire	Park Avenue, Bradford	Kent 251 & 275; Yorks 217 & 192-4	FE Woolley 81; JC Hubble 55; E Humphreys 42; MW Booth 6-108; J Seymour 69; Mr EW Dillon 62; E Humphreys 52; D Denton 85; MW Booth 38*; Blythe 4-64; Mr WA Powell 3-37; GH Hirst 102*; R Kilner 50*; Fielder 3-44	Match Drawn; Kent 3 Points; Yorks 1 Point
5th, 6th & 7th June 1913	Lancashire	Old Trafford, Manchester	Kent 354 & 4-0; Lances 196 & 159	J Seymour 107; FE Woolley 77; E Humphreys 61; H Dean 6-93; JT Tydesley 65; J Sharp 45; WJ Fairservice 5-58; Mr AH Hornby 43; W Huddleston 34; WJ Fairservice 5-44	Kent won by 10 wickets; Kent 5 Points; Lancs 0 Points

Summary of Results

Date	Opposition	Venue	Match Scores	Individual Contributions	Result
9th, 10th & 11th June 1913	Worcestershire	War Memorial Ground, Amblecote	Worcs 156 & 43 Kent 254	FL Bowley 92; FA Pearson 37; FE Woolley 6-31 C Blythe 7-21; FE Woolley 3-21 FE Woolley 99; HTW Hardinge 50; WJ Fairservice 32; F Chester 6-95	Kent won by and innings & 55 runs Kent 5 Points Worcs 0 Points
16th, 17th & 18th June 1913	Essex	The Angel Ground, Tonbridge	Kent 285 & 279-4 dec Essex 161 & 277	HTW Hardinge 83; FE Woolley 72; J Seymour 47; B Tremlin 4-70 JC Hubble 97*; E Humphreys 53; HTW Hardinge 50; J Seymour 46 Rev FH Gillingham 45; PA Perrin 34; C Blythe 5-46 Mr CD McIver 76; PA Perrin 57; FL Fane 33; A Fielder 8-120	Kent won by 126 runs Kent 5 Points Surrey 0 Points
19th, 20th & 21st June 1913	Warwickshire	The Angel Ground, Tonbridge	Warwicks 262 & 16 Kent 132 & 147-4	CS Baker 59; C Charlesworth 47; P Jeeves 30 FE Woolley 5-44 C Blythe 5-8; FE Woolley 5-8 Mr FR Foster 6-62 FE Woolley 76	Kent won by 6 wivkets Kent 5 Points Warwicks 0 Points
23rd, 24th & 25th June 1913	Gloucestershire	Ashley Down, Bristol	Kent 220 & 113 Glos 202 & 132-4	J Seymour 62; FE Woolley 50; E Humphreys 32; EG Dennett 4-57; GL Jessop 4-64 E Humphreys 52; EG Dennett 8-63 H Smith 54; Mr COH Sewell 37; LL Cranfield 33; C Blythe 5-65 Mr CS Barnett 49*	Gloucestershire won by 6 wickets Kent 0 Points Glos 5 Points

Summary of Results

Date	Opposition	Venue	Match Scores	Individual Contributions	Result
26th, 27th & 28th June 1913	Hampshire	United Services Ground, Portsmouth	Hants 261 & 191; Kent 527	G Brown 71; HAW Bowell 35; C Blythe 4-35; FE Woolley 3-64; CP Mead 76; G Brown 50; HTW Hardinge 168; J Seymour 124; FE Woolley 105; Mr EW Dillon 48; Mr A Jaques 5-101; AS Kennedy 3-116	**Kent won by an innings & 75 runs** Kent 5 Points Hants 0 Points
30th June, 1st & 2nd July 1913	Nottinghamshire	Trent Bridge, Nottingham	Notts 266 & 234; Kent 279 & 149	JR Gunn 92; G Gunn 40; WW Whysall 38; A Fielder 4-67; Mr AP Day 4-46; JR Gunn 55; WW Whysall 39; TW Oates 34; A Fielder 5-80; Mr JR Mason 75; E Humphreys 68; DW Jennings 48; C Blythe 37; EB Alletson 4-37	**Nottinghamshire won by 62 runs** Kent 0 Points Notts 5 Points
3rd, 4th & 5th July 1913	Surrey	The Oval, Kennington	Surrey 236 & 211; Kent 331 & 118-4	EG Goatly 80; EG Hayes 62; HS Harrison 38; FE Woolley 5-70; JB Hobbs 49; A Sandham 48*; TW Hayward 41; C Blythe 6-74; FE Woolley 177; DW Jennings 40; T Rushby 4-71; HTW Hardinge 36; E Humphreys 33;	**Kent won by 6 wickets** Kent 5 Points Surrey 0 Points
7th, 8th & 9th July 1913	Warwickshire	Edgbaston, Birmingham	Warwicks 159 & 161; Kent 371	CS Baker 35; JH Parsons 31; C Blythe 5-47; FE Woolley 5-75; C Charlesworth 43; FE Woolley 4-45; WJ Fairservice 3-27; A Fielder 3-70; J Seymour 106; JC Hubble 75; DW Jennings 72; Mr CE Hatfeild 33; P Jeeves 3-90	**Kent won by an innings & 51 runs** Kent 5 Points Warwicks 0 Points

Summary of Results

Date	Opposition	Venue	Match Scores	Individual Contributions	Result
14th, 15th & 16th July 1913	**Worcestershire**	Nevill Ground, Tunbridge Wells	**Kent 252** Worcs 131-3	E Humphreys 80; FH Huish 47; Mr EW Dillon 38; JA Cuffe 4-64	**Match Drawn** Not counted for County Championship table
17th, 18th & 19th July 1913	Yorkshire	Nevill Ground, Tunbridge Wells	**Yorkshire 100** Kent 135	C Blythe 5-30; FE Woolley 4-40 J Seymour 75; W Rhodes 5-42; A Drake 3-23	**Match Drawn** Kent 3 Points Yorks 1 Point
21st, 22nd & 23rd July 1913	Lancashire	Mote Park, Maidstone	**Lancs 158** & 88 Kent 220 & 27-1	JWH Makepeace 88; C Blythe 5-60; WJ Fairservice 3-33 JWH Makepeace 39* FE Woolley 6-33; C Blythe 4-55 E Humphreys 86; WJ Fairservice 31; H Dean 5-108; JS Heap 4-42	**Kent won** by 9 wickets Kent 5 Points Lancs 0 Points
24th, 25th & 26th July 1913	Middlesex	Mote Park, Maidstone	**Middx 56** & 86 Kent 79 & 64-3	C Blythe 5-17; FE Woolley 3-31 C Blythe 6-48; FE Woolley 4-31 FE Woolley 31; JT Hearne 6-21; FA Tarrant 4-54	**Kent won** by 7 wickets Kent 5 Points Middx 0 Points

Summary of Results

Date	Opposition	Venue	Match Scores	Individual Contributions	Result
28th, 29th July & 29th July 1913	Gloucestershire	Bat & Ball Ground, Gravesend	Glos 144 & 176 Kent 249 & 72-2	Mr GL Jessop 87; Mr DW Carr 5-26; A Fielder 5-55; Mr COH Sewell 58; Mr DW Carr 5-74; E Humphreys 59; HTW Hardinge 50; JC Hubble 38; Mr EW Dillon 33; IJ Cranfield 3-31; TH Gange 3-70; IJ Cranfield 2-17;	**Kent won by 8 wickets** Kent 5 Points Glos 0 Points
31st July, 1st & 2nd August 1913	Essex	The County Ground, Leyton	Kent 384 & 168 Essex 206 & 286	E Humphreys 131; J Seymour 48; FE Woolley 48; C Buckenham 4-123; Mr JWHT Douglas 3-60; J Seymour 36; C Buckenham 5-58; Mr CD McIver 80; Mr JWHT Douglas 45; Mr DW Carr 4-71; JR Freeman 69; Mr CD McIver 53; CAG Russell 51; Mr DW Carr 3-84; A Fielder 3-100	**Kent won by 50 runs** Kent 5 Points Essex 0 Points
4th, 5th & 6th August 1913	Sussex	St Lawrence Cricket Ground, Canterbury	Kent 215 & 359 Sussex 212 & 122	Mr EW Dillon 63*; HTW Hardinge 47; RR Relf 5-47; HTW Hardinge 71; Mr EW Dillon 62; WJ Fairservice 48; FH Huish 42; FE Woolley 41; J Seymour 31; NJ Holloway 3-76; J Seymour 3-50; AE Relf 89; J Vine 46; A Fielder 7-41; Mr DW Carr 5-28; A Fielder 3-38	**Kent won by 240 runs** Kent 5 Points Sussex 0 Points

Summary of Results

Date	Opposition	Venue	Match Scores	Individual Contributions	Result
7th, 8th & 9th August 1913	**Nottinghamshire**	St Lawrence Cricket Ground, Canterbury	**Notts 308 & 28-5 Kent 294**	WRD Payton 65; GM Lee 63; Mr AW Carr 58; Mr DW Carr 5-116; C Blythe 4-14 HTW Hardinge 79; J Seymour 67; FE Woolley 50; TG Wass 7-113; J Iremonger 3-108	**Match Drawn** Kent 1 Point Notts 3 Points
11th, 12th & 13th August 1913	**Surrey**	The Oval, Kennington, London	**Kent 102 & 338 Surrey 480**	Mr AP Day 35; Mr EW Dillon 33; JW Hitch 8-48 Mr EW Dillon 135; Mr AP Day 63; E Humphreys 42 JW Hitch 5-115; Mr EC Kirk 4-107 JB Hobbs 115; EG Goatly 76; Mr MC Bird 55; HS Harrison 55; FE Woolley 3-128	**Surrey won by an innings & 40 runs** Kent 0 Points Surrey 5 Points
14th, 15th & 16th August 1913	**Somerset**	The County Ground, Taunton	**Kent 221 & 335-9 dec Somerset 86 & 90-1**	JC Hubble 40; DW Jennings 33; JJ Bridges 6-44 FE Woolley 101*; J Seymour 82; HTW Hardinge 75 JC White 5-120; CJ Bowring 3-24 A Fielder 7-50 Mr PR Johnson 55* W Hyman 35	**Match Drawn** Kent 3 Points Somerset 1 Point
18th, 19th & 20th August 1913	**Leicestershire**	St Lawrence Cricket Ground, Canterbury	**Kent 201 & 349 Leics 192 & 94**	J Seymour 61; FE Woolley 47; G Geary 5-61; S Coe 3-7 HTW Hardinge 154; J Seymour 39; Mr EW Dillon 32 G Geary 3-88 W Shipman 38; C Blythe 7-54 C Blythe 6-40; WJ Fairservice 3-16	**Kent won by 264 runs** Kent 5 Points Leics 0 Points

Summary of Results

Date	Opposition	Venue	Match Scores	Individual Contributions	Result
21st, 22nd & 23rd August 1913	Hampshire	Crabble Athletic Ground, Dover	Kent 424 & 234-4 dec Hants 300 & 200	HTW Hardinge 117; E Humphreys 105; J Seymour 85 JA Newman 4-83; HTW Hardinge 105*; J Seymour 77 HAW Bowell 79; Lt CH Abercrombie 44; Hon LH Tennyson 38; CP Mead 33; C Blythe 4-74 HAW Bowell 70; Mr EJM Sprot 58; CP Mead 30 C Blythe 4-43; FE Woolley 4-20	**Kent won by 158 runs** Kent 5 Points Hants 0 Points
25th, 26th & 27th August 1913	Northamptonshire	Crabble Athletic Ground, Dover	Northants 207 & 294 Kent 240 & 262-5	Mr SG Smith 51; Mr JS Denton 41; Mr DW Carr 6-88; C Blythe 4-72 Mr SG Smith 108; GJ Thompson 67; Mrs JS Denton 35 A Fielder 4-58 HTW Hardinge 107; E Humphreys 58; GJ Thompson 5-72 J Seymour 114*; E Humphreys 54; Mr AP Day 54	**Kent won by 5 wickets** Kent 5 Points Northants 5 Points
28th, 29th & 30th August 1913	Middlesex	Lord's Cricket Ground St John's Wood London	Kent 236 & 124 Middx 131 & 234	HTW Hardinge 110; JT Hearne 4-50; Mr H Weston 3-81 E Humphreys 49; Mr AP Day 33; JW Hearne 4-34; Mr H Weston 3-27; FA Tarrant 3-18 C Blythe 4-37; Mr AP Day 4-58; JW Hearne 96; Mr WP Robertson 47; E Humphreys 3-28; Mr DW Carr 3-84	**Kent won by 5 runs** Kent 5 Points Middx 0 Points
1st, 2nd & 3rd September 1913	**Mr Lionel Robinson's XI** *	Buckenham Hall, Attleborough Norfolk	**Mr Robinson's XI 236 & 71-5 Mr Mason's XI 216**	Mr BJT Bosanquet 79 Mr DW Carr 5-41 C Blythe 3-24 E Humphreys 69; J Seymour 48; SF Barnes 7-88	**Match Drawn**

Summary of Results

Date	Opposition	Venue	Match Scores	Individual Contributions	Result
8th, 9th & 10th September 1913	Lord Londesborough's XI	Marine Parade, Scarborough	Lond's XI 328 & 220; Kent 109 & 102	Mr GL Jessop 116; JW Hearne 102; AE Relf 32; DW Carr 4-79; A Fielder 3-83; JW Hearne 43; HL Simms 36; Mr DW Carr 4-41; JC Hubble 51; MW Booth 5-38; Mr LHW Troughton 34; SF Barnes 6-39; JW Hitch 3-34	Lord Londesborough's XI won by 337 runs
15th, 16th & 17th September 1913	Rest of England **	The Oval, Kennington, London	Kent & Yorks 154 & 67; The Rest 266	MW Booth 38; SF Barnes 4-59; Mr SG Smith 3-53; SF Barnes 7-20; CP Mead 43; SG Smith 32; MW Booth 3-26; E Humphreys 3-41	The Rest of England won by an innings & 45 runs

Notes

* Mr Lionel Robinson's XI vs Mr JR Mason's XI – although designated as first class, this match is not included as a Kent match in the club archives.
  JR Mason's XI: HTW Hardinge, E Humphreys, J Seymour, Mr LHW Troughton, Mr HZ Baker, Mr JR Mason, Mr GVJ Weigall, FH Huish, Mr DW Carr, C Blythe & A Fielder.

** This was the traditional Champions vs The Rest of England match. Because of injuries, Kent could not put a representative side out and the match was played with six from Yorkshire and five from Kent.

The Fallen

The following players appeared for or against Kent during the 1913 season and died in the service of their country during the 1914–1918 War.

County	Player	Rank/Regiment	Date/Age	Place
Kent	**Blythe** Colin	Sergeant Kent Fortress Engineers	08/11/1917 Aged 38	Passchendaele Belgium
	Hatfeild MC Charles Eric	Captain East Kent Regiment	21/09/1918 Aged 31	Cambrai France
	Jennings David William	Corporal Kent Fortress Engineers	06/08/1918 Aged 29	Tunbridge Wells
Essex	**Davies** Geoffrey Boissell	Captain 11th Essex Regiment	26/09/1915 Aged 22	Hulluch France
Gloucestershire	**Nason** John William Washingtonier	Captain Royal Flying Corps	26/12/1916 Aged 27	Vlamertinghe Belgium
Hampshire	**Abercrombie** Cecil Halliday	Lieutenant Royal Navy	31/05/1916 Aged 30	Jutland
	Jaques Arthur	Captain West Yorkshire Regiment	Aged 27	Loos France
	Sandeman George Amelius Crawshay	Captain Royal Hampshire Regiment	26/04/1915 Aged 32	Zonnebeke Belgium
MCC	**Thomson** Edmund Peel	Major Royal Munster Fusiliers	21/12/1914 Aged 40	Festubert France
	Raphael John Edward	Lieutenant King's Royal Rifles	11/06/1917 Aged 35	Remy Belguim
Northants	**Ryan** MC James Henry Aloysius	Captain 1st Liverpool Regiment	25/09/1915 Aged 23	Loos France

Nottinghamshire	**Riley** William	Gunner RGA	09/08/1917 Aged 30	Coxyde Belguim
Oxford University	**Shaw** Edward Alfred	Captain (temp) Oxford & Bucks Light Infantry	07/10/1916 Aged 24	Le Sars France
Somerset	**Hancock** DSO Ralph Escott	Lieutenant Devonshire Regiment	29/10/1914 Aged 26	La Bassee France
Warwickshire	**Jeeves** Percy	Royal Warwickshire Regiment	22/07/1916 Aged 28	Montauban France
Worcestershire	**Burns** William Beaumont	2nd Lieutenant Worcestershire Regiment	07/07/1916 Aged 32	Contalmaison France
	Nevile Bernard Philip	Captain Lincolnshire Regiment	11/02/1916 Aged 27	Ypres Belgium
	Collier Charles George Alfred	Staff-Sergeant Army Ordnance Corps	25/08/1916 Aged 30	Marmetz France
Yorkshire	**Booth** Major William	2nd Lieutenant West Yorkshire Regiment	01/07/1916 Aged 29	La Signy Farm France
Lord Londesborough's XI	**Bird** Wilfred Stanley	Lieutenant King's Royal Rifle Corps	09/05/1915 Aged 31	Richebourg St Vast France

Claud Woolley and Colin Blythe

The Players of 1913
Mr DW Carr. J Seymour, Mr LHW Troughton, DW Jennings, WJ Fairservice
Mr AP Day, Mr EW Dillon, Mr JR Mason
Mr WA Powell, Mr CE Hatfeild
JC Hubble, FE Woolley, E Humphreys C Blythe
HJB Preston, A Fielder, WTW Hardinge, GC Collins, FH Huish

The Players of The 1913 Season

Player	Bat	Bowl	Age	Born	Debut	First Class Career	Kent Cap
Blythe, Colin	RHB	SLAO	34	Deptford	1899	1899 to 1914	1900
Carr, Douglas Ward	RHB	RLBG	41	Cranbrook	1909	1909 to 1914	1909
Collins, George Christopher	LHB	RFM	24	Gravesend	1911	1911 to 1928	1920
Day, Arthur Percival	RHB	RFM/LB	28	Blackheath	1905	1905 to 1925	1905
Dillon*, Edward Wentworth	LHB	RLB	32	Penge	1900	1900 to 1923	1901
Fairservice, William John	RHB	ROB/RM	32	Nunhead	1902	1902 to 1921	1903
Fielder, Arthur	RHB	RF	36	Plaxtol	1900	1900 to 1914	1903
Hardinge, Walter Thomas William	RHB	SLAO	27	Greenwich	1902	1902 to 1933	1907
Hatfeild, Charles Eric	LHB	SLAO	26	Margate	1910	1910 to 1914	
Hubble, John Charlton	RHB	WK	32	Wateringbury	1904	1904 to 1929	1906
Huish, Frederick Henry	RHB	WK	43	Clapham	1896	1895 to 1914	1896
Humphreys, Edward	RHB	SLAO	31	Ditton	1899	1899 to 1920	1901
Jennings, David William	RHB		24	Kentish Town	1909	1909 to 1914	1911
Mason**, John Richard	RHB	RFM	39	Blackheath	1893	1893 to 1914	1893
Powell, William Allan	RHB	RF	28	Blundellsands	1912	1912 to 1921	
Preston, Henry John Berridge	RHB	RM	29	Bareilly, India	1907	1907 to 1913	1910
Seymour, James	RHB	ROB	33	West Hoathly	1902	1902 to 1926	1902
Troughton***, Lionel Holmes Wood	RHB	RM	34	Seaford	1907	1907 to1923	1914
Woolley, Frank Edward	LHB	SLAO/LM	26	Tonbridge	1906	1906 to 1938	1906

* Captain 1909 to 1913
** Captain 1898 to 1902
*** Captain 1914 to 1923

Amateurs *in italics*

RHB = Right Hand Bat; LHB = Left Hand Bat; RFM = Right Arm Fast Medium; RLB = Right Arm Leg Breaks
ROB = Right Arm Off Breaks; RF = Right Arm Fast; WK = Wicketkeeper; LM = Left Arm Medium
SLAO = Slow Left Arm Orthodox; RM = Right Arm Medium; RM = Right Arm Medium; RLBG = Right Arm Leg Breaks
& Googlies

Kent 1913 Batting & Fielding Averages: County Championship Only

Name	M	Inns	NO	Runs	HS	Ave	100	50	Ct	St
HTW Hardinge	28	50	6	1949	168	44.29	7	9	9	
FE Woolley	26	40	5	1507	177	43.05	3	9	29	
J Seymour	28	48	6	1804	124	42.95	5	10	43	
E Humphreys	27	47	4	1554	131	36.13	2	13	13	
Mr EW Dillon	26	39	5	871	135	25.61	1	4	33	
Mr JR Mason	3	5	0	122	75	24.40	0	1	5	
JC Hubble	26	39	2	818	97*	22.10	0	3	24	
Mr AP Day	10	16	2	307	63	21.92	0	2	10	
DW Jennings	10	15	0	277	72	18.46	0	1	6	
FH Huish	28	39	6	505	47	15.30	0	0	58	26
Mr WA Powell	6	7	0	105	48	15.00	0	0	2	
Mr CE Hatfield	11	12	0	177	33	14.75	0	0	8	
WJ Fairservice	19	24	4	292	48	14.60	0	0	5	
C Blythe	28	36	5	246	37	7.93	0	0	13	
A Fielder	22	29	17	94	16	7.83	0	0	9	
Mr DW Carr	8	12	1	83	25*	7.54	0	0	3	
GC Collins	1	2	0	15	13	7.50	0	0	0	
HJB Preston	1	1	1	8	8*	N/A	0	0	1	

Kent 1913 Bowling Averages: County Championship Only

Name	Overs	Mdns	Runs	Wkts	Ave	BB	5wI	10wM
J Seymour	2.5	0	3	1	3.33	1-0	0	0
C Blythe	966.4	259	2254	145	15.54	7-21	14	3
FE Woolley	586.4	162	1462	83	17.61	6-31	7	1
Mr WA Powell	48	9	146	8	18.25	3-37	0	0
Mr DW Carr	254.1	38	872	47	18.55	6-88	5	1
A Fielder	629.2	103	1971	105	18.77	8-120	8	2
WJ Fairservice	383.4	125	892	47	18.97	5-40	3	1
Mr AP Day	213.1	37	594	22	27.00	4-46	0	0
E Humphreys	161	31	437	16	27.31	3-28	0	0
Mr JR Mason	18	5	61	2	30.50	2-34	0	0
Mr EW Dillon	21	1	109	2	54.50	1-34	0	0
GC Collins	1	1	0	0	-			
DW Jennings	1	0	2	0	-			
Mr CE Hatfeild	9.1	1	27	0	-			
HJB Preston	5	0	35	0	-			

Played: 28

Won: 20   Sussex (2), Leicestershire (2), Somerset (Catford), Northamptonshire (2), Lancashire (2), Worcestershire (Amblecote), Essex (2), Warwickshire (2), Middlesex (2), Gloucestershire (Gravesend), Surrey (Blackheath), Hampshire (2)

Lost: 3   Gloucestershire (Bristol), Nottinghamshire (Trent Bridge), Surrey (The Oval)

Drawn: 4   Yorkshire (2), Nottinghamshire (Canterbury), Somerset (Taunton)

No Result: 1   Worcestershire (Tunbridge Wells)

Kent 1913 Batting & Fielding Averages: First Class (Kent matches only)

Name	M	Inns	NO	Runs	HS	Ave	100	50	Ct	St
FE Woolley	28	43	6	1737	224*	46.94	4	9	30	
HTW Hardinge	30	53	6	2018	168	42.93	7	9	9	
J Seymour	31	53	6	1932	124	41.10	5	11	45	
E Humphreys	30	52	4	1587	131	33.06	2	13	14	
Mr EW Dillon	28	42	5	944	135	25.51	1	4	33	
Mr AP Day	10	16	2	307	63	21.92	0	2	10	
JC Hubble	28	43	2	886	97*	21.60	0	4	25	
Mr JR Mason	4	7	0	124	75	17.71	0	1	8	
DW Jennings	11	17	0	293	72	17.23	0	1	7	
Mr LHW Troughton	2	3	0	49	34	16.33	0	0	1	
Mr CE Hatfeild	13	15	0	222	33	14.80	0	0	9	
FH Huish +	31	44	6	551	47	14.50	0	0	69	30
WJ Fairservice	20	26	4	307	48	13.95	0	0	7	
Mr WA Powell	8	10	0	114	48	11.40	0	0	2	
Mr DW Carr	9	14	2	91	25*	7.58	0	0	4	
GC Collins	1	2	0	15	13	7.50	0	0	0	
C Blythe	31	41	5	263	37	7.30	0	0	15	
A Fielder	25	34	20	102	16	7.28	0	0	10	
HJB Preston	1	1	1	8	8*		0	0	1	

Kent 1913 Bowling Averages: First Class (Kent matches only)

Name	Overs	Mdns	Runs	Wkts	Ave	BB	5wI	10wM
J Seymour	2.5	0	3	1	1.50	1-0	0	0
C Blythe	1043.1	275	2493	160	15.48	7-21	15	3
Mr DW Carr	275.1	41	992	55	17.71	6-88	5	1
FE Woolley	618.4	173	1522	83	18.11	6-31	7	1
Mr WA Powell	77	16	229	11	19.08	3-37	0	0
WJ Fairservice	405.4	127	963	49	19.26	5-40	3	1
A Fielder	704.5	114	2222	113	19.49	8-120	8	2
Mr JR Mason	29.2	6	118	5	19.66	2-17	0	0
E Humphreys	209	37	601	26	22.25	3-28	0	0
Mr AP Day	213.1	37	594	22	25.82	4-46	0	0
Mr EW Dillon	21	1	109	2	36.33	1-34	0	0
GC Collins	1	1	0	0				
DW Jennings	1	0	2	0				
Mr CE Hatfeild	17.5	2	60	0				
HJB Preston	5	0	35	0				

Played 32

Won 21w Sussex (2), Leicestershire (2), Somerset (Catford), Northamptonshire (2), Lancashire (2), Worcestershire (Amblecote) , Essex (2), Warwickshire (2), Middlesex (2), Gloucestershire (Gravesend), Surrey (Blackheath), Hampshire (2), Oxford University.

Lost 6 Marylebone Cricket Club, Gloucestershire (Bristol), Nottinghamshire (Trent Bridge), Surrey (The Oval), Lord Londesborough's XI (Scarborough), The Rest (The Oval)*

Drawn 4 Yorkshire (2), Nottinghamshire (Canterbury), Somerset (Taunton)

No Result 1 Worcestershire (Tunbridge Wells)

* The traditional Champion County vs The Rest at the Oval was played by a combined Kent and Yorkshire side and does not appear in the official records of Kent's first-class season. This match is excluded from the averages shown above.

Bibliography

Altham, HS, *A History of* Cricket, Allen & Unwin, London, 1926

Arlott, John, *Arlott on Cricket – His Writings on The Game*, Willow Books, London, 1984

Arnot, Chris, *Britain's Lost Cricket Grounds: The Hallowed Homes of Cricket That Will Never See Another Ball Bowled*, Aurum, London, 2011

Arrowsmith, RL, *A History of County Cricket: Kent*, Arthur Barker Limited, London, 1971

Birley, Derek, *A Social History of English Cricket*, Aurum Press, Bodmin, 2000

Birley, Derek, *The Willow Wand: Some Cricket Myths Explored*, Aurum Press, London, 2000 (original 1979)

Brodribb, Gerald, *Felix on the Bat: Being a Memoir of Nicholas Felix*, Eyre & Spottiswoode, London, 1962

Blunden, Edmund, *Cricket Country*, Pavilion Library, London, 1985 (original 1944)

Boyle, John, *Portrait of Canterbury*, Phillimore, Canterbury, 1974

Bright-Holmes, John, *The Joy of Cricket*, Unwin, London, 1985

Brooke, Robert, *A History of the County Cricket Championship*, Guinness, Bath, 1991

Brooke, Robert, *FR Foster: The Fields Were Sudden Bare*, ACS Publications, 2011

Butler, Derek, *Canterbury – A Second Selection in Old Photographs*, Sutton Publishing, Canterbury, 1993

Carlaw, Derek, *Finding Young Talent*, KCCC Annual 2003, pp 60–67

Carlaw, Derek, *Kent in the USA September / October 1903*, KCCC Annual 2004, pp 63–66

Clough, Dr PWL, *Colin Blythe: Biography of a Bowler*, KCCC Annual 1981, pp 61–66

Coldham, James D, *Lord Harris*, George Allen & Unwin, London, 1983

Dockrell, Morgan, *Frank E. Woolley 1887–1978*, KCCC Annual 1979, pp 55–64

Ellis, Clive & Pennell, Mark, *Trophies and Tribulations: Forty Years of Kent Cricket*, Greenwich Publishing, Trowbridge, 2010

Evans, John, Carlaw, Derek and Milton, Howard, *Images of Kent Cricket: The County Club in the Twentieth Century*, Breedon Books, Derby, 2000

Frindall, Bill, *England Test Cricketers*, Willow Books, London, 1989

Frith, David, *The Golden Age of Cricket 1890–1914*, Omega Books, Ware, 1978

Green, Benny, *The Wisden Book of Cricketers' Lives*, Queen Anne Press, London, 1989

Griffiths, John F, *Colin ("Charlie") Blythe*, KCCC Annual 1977, pp 59–63

Guha, Ramachandra, *The Picador Book of Cricket*, Picador, London, 2006

Harker, Sydney, *The Book of Gravesham*, Barracuda Books, Buckingham, 1979

Harris, Lord George, *A Few Short Runs*, John Murray, London, 1921

Harris, Lord George, *The History of Kent County Cricket*, Eyre & Spottiswoode, London, 1907

Hattersley, Roy, *The Edwardians*, Abacus, London, 2004

Hayes, Dean, *Kent Cricketing Greats*, Spellmount Ltd, Tunbridge Wells, 1990

Hougham, Terry, *Canterbury in old picture postcards volume 2*, Canterbury, 1992

Hoult, Nick, *The Daily Telegraph Book of Cricket*, Aurum Press, London, 2009

Hughes, Simon, *And God Created Cricket: An Irreverent History of the English Game and How Other People (like Australians) Got Annoyingly Good at It*, Doubleday, London, 2009

Kent CCC, *1914 "Blue Book"*, Gibbs and Sons, Canterbury, 1914

Lazenby, John, *Test of Time – Travels in Search of a Cricketing Legend,* John Murray, London, 2005

Lee, Christopher, *Through the Covers: An Anthology of Cricket Writing*, Oxford University Press, Oxford, 1997

Lemmon, David, *The Wisden Book of Cricket Quotations*, MacDonald Queen Anne Press, London, 1990

Major, John, Sir, *More Than a Game: The Story of Cricket's Early Years*, Harper Press, London, 2007

Malies, Jeremy, *Great Cricketers from Cricket's Golden Age*, Robson Books, London, 2000

Manners, David, *Canterbury Stage by Stage – the City's Theatrical Past,* David Manners, Herne Bay, 2011

March, Russell, *Cricketers of Vanity Fair*, Webb & Bower, Exeter, 1982

Milton, Howard, *Kent Cricketers 1834–1983*, Association of Cricket Statisticians, Haughton Mill, Retford, Nottinghamshire, 1983

Milton, Howard, *Kent Cricket Records 1815–1993*, Linslow Books, 1994

Milton, Howard, *Cricket Grounds of Kent*, The Association of Cricket Statisticians, West Bridgford, Nottingham, 1992

Milton, Howard, *The Bat and Ball Ground: A First-Class Cricket History*, Gravesend Cricket Club, 1999

Moore, Dudley, *The History of Kent County Cricket Club*, Christopher Helm, London, 1989

Morrah, Patrick, *Alfred Mynn and the cricketers of his time*, Constable, London, 1986 (original 1963)

Morrah, Patrick, *The Golden Age of Cricket*, Eyre & Spottiswoode, London, 1967

Ogley, Bob, *Kent: A Chronicle of the Century Volume 1: 1900–1924,* Froglets Publications, Westerham, 1996

Osborn, T, *The History of the Mote Cricket Club*, Kent County Council, West Malling, 1990

Parker, Grahame, *Gloucestershire Road, A History of Gloucestershire CCC,* Pelham 1983

Pardon, Sydney H, *John Wisden's Cricketers' Almanack for 1914*, John Wisden & Co. London, 1914

Peebles: Ian, *Woolley: The Pride of Kent*, Hutchinson & Co & The Cricketer Ltd, London, 1969

Pentelow, JN (ed), *CRICKET: A Weekly Record of the Game,* Volume II (New Series) 1913, Cricket & Sports Publishers, London 1913

Plumptre, George, *The Golden Age of Cricket*, MacDonald Queen Anne Press, London, 1990

Pope Anne, *Tell us about when you were young – living in Canterbury and its villages 1900–1939,* Canterbury Environment Centre, Canterbury, 1997

Porter, Clive W, *Kent Cricket Champions,* Limlow Books, Royston, 2000

Powell, William A, *Images of Sport: Kent County Cricket Club*, Tempus, Stroud, 2000

Powell, William A, *Cricket Grounds Then and Now*, Dial Press, London 1994

Robertson, David, Milton, Howard & Carlaw, Derek, *Kent County Cricket Club: 100 Greats*, Tempus, Stroud, 2005

Carlaw, Derek, *Kent County Cricket Club: 50 of the Finest First-Class Matches*, Tempus, Stroud, 2006

Ruygrok, Peter, *A wonderful Kent hero from cricket's Golden Age*, KCCC Annual 2001, pp 245–248

Sackville-West, Vita, *The Edwardians*, Virago, London, 1930

Sampson, Aylwin, *Grounds of Appeal: The Homes of First-Class Cricket*, Robert Hale, London, 1981

Scoble, Christopher, *Colin Blythe: lament for a legend*, SportsBooks, Cheltenham, 2005

Scott, Leslie, *Bats, Balls & Bails – The Essential Cricket Book*, Bantam Press, London, 2009

Smart, John Blythe, *The Real Colin Blythe*, Blythe Smart Productions, Kingsbridge, 2009

Tassell, Bryan*, Band of Brothers 1858–1958,* Private Publication, 1958

Taylor, Chris H, *The Story of Canterbury Cricket Week 1842–1992*, Geerings, Ashford, 1991

Thomson, AA, *Hirst and Rhodes*, Pavilion Library, London, 1986

Tunbridge Wells CC, *The Nevill Cricket Ground Centenary 1898–1998*, Ditchling Press, 1998

Warner, HW, *Looking Back: Brief Reviews of Past Seasons – 1913*, KCCC Annual 1971

Warner, Oliver, *Cricketing Lives: Frank Woolley*, Phoenix House, London, 1952

Webber, Roy, *County Cricket Championship: A History of the Competition from 1873*, Phoenix, Sports Books, London, 1957

Wilson, AN, *After The Victorians: The World Our Parents Knew*, Arrow Books, London, 2006

Williams, Marcus (ed), *Double Century: 200 Years of Cricket in The Times*, Collins Willow, London, 1985

Woolley, Frank, *The King of Games*, Stanley Paul & Co, London, 1936

Woolley, Frank, *Early Memories*, The Cricketer, London, 1976

Index

Notes

This Index has been compiled to include the many references to the various players and other people, places and events that appear on the pages of this book outside of the context of an individual match or the chapter on the background to the 1913 Season, although it does include reference to match venues. It therefore excludes references to Kent players in respect of their performance in an individual match. This also applies to players of the opposition unless the chapter includes a photograph of the particular individual.

Page numbers in italics indicates a photograph